Alain de Botton

中英双语插图本

哲学的慰藉

The Consolations of Philosophy

〔英〕阿兰·德波顿 著　资中筠 译

上海译文出版社

哲 学 的 慰 藉

〔英〕阿兰·德波顿 著

资中筠 译

我的作品在中国

Alain le Botton 阿兰·德波顿

我很清楚地记得我的首度中国之行。抵达北京时是2004年5月的一个清晨,我的几位中国编辑亲自前往机场迎接,随身带着我所有作品的中文版。从机场前往市区的路上,我的编辑向我解释,对于将我的作品引进中国市场她真是既充满期待又有些担心。她说,要想让中国读者接受一个全新的欧洲作家的作品真的很难,除非是那些教你如何取得商业成功或是如何操作电脑软件的书。不过,我的中国编辑也充满信心。因为中国读书界自有一群严肃的读者,他们渴望读到内容深刻、发人深省的优秀作品。结果,我的中国之行就演变成一连串的图书推广活动:接受采访、

1

在媒体上露面以及在书店里朗读和签售。虽说大家事先都有过各式各样的疑虑，不过好消息还是接踵而至：我的作品确实在中国卖出去了。《拥抱逝水年华》——一本描写以晦涩著称的法国作家普鲁斯特的书竟然卖了两万册！

写书的人可以分成两种：一种人搞不懂为什么他的大著地球人没有人手一册；另一种人则不敢相信自己的好运：竟然有人肯巴巴地花钱买他的书而且认真读过。我属于后一个阵营，所以对于我的书竟然能在中国赢得这么多读者，我深怀感激。我有个网站（www.alaindebotton.com），我每天都能看到中国读者的留言，他们想跟我交流几句，想表达他们对我作品的喜爱。写作是桩难上加难的营生，可是拥有这么热心的中国读者，感觉确实容易了很多。

反观我已经出版的几本书，我有时仍不免有些犯嘀咕：我到底属于哪一类作家——究竟是什么将这些只言片语连缀到一起，成为一本完整的书。从一开始写作，我就缺乏一个明确的定位。在明确知道我想成为哪一类作家之前我只知道我不可能成为哪一类作家。我知道我不是诗人，我也知道我不是个真正的小说家（我讲不来故事，我"发明"不了人物）。而且我知道我也做不来学者，因为我不想墨守那一整套学术规范。

后来,我终于发现了自觉正好适合自己的定位:随笔作家。据我个人的理解,所谓随笔作家,就是既能抓住人类生存的各种重大主题,又能以如话家常的亲切方式对这些主题进行讨论的作家。如果一位随笔作家来写一本有关爱的书,他也许会对爱的历史和心理稍作探究,不过他最终必须得用一种个人化的调子来写,使读者读起来就像跟朋友娓娓谈心。这种朋友般的阅读感受对我而言非常重要:我希望我的书读起来就像跟朋友谈心,不想拿大学问的帽子来充门面、唬人。

初习写作,我还认识到我喜欢写得尽可能简单朴素。这当然也挺冒险的,因为虽说你是刻意写得朴素,可难免也会冒乏味和幼稚之讥。不过我在自己的学习过程中发现,要想附庸风雅、假充聪明实在是再简单不过的事儿了,你只需故作高深,让人弄不懂你就成。如果有本书我看不懂,也许就意味着作者比我更聪明——这是我们作为读者都未能免俗的一种普遍的受虐欲心理。我则宁肯抵挡住这种诱惑,用日常生活中的语言来写作,因为我讨论的主题本身就是跟每个人息息相关的:恋爱、旅行、身份焦虑、美与丑以及分离与死亡的经验等等。

除了要写让人看得懂的书之外,我还立志要写在某些方面能对人有所助益的书。有一种观念认为好书就不该（没义务）对人有任何用处，为艺术而艺术嘛——并非为了实际的进步或是事业的成功而艺术。在一定程度上我也认同这种观念。为了完全改变自己而去啃那些严肃的书籍确实愚不可及，不过，我也认为，抱定为了更好地理解自己以及自己所处环境的目的去读书，是至关重要的。最好的书能清楚地阐明你长久以来一直心有所感，却从来没办法明白表达出来的那些东西。

恋爱和阅读之间或许真有某种重要的关联，两者提供的乐趣差堪比拟，我们感到的某种关联感或许就是基于这个根源。有些书跟我们交流的方式与我们的爱人同等热烈，而且更加诚实可靠。这些书能有效地防止我们因自觉并不完全属于人类大家族而滋生的伤感情绪：我们觉得孑然孤立，谁都不理解我们。我们身上那些更加隐秘的侧面——诸如我们的困惑、我们的愠怒、我们的罪恶感——有时竟然在某一书页上跟我们撞个正着，一种自我认同感于是油然而生。那位作者用确切的文字描述了一种我们原以为只有我们自己才有所会心的情境，一时间，我们就像两个早早地去赴约吃饭的爱人，兴奋不已地发现两人间竟有这么多的共同点（陶醉之下，只能嚼几口眼前的开胃小食，哪有心思再去吃什么正餐），我们也会把书暂时放下，带点乖张地微笑着盯着书脊不放，仿佛在说，"何等幸运，邂逅此君。"

马塞尔·普鲁斯特曾表达过类似的意思，他说，"事实上，每个读者只能读到已然存在于他内心的东西。书籍只不过是一种光学仪器，作者将其提供给读者，以便于他发现如果没有这本书的帮助他就发现不了的东西。"不过，书的价值还不止于描绘我们在自己的生活中习见的那些情感和人物，好书对我们各种感情的描绘远胜过我们自己的体会，它处理的感知和认识虽确属我们所有，却又是我们根本无力予以明确表达的：它比我们更了解我们自己。

我读书时总抱着非常个人的理由：为了帮我更好地生活而读书。我十五六岁时开始认真地读书，当时最喜欢读的就是爱情故事。我把书中的人物都想象成我的生活中真实存在的活人：我读得如饥似渴，又感同身受。这足可以解释文学何以能够为失恋的人儿带来舒解和慰藉。在文艺作品中认出我们自己，可以使我们换一种达观的态度看待我们自身的困境，因为我们可以学着站在普世的高度看问题，这正是作家们为了创作而采取的立场。

学着读书——写作又何尝不是——也就等于接受这样

一个现实:我们的个性并非如我们乐于想象的那般密不透风,我们自以为只归我们独有的很多东西其实根本没那么私密——当然并不是说它们就是客观超然的,像你在快餐店里招呼侍应生那么不带感情色彩,而是说它们其实都是人类所共有的东西。我们在发现自己并非如此孤立的同时也要付点代价:我们也并非如我们想象的那般与众不同。

我自己在读书时总是很自私:我不想只是为了读书而读书。我读书是为了学习,是为了成为一个更好、更有自知之明、更多才多艺的人。我几乎从来都不为了"取乐"而读书。

我希望这能有助于解释我为什么写了这些书——写这些书是期望它们能有助于我们更好地理解我们人类的处境。中国竟然也有些读者愿意跟随我探索的旅程,幸何如哉!

2008 年 10 月于伦敦

(冯涛　译)

目 录

哲学不只是慰藉(推荐序)

译 序

哲学不只是慰藉(推荐序)

周国平

德波顿的《哲学的慰藉》一书选择西方哲学史上六位哲学家,从不同角度阐述了哲学对于人生的慰藉作用。人生中有种种不如意处,其中有一些是可改变的,有一些是不可改变的。对于那些不可改变的缺陷,哲学提供了一种视角,帮助我们坦然面对和接受,在此意义上,可以说哲学是一种慰藉。但是,哲学不只是慰藉,更是智慧。二者的区别也许在于,慰藉类似于心理治疗,重在调整我们的心态,智慧调整的却是我们看世界和人生的总体眼光。因此,如果把哲学的作用归结为慰藉,就有可能缩小甚至歪曲哲学的内涵。当然,智慧与慰藉并非不能相容,总体眼光的调整必然会带来心态的调整,在此意义上,则可以说哲学是一种最深刻的慰藉。

全书中,我读得最有兴味的是写塞内加的一章。部分的原因可能是,这一章比较切题,斯多葛派哲学家本身就重视哲学的慰藉作用,塞内加自己就有以《慰藉》为题的著作。作为罗马宫廷的重臣,此人以弄权和奢华著称,颇招时人及后世訾议。不过,他到底是一个智者,身在大富大贵之中,仍能清醒地视富贵为身外之物,用他的话来说便是:"我从来没有信任过命运女神。我把她赐予我的一切——金钱,官位,权势——都搁置在一个地方,可以让她随时拿回去而不干扰我。我同它们之间保持很宽的距离,这样,她只是把它们取走,而不是从我身上强行剥走。"不止于此,对于家庭、儿女、朋友乃至自己的身体都应作如是观。塞内加的看法是:人对有准备的、理解了的挫折承受力最强,反之受伤害最重。哲学的作用就在于,第一,使人认识到任何一种坏事都可能发生,从而随时作好准备;第二,帮助人理解已经发生的坏事,认识到它们未必那么坏。坏事为什么未必那么坏呢?请不要在这里揣坏事变好事之类的通俗辩证法,塞内加的理由见于一句精辟之言:"何必为部分生活而哭泣?君不见全部人生都催人泪下。"叔本华有一个类似说法:倘若一个人着眼于整体而非一己的命运,他的行为就会更像是一个智者而非一个受难者了。哲人之为哲人,就在于看到了整个人生的全景和限度,因而能够站在整体的高度与一切个别灾难拉开距离,达成和解。塞内加是说到做到的。他官场一度失意,被流放到荒凉的科西嘉,始终泰然自若。最后,暴君尼禄上台,命他自杀,同伴们一片哭声,他从容问道:"你们的哲学哪里去了?"

蒙田是我的老朋友了,现在从本书中重温他的一些言论,倍感亲切。作者引用了蒙田谈论性事的片断,评论道:"他把人们私下都经历过而极少听到的事勇敢地说出来……他的勇气基于他的信念:凡是能发生在人身上的事就没有不人道的。"说得好,有蒙田自己的话作证:"每一个人的形体都承载着全部人的状况。"然而,正因为此,这一章的标题"对缺陷的慰藉"就很不确切了。再看蒙田的警句:"登上至高无上的御座,仍只能坐在屁股上。""国王与哲学家皆拉屎,贵妇人亦然。"很显然,在蒙田眼里,性事、屁股、拉屎等等哪里是什么缺陷啊,恰好是最正常的人性现象,因此我们完全应该以最正常的心态去面对。一个人对于人性有了足够的理解,他看人包括看自己的眼光就会变得既深刻又宽容,在这样的眼光下,一切隐私都可以还原成普遍的人性现象,一切个人经历都可以转化成心灵的财富。

在当今这个崇拜财富的时代,关于伊壁鸠鲁的一章也颇值得一读。这位古希腊哲学家把快乐视为人生最高价值,他的哲学因此被冠以享乐主义的名称,他本人则俨然成了一切酒色之徒的祖师爷,这真是天大的误会。其实,他的哲学的核心思想恰恰是主张真正的快乐对于物质的依赖十分有限,无非是食、住、衣的基本条件。超出了一定限度,财富的增加便不再能带来快乐的增加了。奢侈对于快乐并无实质的贡献,往往还导致痛苦。事实上,无论是伊壁鸠鲁,还是继承了他的基本思想的后世哲学家,比如英国功利主义者,全都主张快乐更多地依赖于精神而非物质。这个道理一点也不深奥,任何一个品尝过两种快乐的人都可以凭自身的体验予以证明,沉湎于物质快乐而不知精神快乐为何物的人也可以凭自己的空虚予以证明。

本书还有三章分别论述苏格拉底、叔本华、尼采,我觉得相比之下较为逊色,没有把他们的精华很好地呈现出来。部分的原因也许在于,这三人的哲学是更不能以慰藉论之的。尤其尼采,他的哲学的基本精神恰恰是反对形形色色的慰藉,直面人生的悲剧性质,以此证明人的高贵和伟大。一本好的通俗哲学读物的作用是让我们领略哲学的魅力,吸引我们走进哲学之门,本书无疑起到了这样的作用。至于在入门之后,怎样深入堂奥,与历史上这一个或那一个独特的灵魂深交,就要靠读者自己的修行了。

2008 年 12 月 11 日于北京

译　　序

　　由于精力与时间有限，我一般不轻易接受翻译的约稿。因此译文出版社的朋友最初提出要我承担他们准备出的一套丛书中的一本时，我本能地倾向于推辞。但是当他们把阿兰·德波顿的《哲学的慰藉》一书送到我手上后，翻阅之下，立刻就被吸引住了。首先是文字，后来才是内容。说来惭愧，我也算是主修英国文学出身，在大学上的基本课程是从莎士比亚到维多利亚时代的文学作品。较之诗歌、戏剧，我自己更偏好小说和散文。但是一出校门，我的工作就与文学绝缘，也做了不少翻译工作，却多为政治性的文献、资料以及口译，少有文采可言。近20年来，专业是国际政治研究，所读书刊文章很少在文字上有特点，而且大量是美国人的著作。在这个领域内我所读到的真正上乘的英文是丘吉尔关于第二次世界大战的回忆录，虽不是文学作品，却在遣词用字上有不可言传之妙。当然，丘吉尔除了政治家的身份外，作为写作家的英文也是享有盛名的，不必我赘言。

　　这一次，这本小书的文字使我有他乡遇故知的感觉。那种特别英国式的散文风格，简洁而优雅，机智而含蓄，能用小字眼就不用大字眼，惯以轻描淡写代替浓墨重彩，给读书留有回味的余地，这些都深得英国古典散文的传承。我一向认为，一种臻于上乘的文字首先是本土的，不是洋腔洋调的，中文如此，其他国家文字也如此。例如纯粹英国英文与带点法国味或德国味（指文风，不是口音）的英文就不一样，哪怕后者非常流畅而正确。（现在国内流传的美国式英文又当别论，其实美国真正的大作家也有文字不俗的。）因为每一个有悠久文明的民族的语言都是经过千锤百炼，形成自己特殊的审美和表达方式。每一种文字本身又有文、质、雅、俗之分。凡精美的文字，大多读来明白晓畅，看来朴素无华，修辞却极有讲究，越是如此，要精确传神地译成别国文字就越加难乎其难。正是这本小书的这一特点对我产生了极大的吸引力，对自己的中文形成一种挑战，使我跃跃欲试，于是就知难而上了。

当然，本书的吸引力与难译之处不仅在于文字，更在于内容。这是一本以介绍几位哲学家及其思想的非学术性书，既像写自己读书心得的随笔，又像普及知识的"科普"作品。人物的挑选、切入的角度和思想的诠释都凭作者的个人兴趣和理解。对某位哲学家的言论是否引用得当，诠释是否到位，专家们可以提出各种批评和质疑。但是如果不以学术性著作来要求（本来就不是），我觉得本书决不是"戏说"，表达方式虽然活泼俏皮，作者的态度却是相当严肃的。可以相信，他对所涉及的哲学著作是认真读过，经过自己思考的。

在作者看来,哲学最大的功能就是以智慧来慰藉人生的痛苦。这痛苦有主观自找的,例如名缰利锁,欲壑难填;有外界强加的,例如天灾人祸,种种不公平的遭遇。但是在哲学家那里都可以找到解脱之道:苏格拉底以通过理性思辨掌握真理的自信直面压倒优势的世俗偏见,虽百死而不悔。塞内加参透人事无常,对命运作最坏的设想,因而对任何飞来横祸都能处变不惊。伊壁鸠鲁认为人生以追求快乐为目的,但是他对快乐有自己的理解:摈弃世俗的奢华,远离发号施令的上级,布衣简食,良朋为伴,林下泉边,悠哉游哉!蒙田(姑从德波顿,把他也列入哲学家)自己大半生在藏书楼中度过,却贬低书本知识,因厌恶上流社会的矫揉造作,而走向了另一极端——让饮食男女的原始本能登大雅之堂;他痛恨当时学界言必称希腊的引经据典之风,提倡用百姓自己的话代替"亚里士多德如是说",这样,因能力、知识不足而自卑者可以从中得到慰藉。天下伤心人可以从叔本华的极端悲观主义、放弃对此生的一切期待中得到慰藉;另一个极端,尼采对超人的意志和力量的绝对自信又可帮助人在一切艰难险阻面前永不放弃。

作者并没有表明他对任何一种哲学的倾向性,对其中有一些也以调侃的笔法透露了一点质疑。但是从作者的角度看,这些哲学家的思想虽然相距甚远,甚至相对立,却有一个一以贯之的共同点,那就是哲学一词希腊文的原义:"爱智慧",而且用这种智慧来慰藉人生的种种悲苦。这也是本书的切入点,因此以此为题。下面这段话最好地概括了作者自己的旨趣和写这本书的真意：

> 广而言之，以这位希腊哲学家（苏格拉底）为最高象征的主题似乎在召唤我们担负起一项既深刻又可笑的任务，那就是通过哲学求得智慧。尽管古往今来被称作哲学家的思想者千差万别（他们如果聚集在一场大型酒会上，不但互相话不投机，而且很可能几杯酒下肚就要拳脚相向），还是有可能在相隔几世纪之间找到一小群情貌略似的人，其共同点就是忠于"哲学"一词希腊文的原义——"爱智慧"。人以群分，把这一小群人归在一起的共同爱好在于就人生最大的痛苦的根源向我们说一些宽慰而切合实际的话。我愿从斯人游！

不论哲学家的主张如何，他们共同的特点是不随俗、不从众、不畏权势，通过独立的深思熟虑而得出自成体系的对宇宙、对人生的看法。一旦形成，就身体力行，以大无畏的精神捍卫、宣扬之。本书以苏格拉底之死开篇，开宗明义用这种精神统领全书：

> "这位哲学家宁愿失欢于众，获罪于邦，而决不折腰。他决不因别人指责而收回自己的思想。而且，他的自信不仅是出于一时冲动或者匹夫之勇，而是来自更深层次的、根植于哲学的源泉。哲学给苏格拉底以坚定的信仰，使他面对千夫所指能够保持合乎理性的而不是歇斯底里的自信。"
>
> "这种思想的独立性给我以启迪和激励。它向我展示了

一种力量，可以抗衡在行动和思想上曲意迎俗的习性。在苏格拉底的生死之间包含着一种召唤，唤起人聪慧的怀疑精神。"

这一贯穿全书的追求真理的精神和独立人格，也许正是作者要与读者分享与共勉的启迪。

其实，这种精神在东西方的哲人那里是相通的（我得赶紧声明，我决不是要把东西方的哲学作牵强附会的比附，那正是我反对的）。如"三军可以夺帅，匹夫不可夺志"（《论语》），"自反而缩①，虽千万人，吾往矣！"（《孟子》），都是指的只要自信真理在我，就坚持到底，无所畏惧。压力可能来自掌握生杀予夺之权的统治者，也可能来自世俗的无知和成见，还可能来自自己本身对名利的欲望，这些同样都是压制理性探索的死敌。中国春秋时代的先哲主张各异，同时也都拥有那份自信，那种依靠自己的智慧独立思考的精神，因此才有光耀千秋的"百家争鸣"的局面。而从伊壁鸠鲁对待权势财富的态度来看，也能找到中国读书人的不为五斗米折腰而归隐田园、崇尚淡泊宁静、归真返璞的影子，还有魏晋名士特立独行的风骨。书中所描绘的尼采对人生必须经过苦难的看法，有点"天将降大任于斯人也，必先苦其心志……"的味道。从这个意义上讲，哲学作为一种超越世俗的精神，在各民族的智者那里是相通的。

---

① "缩"，直也，"自反而缩"就是自信理在我。——译者

作者阿兰·德波顿近年来在欧洲已经崭露头角,但是在我国还没有进入读者的视野。我本人也是在接手本书的翻译后才对他略作了解。首先使我意外的是他的年轻——生于1969年,写此书时才三十出头,而书中所显示的学养、见识和开阔的视野给我的第一印象似乎应在中年以上。继而一想,也不奇怪,我国上个世纪二三十年代成名的作家、思想家、学问家也不过这个年龄,而这些前辈在深厚的国学功底之外还有西学。实际上一个人的文化底蕴应该在二十岁左右,甚至更早,就已奠基。德波顿生于瑞士,由于其父母特别喜欢英国,八岁就被送到伦敦上寄宿学校,四年后全家人移居伦敦。他最早学的是法语,现在写作以英语为主,同时通晓法、德、西班牙语。从这本书来看大约至少能读希腊文和拉丁文。十八岁入剑桥大学,正式学历为剑桥大学历史系毕业。他自称大学时代只有两样追求:爱情和创作。前者很不成功,促成了后者的成功,因而他深信失恋与文学是并行的。对学校的课程他一点也不感兴趣,好在学业比较宽松,他有足够的时间随心所欲地博览群书,自学成才。整个大学期间他主要依靠大学图书馆和附近一家书店,在那里他父母给他开了一个账户,随他自由买书(后来他买书之多令他父母后悔当初的慷慨)。他读书不是被动地接受知识,而是为寻找一种表达方式,为此徜徉于文学、艺术、美学、哲学、心理分析之间,上下古今求索,从中邂逅知音,产生共鸣,在跨越千年的著作里欣然找到先得我心之感,逐步接近了自己的目标。这样,上大学不是为求学位,只不过提供他一个读书的氛围;而读书不是为了日后求职,只是帮他找到自己独特的创作模式。所以,他不愿把他的写作归入任何一类:小说、历史、哲学……最多能称之为"随笔",以个人的声音谈人生的重大题材。

德波顿在各种报刊杂志发表的文章很多,二十三岁开始出版第一部作品,是小说体裁,以后两部也是小说。但是正如前面讲的,他写小说力求打破讲故事和表现情景的传统模式,探索情景背后的所以然,要弄明白各种人际关系后面的动力是什么。他最喜爱的、能引起共鸣的作家之一是普鲁斯特。他的第四部著作:《拥抱逝水年华》是从文学通向哲学的桥梁,这本书使他名声大噪。由此引出下一部:《哲学的慰藉》。如果说他的小说是寓哲学探索于文学创作之中,那么这本书则是用文学笔法写哲学。为什么在漫长的哲学史上偏取这几个人? 作者说就因为这几个人他能读懂,令他喜欢,岂有他哉! 更深一层的意思就是他认为哲学家的伟大不在于高深莫测,而在于能与常人对话。他以自己驾驭文字的才华把通常是枯燥晦涩的哲学思想写得生动活泼而通俗易懂,目的就是要把哲学从高头讲章拉下来,进入平常百姓的日常生活之中。另一方面,他又通过哲学家之口告诉人们思想的重要,人生道路上遇到种种问题,不假思索凭本能作出反应,与通过思考,理性地对待,结果是大不相同的。他认为在世俗的世界里只有哲学能解人生痛苦之谜。但是哲学著作又多艰深难懂,令普通人望而生畏。

而在他看来,哲学如龙虾,外面有一层硬壳,还有应该剔除的污垢,但是里面的肉却是美味而营养丰富的。《哲学的慰藉》的作用就如给龙虾剥壳的钳子和掏肉的长钩。他思接千载,驰骋跳跃于古今之间,把古人的思维展示在现代人物和时髦的生活方式之中,不由人不得出结论:人性在某些方面是永恒的,因而有些哲理也是永恒的。

从作者自述的意图来看,他是成功了。能把这门艰深的学问写成这样有趣,引人入胜,实属难得,可以称得上是深入浅出之作——我一向认为"深入浅出"是有学术含量的文章的高难境界。不研究哲学的人读了这本书可以增加知识,得到启发,甚至进一步对人生有所感悟。年轻人也许会从此爱上哲学,决心进一步登堂入室。至少,也可以作为优美的文学随笔来读。当然,作者对这些哲学家的理解程度可能深浅不一,对有的概括比较准确,而对有的可能有失偏颇。这也是见仁见智的问题。读者自可做出批判,得出自己的看法。

这本书的确很难归类,无以名之,名之曰才子书。欧洲知识分子有一个得天独厚的优势,就是浸润在有深厚历史积淀、丰富多彩、和而不同的文化之中。他们通晓几种欧洲语言是寻常事,不少人自幼就有机会在这片古老而现代的大地上遍游名胜古迹。欧洲的教育制度虽然也受现代专业化的影响,但在人文领域内的通才教育传统和氛围还是比高度功利化、市场化的美国教育制度多一些文化底蕴。德波顿正是从这种文化土壤中生长的幸运儿。他自称早年受的是严格而规范的教育(大概这是父母决心送他到英国上学的原因),上大学之前到法国游历了一年,爱上了法国文化的浪漫主义气质,因此到了大学,力图摆脱英国式传统的束缚,寻求自由创作。事实上,惟其他有了严格规范的底子,才能在十八岁之后这样自由自在地思而学、学而思,有能力钻进那龙虾的硬壳,尽情地吸收欧洲文明的营养,并与他人分享。他力求简洁的文字也是这种锤炼的结果。有人说他思想接近"前卫"、"后现代",他特别表示不能认同那种佶屈聱牙的文风。他在书中还借蒙田之口要读者不要被那些晦涩难懂的书唬住,那多半是作者缺乏清楚表达的能力之故。这一点也令我感到古今中外相通,切中时弊。看得出德波顿的活泼、晓畅的文风也正是得力于早先的规范的训练。总之,天赋的灵气加适宜的土壤再加机遇,成就了这位才子型人物。

译者自知对哲学是门外汉,有关知识没有超出常识范围,翻译此书有些诚惶诚恐,力图避免望文生义,或出硬伤,贻笑方家。现将翻译本书的原则和体例作一说明:书中涉及六位哲学家,其著作的原文有希腊、拉丁、法、德四种语言。从书后索引看,作者不论是间接叙述或直接引语绝大部分都来自这些著作的英译本,书中只有个别地方引了原文。译者的原则是只对本书的英文负责,一切引语也从书中的英文译出,不负责查对原著。有不少著作国内已有中译本,但我还是根据本书的文字自己译出,没有抄录已有的中译本。一则是为了与全书译文的风格保持一致,二则更重要的是，中译版本有时不止一个，偶然碰巧发现同一引文，往往与书中的英文并不完全吻合。除非一一查对原文，并且比较各种译文版本，得出自己的判断（那就是另一种专业研究工作了），否则只能一律以本书为准。惟有《圣经》例外，因为中文《圣经》有其特殊的语言，书中引语除个别无法查到的之外，大多照抄中国基督教协会印发的《新旧约全书》中文本，即便文字有些古怪。关于人名地名，约定俗成众人皆知的，当然不成问题（如苏格拉底）。但是约定俗成也有不同范围，有的在圈内认为已有定论，而圈外人就不一定知道。本人自知非哲学界人士，对此没有把握。在查阅有关资料中常发现译名也有不同版本。有些常见的名字就存在不同译法，例如 Seneca 至少有塞内加和塞尼卡两种译法。本书关于人名、地名翻译的参照本有：《希腊哲学史》第 2 卷（汪子嵩等著，人民出版社，1997 年）、《大英百科全书》中文版，以及新华社出的外国人名、地名译名手册。查不到的只好揣译。全书译名的统一工作则偏劳责编衷雅琴女士了。

在翻译过程中遇有疑难问题曾请教叶秀山、周国平等哲学界专家，承蒙他们热心、认真、及时指教，助我解惑。由于本人不懂希腊文和拉丁文，曾请叶秀山先生帮忙。第四章第四节的希腊文根据叶秀山先生提供的牛津版英译本《亚里士多德全集》第 2 卷（乔纳森·巴恩斯主编）引文译出，同一节中的一段拉丁文引语则由出版社请冯象先生帮忙译出。在此一并致谢。

第一章

对与世不合的慰藉

（一）

几年前,在纽约一个苦寒的冬日,我在赶赴伦敦的班机前还有一下午可以闲逛,信步走去,不觉来到了大都会美术博物馆楼上的画廊。那里灯火通明,一片寂静,只有地板下的暖气低吟,令人心神悠然。我在印象派的画廊里看画看腻了,正想寻找一间咖啡厅,喝一杯我当时特别喜爱的一种美式巧克力牛奶,蓦然间一幅画映入眼帘,从说明来看,这幅画是雅克-路易·大卫作于1786年秋,时年38岁。

画上被雅典人民判处死刑的苏格拉底在悲痛欲绝的朋友围绕中正准备喝那杯毒药。公元前 399 年的春天,3 名雅典公民对这位哲学家提起诉讼,告他不敬城邦之神、传播异端宗教、腐蚀雅典青年——罪名重大,非判死刑不可。

　　苏格拉底的申辩以其非凡的镇静自若流传后世。法庭给他机会当众放弃他的哲学,但是他选择了所信仰的真理而不肯随俗,根据柏拉图的叙述,他意气昂然对法官说:

　　　　只要我一息尚存,官能健全,我决不会停止哲学实践,不会停止对你们进行劝导,不会停止向我遇到的每一个人阐明真理……所以,诸位,不论你们是否释放我,你们知道我是不会改变我的行为的,虽百死而不悔。

于是,他就给带到一所雅典的牢狱中等待生命的终结。他的死标志着哲学史上一个特定的时刻。

这一事件的意义之重大,也许以此为题的绘画频繁出现足以为证。1650年法国画家夏尔-阿方斯·迪弗雷努瓦绘《苏格拉底之死》,此画现悬挂于佛罗伦萨的帕拉蒂画廊(那里没有咖啡厅)。

艾蒂安·德·拉瓦莱-普桑,1760年

对苏格拉底之死的兴趣到18世纪臻于极至,尤其是狄德罗在其《论戏剧诗》中专门有一段话提到这一事件蕴含着丰富的可以入画的意境,其后就更加引起关注。

雅克-路易·大卫是在1786年春从一名富有的国会议员,才华过人的希腊学者,夏尔-米歇尔·特吕代纳·德·

雅克·菲利普·约瑟夫·德·圣康坦,1762年

拉萨布利埃手中接受这一任务的。报酬极为优厚:预付6000里弗赫,交货时再付3000里弗赫(路易十六给那幅更大的画《贺拉斯兄弟之誓》才付了6000里弗赫)。当1787年这幅画在沙龙里展出时,立即被

5

皮埃尔·佩龙,1790 年

公认为以苏格拉底之死为题材的画中的极品。乔舒亚·雷诺兹爵士认为"这是自西斯廷教堂天顶画①和拉斐尔的罗马教皇居室壁画以来最精美、最令人仰慕的艺术成就。这幅画足以让伯里克利②时代的雅典人感到荣耀"。

我在博物馆的纪念品商店买了 5 张大卫的那幅画的明信片。后来,在飞过冰封的纽芬兰上空时(当时晴空万里,一轮明月把大地照出耀眼的绿光),我拿出一张来看,一边嚼着服务小姐在误以为我打瞌睡时放在我前面小桌上的淡而无味的饭菜。

画上柏拉图坐在床脚,手里拿着一支笔,身旁放着一卷纸,他是这场城邦冤案的沉默的见证人。他在苏格拉底死时 29 岁,但是大卫把他画成了一位老人,须发皆灰,神色凝

---

① Cappella Sistina,是米开朗琪罗奉罗马教皇尤里乌斯二世之命在罗马西斯廷教堂的穹顶作的大型雕塑,于 1512 年尤里乌斯死后完成。梵蒂冈宫壁画是拉斐尔在罗马教皇的居室画的大型壁画,也是奉尤里乌斯教皇之命,也是在他死后(1514—1517)完成。这两件作品都被认为是代表文艺复兴时期的艺术巅峰之作。——译者

② Pericles(约前 495—前 429),古希腊雅典国家的统治者,他的名字代表雅典极盛时期。在他死前两年相继发生伯罗奔尼撒战争和鼠疫,雅典从此由盛而衰。——译者

重。走廊里是苏格拉底的妻子桑娣帕，由两名狱卒陪送从牢房里走过来。有7位朋友处于不同程度的悲戚之中。苏格拉底最亲密的伙伴克里托坐在他身旁深情而关切地凝视着这位大师。但是哲学家本人腰杆笔挺，上身和胳膊如运动员般健壮，神情既无畏惧也无悔意。众多的雅典人骂他是笨蛋，却丝毫没有动摇他的信仰。起初大卫准备画苏格拉底正在仰药自尽的情景，但是诗人安德烈·谢尼埃提出了可以表现更大的戏剧张力的建议：画上的苏格拉底正宣讲完一个哲学论点，同时泰然伸手拿起那将要结束他生命的毒杯，这既象征着对雅典法律的服从，又象征着对自己内心的召唤始终不渝。现在我们看到的就是生命完成升华的那一刻。

这张明信片之所以使我如此震撼，或许是由于它所描述的行为和我自己的成鲜明对比。我在与人谈话时总是重视取悦于人甚于讲真话。为了讨好别人我常常为索然无味的笑话大笑，就像家长对待学校恳亲会演出的开幕式一样。对待陌生人，我常采取饭店守门人对待有钱顾客那种奉承的态度——那是出于讨好所有人的欲望而表现出的过分殷勤。我从不对大多数人认同的观点公开表示怀疑。我努力博取大人物的赏识，每当同他们见过面后，总要久久心怀忐忑，担心他们是否看得上我。经过海关，或是开车在路上遇到与警车并行时，我总有一种莫名其妙的希望，想让穿制服的人对我有好印象。

但是这位哲学家宁愿失欢于众,获罪于邦,而决不折腰。他决不因别人指责而收回自己的思想。而且,他的自信不仅是出于一时冲动或者匹夫之勇,而是来自更深层次的、根植于哲学的源泉。哲学给苏格拉底以坚定的信仰,使他面对千夫所指能够保持合乎理性的而不是歇斯底里的自信。

那一夜,在冰封大地的上空,这种思想的独立性给我以启迪和激励。它向我展示了一种力量,可以抗衡在行动和思想上曲意迎俗的习性。在苏格拉底的生死之间包含着一种召唤,唤起人聪慧的怀疑精神。

广而言之,以这位希腊哲学家为最高象征的主题似乎在召唤我们担负起一项既深刻又可笑的任务,那就是通过哲学求得智慧。尽管古往今来被称作哲学家的思想者千差万别(他们如果聚集在一场大型酒会上,不但互相话不投机,而且很可能几杯酒下肚就要拳脚相向),还是有可能在相隔几世纪之间找到一小群情貌略相似的人,其共同点就是忠于"哲学"一词希腊字根的原义——*philo*①; *sophia*②。人以群分,把这一小群人归在一起的共同爱好在于就人生最大的痛苦的根源向我们说一些宽慰而切合实际的话。我愿从斯人游!

---

① 意为"爱"。——译者
② 意为"智慧"。——译者

（二）

每个社会都有一套观念，应该相信什么，如何待人接物，否则就会遭到怀疑，不容于众。这些社会规范有的是用法律条文明文规定的；更多的则是在一个庞大的伦理和实践的判断体系中本能地遵循的，这个体系叫做"常识"，它命令我们穿什么衣服，采用什么理财标准，尊重什么样的人，遵守什么礼节，以及过什么样的家庭生活。如果对这些规范提出疑问，就会被视为怪异，甚至故意挑衅。常识之所以被悬置起来而不容置疑，是因为人们把它的判断都视为天经地义，不必加以审视。

例如，在平常的谈话中提出问题：我们社会认为工作的目的应该是什么；或是问一对新婚夫妇他们决定结婚的动机是什么；或是向度假的人打问他们旅行的详细设想，都是不合规矩的。

古希腊人也有那么多的常识规范，并同样固执地恪守这些规范。有一个周末，我在布卢姆斯伯里一家二手书店中浏览，看到一套本意是作为儿童读物的历史丛书，里面有许多照片和精美的插图。这套丛书包括《埃及古镇探秘》、

《古堡探秘》等等，我在购买一部关于有毒植物的百科全书的同时，也买了一本《古希腊城镇探秘》。那里面有公元前5世纪希腊城邦中普通的服装。

书中解释说古希腊人信奉多神：爱神、猎神、战神，以及司收成、司火与海之神。他们在进行某种探险之前都要向诸神祈祷，或在神殿里祈祷，或在家中供奉一个小的神龛，还要杀牲口祭祀。牺牲是很昂贵的：祭雅典娜要用一头牛，祭阿耳特弥斯（月神和狩猎女神）和阿佛洛狄特（爱与美的女神）用一头山羊，祭阿斯克勒庇俄斯（医药神）用一只母鸡或公鸡。

希腊人以多蓄奴隶为荣。在公元前5世纪，仅在雅典就有8至10万奴隶，平均每个自由人有3名奴隶。

古希腊人也曾是尚武的，崇拜战场上的勇敢。要做一个公认为合格的男人必须会砍掉敌人的脑袋。如盘子上画的一名雅典士兵正在结束一个波斯人的性命，表明这是正当的行为(此画作于第二次波斯战争之时)。

　　妇女完全在父权和夫权的压制之下。政治和公共生活都没有她们的份,她们既不能继承财产也不能拥有钱财。通常在 13 岁出嫁,丈夫由父亲指定,感情上是否合得来不在考虑之中。

　　所有这一切对苏格拉底同时代人来说都不足为奇。如果有人问他们为什么要杀鸡祭祀阿斯克勒庇俄斯,或是为什么男人一定要杀人才算好样的,他们一定会愕然,或者愤然。这同问为什么冬去春来,或者为什么冰是冷的一样荒唐。

　　但是阻止我们对现状怀疑

的不仅是他人的敌意。我们自己内心的想法可能同样强有力地扼杀我们怀疑的意志，那就是认为既然社会传统规范已经为大多数人遵循了这么长时间，那一定是有道理的，尽管我们不知道那道理到底是什么。我们社会竟然有严重错误，而注意到这一事实的又只有我们自己，那简直不可思议。于是我们抑制自己的怀疑而随大流，因为我们不能想象自己竟然是发现至今不为人知的、艰难的真理的先驱。

正是为了克服自己的怯懦，我们才求助于这位哲学家。

（三）

1. 生平

他于公元前 469 年生于雅典,据说父亲索弗若尼斯库斯是一名雕塑家,母亲斐娜拉底是接生婆。苏格拉底年轻时是哲学家阿基劳斯的学生,从此毕生以哲学为业,却从不把他的哲学思想写下来。他教学从来不收学费,于是很快陷于贫困,不过他对物质财富毫不在意。他一年到头就穿那一件袍子,而且几乎总是打赤脚(有人说他生来蔑视鞋匠)。在他死前已经结婚成家并有三个儿子。他的妻子桑娣帕以凶悍著称(有人问他为什么娶她,他说驯马人需要在最烈性的马身上练习)。他很多时间都花在室外,在雅典的公共场所同朋友谈话。他们欣赏他的智慧和风趣,却很少有人能欣赏他的外表。他身材矮小,大胡子、秃顶,走起路来步子奇怪地摇晃,他那张脸被熟人打过各种比方:螃蟹、猩猩或者怪物,他扁鼻子、大嘴,杂乱的眉毛下一双鼓出的肿泡眼。

但是他最奇特之处还在于行为习惯：他经常走到各种阶层、各种年龄的雅典人跟前贸然发问，根本不管人家会觉得他怪异或者会发火，要他们用确切的词语解释他们为什么相信某些常识，或者他们认为生命的意义是什么。正如一位曾遭他突然袭击的将军所描述的：

> 毫无例外，任何人只要面对苏格拉底，而且开始谈话，不管他起初的话题离得多远，苏格拉底总是能在谈话过程中牵着他的鼻子走，直到最终把他套牢在一个话题之中：让他讲述现在的生活方式，以及过去是如何度过的。一旦给套住了，那么苏格拉底在把他从各个角度彻底审问个遍之前是不会放他走的。

气候和城市布局也助长他这种习惯。雅典一年中有半年天气温暖，增加了在室外萍水相逢就随便交谈的机会。在北方，一般的活动都是在泥筑围墙之内，阴暗、烟雾弥漫的室内进行的，而在阿提卡得天独厚的蓝天之下不需要任何遮蔽。

在熙熙攘攘的正午过后，忧思忡忡的夜晚尚未到来之前，午后的时光特别令人心旷神怡，此时悠然自得地在古希腊的集市上闲逛，在

彩绘的或是饰有厄琉特里奥的浮雕宙斯像的拱顶之下,圆柱之间,同素不相识的过客闲聊,是很平常的事。

城市的规模也正适合居民宴饮交际。大约 24 万人居住在雅典城内及其港口。从位于城市一头的皮雷埃夫斯(一译比雷埃夫斯)步行到另一头埃基厄斯城门,1 小时足够了。这里的居民互相之间的感觉就像是学校的同学,或是共同参加一场婚礼的客人。并不是疯子或是醉汉才在公共场合找陌生人交谈。

我们之所以对现状不予质疑,除了气候和城市规模的因素外,主要是因为我们把大众喜爱和正确混为一谈了。这位赤脚哲学家提出了无数问题,就是为了论定大众喜爱的是否恰巧是正确的。

2. 常识的统治

许多人都被他提出的问题搅得发狂。有的人奚落他,还有少数人恨不得杀了他。在公元前 423 年春季,狄俄尼索斯剧院首演的《云》一剧中,喜剧作家阿里斯托芬为雅典人塑造了一名角色,就是他们中间的这位哲学家的漫画形象,他对一切常识都无礼地、没完没了地刨根问底,不找出其逻辑之前决不接受。扮演苏格拉底的演员在舞台上出现时坐在一个由吊车高挂在天空的篮子里,因为他自称他的头脑在高处能更好地思考。他终日沉醉于重要的思想之中,没有时间梳洗或做家务,因此衣衫总是散发着恶臭,家里脏得到处都是虫子,但是他至少能思考人生最重要的问题,其中包括:一只跳蚤能跳相当于它身体几倍的高度? 蚊子哼哼是从嘴里还是尾部发声? 虽然阿里斯托芬没有就苏格拉底的问题的结果予以展开,观众看完戏以后一定能感觉到问题与结果之间的关系。

阿里斯托芬所表达的是常见的对智者的批评:他们提问题时比那些从不冒险去系统地分析问题的人离常识的观点越来越远。那位喜剧作家与哲学家的分歧就在于是否满足于通常的解释。对这一问题的估计截然不同。在阿里斯托芬看来,正常的人满足于普通的常识:跳蚤由于身材小所以跳得远,蚊子哼哼声总是从某个地方出来的,而苏格拉底是个疯子,因为他悖乎常理,如饥似渴地追寻复杂的、不合常情的另一种答案。

按照苏格拉底的观点,对这种指责的回答是,在某些问题上——也许不一定是跳蚤问题——常识可能更值得深究。他同许多雅典人简短地交谈后,发现对于如何拥有美好生活有着普遍的看法,多数人视为当然,不容置疑,但是令人惊奇的是,事实上这种看法漏洞百出。而人们谈到这种看法时自信的神态说明他们根本没有觉察到这一点。与阿里斯托芬的期待相反,苏格拉底与之对话的那些人似乎不太明白自己在说什么。

3. 两场谈话

据柏拉图的《拉凯斯篇》记载,有一天下午,这位哲学家遇到了两位受人尊敬的将军:尼西亚斯①和拉凯斯。他们都曾在伯罗奔尼撒战争中与斯巴达人作战,因而赢得雅典城里老人的敬重和青年的仰慕。后来,两位将军都战死疆场——拉凯斯在公元前 418 年的曼丁尼亚战役中牺牲,尼西亚斯则于公元前 413 年死于不走运的远征西西里之役。他们都没有留下任何肖像,不过可以想象,他们可能同帕台农

神殿上一组壁画中的两位马上骑士相似。这两位将军坚定地信仰一种被奉为常识的思想:为了证明一个人勇敢,必须参军,在战场上勇往直前,杀死敌人。但是当苏格拉底在露天广场与他们邂逅时,忍不住要再问他们几个问题:

---

① Nicias,公元前 5 世纪雅典军事家和政治家,其家族拥有银矿开采权,为雅典富户之一。——译者

苏格拉底:拉凯斯,我们来说说什么是勇敢,好吗?

拉凯斯:我说,苏格拉底,这太容易了! 如果一个男人自愿与自己的队伍在一起,直面敌人而不逃跑,那他肯定就是勇敢的。

但是苏格拉底记得在公元前479年普拉蒂亚战役①中,希腊军队在斯巴达执政官保萨尼阿斯带领下,先后退,然后才勇敢地打败了马多尼斯领导的波斯军队。

苏格拉底:据称,普拉蒂亚之役,斯巴达人遭遇(波斯人),不愿面对面作战,退了回去。波斯人在追击中打乱了队伍,然后斯巴达人再转回身去像骑兵那样战斗,从而打赢了那一战役。

拉凯斯不得不再思,然后又提出第二种常识的观点:勇敢是一种坚韧精神。但是苏格拉底指出,坚韧精神可以指向鲁莽的目的。为区别勇敢和胡来,还需要另外的因素。拉凯斯的同伴尼西亚斯在苏格拉底指引下,提出勇敢还应

---

① The battle of Plataea,公元前5世纪希腊与波斯作战之处,先是普拉蒂亚人站在希腊人一边打败波斯人,不过牺牲惨重。公元前480年波斯人进行报复,击溃普拉蒂亚城,次年,希腊巴达人又在此大败波斯,是历史上有名的战役。——译者

该包括知识,知道辨别善恶,而且不能总是只限于打仗。

于是,雅典人极为推崇的一种美德,其标准定义之严重不足就在一场短短的室外谈话中揭露出来了。这场谈话证明,原来的定义没有考虑到战场以外也可以有勇敢,也没有考虑到把知识与坚韧精神结合起来的重要性。这个问题也许看来很小,但是其意义深远。如果在此之前,一位将军所受的教育是命令部队撤退就是懦夫行为,尽管撤退在当时是惟一明智的策略,那么重新定义勇敢之后,就使他的选择余地有所拓宽,并且有了应付批评意见的依据。

在柏拉图的《美诺篇》中还有一则苏格拉底同一个对一种常识观点极端坚信的人的谈话。美诺是一名专横跋扈的贵族,从他的故乡塞萨利亚到阿提卡来访问,他对金钱与美德的关系有他自己的看法。他向苏格拉底解释说,要做一个有道德的人必须十分富有,贫穷总是由于个人有缺陷,而不是出于偶然。

我们现在也看不到美诺的画像,不过我在雅典一家旅馆的大厅里翻阅一本希腊男人的杂志时,我想象他可能同画上那位在灯光照耀的游泳池中饮香槟酒的男人相似。

美诺自信十足地告诉苏格拉底,一个有美德的人就是有许多钱买得起好东西的人。苏格拉底问了他几个问题:

苏格拉底:所谓好东西,你是不是指健康、财富之类?

美诺:我的意思包括获得金银,以及城邦的显要职位。

苏格拉底:你心目中的好东西只是这些?

美诺:是的,我指的是一切诸如此类的东西。

苏格拉底:……你在"获得"一词前面要不要加上"正义、正当"的字眼? 你认为有没有区别? 如果是不正当地获得的,你还称之为美德吗?

美诺:当然不啦!

苏格拉底:那么,似乎正义、节制、虔诚,或者其他的美德应该附加于"获得"(金银)之上……事实上,如果在某种情况下……只有用不正当的手段才能获得金银,因此使人缺少金银财富,那么这匮乏本身就是美德。

美诺:看起来是这样。

苏格拉底:那么拥有这些东西并不比缺少这些东西更体现美德……

美诺:看来是逃不出你的结论了。

片刻间,已经向美诺证明了金钱、权势本身不是美德的必要和充足的条件。富人可能值得仰慕,但这取决于他的财富是怎样获得的,正如贫穷本身并不能表明一个人的道德价值一样。没有必然的理由让一名富人自以为他的资产就保证他的美德;也没有什么必然的理由让穷人觉得贫穷本身就是堕落的表现。

4. 为什么别人可能不知道

话题可能会过时,但是其根本意义是没有时间性的:他人也可能错,尽管他们身居要职,尽管他们所采纳的是几世纪来大多数人的信仰。理由很简单,他们没有用逻辑审视他们的信仰。

美诺和两位将军的观念不健全,因为他们没有先论证其逻辑性就全盘吸收了流行的规范。苏格拉底打了一个比方来指出他们这种被动态度的不合理:活着而不作系统思考就好比制作陶器或制鞋而不遵循技术程序,或者根本不知道有技术程序。谁也不能想象单凭直觉就能做出好的陶器或鞋子来;那为什么认为过一种比这要复杂得多的生活,就不需要对其前提和目标进行持续的思考呢?

也许这是因为我们实际上不认为生活有那么复杂。某些困难的活动从外表就看得出很困难;而有些同样困难的事物却看起来很容易。对如何生活有一个健全的观点属于第二类;制作陶器或制鞋属于第一类。

制陶显然是十分艰巨的工作。首先要把泥土运到雅典,通常是从城南 7 英里处的科利亚斯角的一个大坑中取土。然后放在一个轮子上转,每分钟 50 至 100 转,转速与器皿的直径成反比(东西越小,转速越快)。然后进行擦拭、抹平、抛光和装手柄。

下一步是上一种与碳酸钾混合的优质黏土制成的黑釉。等釉干了以后立即放进开着风口的窑内加温到摄氏800度,烧得颜色变成深红,那是黏土硬化成为氧化铁(Fe_2O_3)的结果。然后再全封闭加温到950度,窑里再加一些湿的树叶以维持潮湿,这样,陶身变成灰黑色,而那层釉呈烧结晶的黑色(磁铁矿 Fe_3O_4)。过几个小时,再把风口打开,把叶子耙出来,让温度降到900度。此时釉仍维持第二次火烧成的那种黑色,而陶身又回到了第一次的深红色。

难怪很少有雅典人不假思索就去自己制作陶器。制陶业的艰难谁都可以充分看到。可惜,达到良好的伦理思想却不是如此,这属于另一类表面简单而内里十分复杂的活动。

苏格拉底鼓励我们不要被那些人的信心十足唬住而泄气,他们根本不理会其中的复杂性,至少不如制陶的工序那么严格就断然得出自己的看法。凡公认为显而易见和"当然"的,很少真是如此。认识到这一点,就可以教会我们想到世界比看起来更有可变性,因为传统的成见往往不是从无懈可击的推理中得出来的,而是从几世纪的混沌头脑中涌现出来的。现存的不一定就是合理的。

5. 如何独立思考?

这位哲学家不但帮助我们设想别人可能是错的,他还教给我们一种简便的方法,可以自己决定什么是对的。需要什么条件才能开始过有思想的生活?很少有哲学家比苏格拉底对此的要求更低了:我们不需要受过多年正规教育,也不一定需要闲适的生活。任何人,只要有好奇心、思维正常,有意对一种常识的观念进行评估,就可以随时在街头同一个朋友开始对话,仿效苏格拉底的方法,不到半小时也许就会得出一两个开创性的新思想。

苏格拉底拷问常识的方法在柏拉图的早期和中期的对话录中随处可见,由于其步骤一贯,很容易用说明书、手册类的语言表达而不走样,并适用于任何被灌输的、或者想要反抗的思想信仰。这一方法告诉我们:一项论断是否正确,不取决于它是否是大多数人的主张,或长期为重要人物所信仰。只有不能被合乎理性地驳倒的论断才是正确的。不能证伪的论断才是真理。如果能够被合乎理性地驳倒,能够被证伪,那么不论有多少人相信,不论相信它的人多伟大,这种论断也是错的,我们应该怀疑它。

苏格拉底式的思辨方法

（1）取一种为世所认定的常识论断：

勇敢的行为要求坚守阵地不后退。

有美德的人需要有钱。

（2）想象一下这一论断可能是错的,尽管说这话的人充满自信。寻找这一论断可能不对的情境。

是否存在在战场上后退的勇士?

是否存在坚守阵地而并不勇敢的人?

一个人能否有钱而无德?

一个人能否无钱而有德?

（3）如果对以上问题找到例外情况,那么原来的定义就是错的,或者至少不准确。

勇敢而后退是可能的。

坚守阵地而并不勇敢是可能的。

有钱而为卑鄙小人是可能的。

贫穷而道德高尚是可能的。

（4）最初的论断必须考虑到以上例外并将之精确细腻

地表达。

在战场上退或进都可以是勇敢行为。

有钱人只有财产取之以道才可称为有美德;而有些无钱的人可能有美德,因为其处境使美德与赚钱不能两全。

(5)如果随后又找到了对以上修正过的论断来说的例外,那么整个过程再重复一遍。真理——就迄今为止人类可以企及的而言——寓于一项看来驳不倒的论断。追求真理,就是发现我们原来差不多认定为是的其实为非。

(6)不论阿里斯托芬如何加以歪曲,思考的产物总是优于直觉的产物。

当然,不经过哲学思辨也有可能获致真理。即使不用苏格拉底的方法,我们也会认识到如果处境使道德与赚钱不能两全,一个没钱的人是可以称为道德高尚的,或者在战场上进退都可以是勇敢行为。但是,除非我们先已对反对的意见作过彻底的逻辑思考,遇到有人不同意我们的意见,我们就会不知如何应付。如果有一位盛气凌人的人物断然表示:金钱是道德的要素,或者只有懦夫才在战场上后退,我们就无言以对。缺乏反击的论据作后盾力量(犹如普拉蒂亚战役和在腐化的社会中致富),我们只能理不直气不壮地、或是蛮横地说,我觉得我是对的,但是不能解释为什么。

意见虽然正确,但不知道如何理性地回应反对的意见,苏格拉底称之为"原始意见",以别于"知识"——那就是不但知道一种看法之所以为真,而且还知道另一种看法之所以为伪。"原始意见"比"知识"逊一筹。苏格拉底把这两种对真理的认知比作著名雕塑家代达罗斯的优美的作品:由直觉得来的认知犹如一尊塑像放在室外的底座上而没有支撑,随时可以被一阵大风刮倒;

而以理智和反诘的论据为支撑的认知则犹如用绳索钉牢在地上的塑像。

苏格拉底的思辨法向我们提供了一种获致结论的途径,这样达成的意见可以经得起狂风暴雨而信心不动摇。

（四）

苏格拉底在 70 岁时遭遇了一场风暴。3 名雅典人——诗人米利图斯、政治家阿尼图斯和演说家莱昂——认定他是一个怪诞的恶人。他们指责他不敬城邦之神,腐蚀了雅典的社会构成,唆使年轻人反对他们的父辈。他们认为应该让他沉默,甚至杀死他。

雅典城邦已经建立起一套分辨是非的程序。赫里阿斯特法庭①位于集市之南,那是一幢庞大的建筑,一头是陪审团员坐的长凳,另一头是公诉人和被告方的讲坛。审判开始先由公诉人讲话,接着被告讲话。然后由 200 到 2500 人组成的陪审团投票或举手表决是非曲直。这种用计算赞成的人数来决定某种主张的是非的办法贯穿于雅典的整个政治和法律生活中。一个月中有两三次,全城的男性公民,大约 3 万人,应邀到集市西南的普尼克斯山头集会,用举手表决的办法决定城邦的重大问题。对于城邦来说,多数人的意见就等同于真理。

---

① the Court of the Heliasts,古雅典法庭,一般由 500 或以上人数的陪审员组成,陪审员从 30 岁以上的男性公民中产生。——译者

审判苏格拉底那天,陪审团有 500 名公民。公诉人一开始就要他们把站在他们面前的这位哲学家当作一个不诚实的人。他上天入地刨根问底,他提出异端邪说,他善于用闪烁的辞藻让弱理战胜强理,他故意通过谈话腐蚀年轻人,对他们施加邪恶的影响。

苏格拉底对这些指控进行申辩。他解释说,他从未对天上或地下的事物提出过理论;他信奉神明,并非异端;他从未腐蚀过雅典的青年,只不过有些逍遥自在的富家子弟模仿了他的提问法,证明某些重要人物无知,使他们感到恼火。即使他误导了任何人,那也是无意的,他没有理由故意对同伴施加坏影响,因为他们有可能反过来伤害他自己。如果他曾无意中误导了什么人,那么正确的程序应该是在私下纠正他,而不是公开审判。

他承认他的生活方式显得有点特别:

> 我对许多人关心的事弃置不顾——赚钱、经营房产、追求军职或文职的荣誉,或其他权力地位,或参加政治团体以及本城邦的政党。

但是,他从事哲学的动机是出于改善雅典人生活的朴素愿望。

我设法劝告你们每一个人少想一些实际利益，而多想一些精神和道德的福祉。

　　他解释说，他已献身于哲学，因此即使陪审团以他放弃哲学活动为释放他的条件，他也不可能放弃：

　　我将继续像平时一样说："我的好朋友，你们是雅典人，属于因智慧和力量而著称于世的最伟大的城邦。可是你们孜孜于争名逐利，而不思考如何理解真理，如何改善自己的灵魂，不觉得惭愧吗？"假如有人争辩说自己不是那种人，还是关心真理和灵魂的，那么我不会放他走或离他而去，而要对他进行盘问，让他经过考验……我将要对所有我遇到的人这样做，不论老、少、本邦人或是外邦人。

　　现在轮到那500名陪审员来决定了。他们经过简短的讨论后，220人决定苏格拉底无罪，280人认为有罪。哲学家苦笑说："我没想到比分那么接近。"不过他没有丧失信心，没有犹豫，没有惊慌；他坚持对一种哲学方案的信仰，虽然他的听众刚刚以56％的多数宣判其为荒谬。

　　如果我们做不到这样的泰然自若，如果我们听了几句对我们的性格或业绩的严厉批评就忍不住掉眼泪，那可能是因为我们相信自己正确的能力主要是由他人的赞许构成的。我们对于不受世人喜爱很在意，不仅是出于实用的理由——例如生存或升迁,更重要的是世人的嘲弄似乎是一种信号,毫不含糊地表明我们已误入歧途。

苏格拉底自然也会承认我们有时可能是错的,我们的观点可以怀疑,但是他会提出一项至关重要的细节来改变我们对真理与不受世人喜爱之间的关系的认识:我们的思想和生活方式的错误决不能简单地以遭到反对来证明。

我们应该关心的不是反对我们的人数,而是他们反对的理由有多充分。所以我们的注意力应该由不受世人喜爱转向解释其所以然。社会上占很大比例的人认为我们是错的,听起来怪吓人的。但是在放弃我们的立场之前先要审视一下他们得出这一结论所用的方法。我们对他们的反对意见给予多少重视,应取决于他们论证方法是否健全。

但是我们似乎被一种相反的倾向所折磨:每个人的话都听,每一句不中听的或是嘲讽的意见都足以使我们心烦意乱。我们往往不能反思一个最主要的也是最令人宽慰的问题:这些阴暗的指责的依据是什么?我们常把经过深思熟虑的诚实的批评者与出于愤世和妒忌的反对意见相提并论。

我们应该花点时间看看批评的背面。如苏格拉底了解到的，尽管经过小心掩饰，其思想的基础可能是极端歪斜的。我们的批评者可能凭着心血来潮摸索到结论，或者出于冲动或偏见，然后利用他们的地位抬高他们的点滴直觉。他们的思想可能就是像喝得醉醺醺的业余制陶人那样建立起来的。

不幸的是，与陶器不同，思想产品的优劣极难一眼就分辨出来。分辨哪一件陶器是醉汉做的，哪一件是清醒的工匠做的并不难。

可是要立即确定以下两个定义的优劣，就要难得多：

ἡ φρόνιμος χαρτερία
ἔστιν ἀνδρεία.[1]
ἀνδρεῖός ἐστι ὃς ἂν ἐν τῇ τάξει
μένων μάχηται τοῖς πολεμίοις.[2]

一种坏思想以权威的方式提出来，往往可以在一段时期内具备好思想的分量，尽管并没有证据说明它是如何产生的。而我们只注意结论，就会养成尊重错了人的习惯。所以苏格拉底敦促我们把注意力放在他们得出结论的逻辑上。即使我们逃避不了遭遇反对的后果，我们至少可以免

---

[1] 希腊文，意为"明智而坚韧不拔谓之勇"。——译者
[2] 希腊文，意为"坚守阵地，疆场杀敌者为勇士"。——译者

去自以为非的那种软弱感。

这一想法最初提出是在审判之前不久。有一次苏格拉底与一位从西西里来雅典访问的著名修辞学教师波卢斯对话。波卢斯有一些令人不寒而栗的政治观点，热切地想以之说服苏格拉底。波卢斯认为对于人来说，幸福生活的核心莫过于做僭主，因为专制统治可以让人随心所欲，把敌人投入监狱，褫夺其财产，处决他们。

苏格拉底彬彬有礼地听着，然后用一系列的论据回答，企图证明幸福在于行善。但是波卢斯不为所动，坚持自己的看法，指出专制君主常常得到大多数民众的尊敬，并举马其顿的国王阿基劳斯为例，他谋杀了他的叔父、侄子和 7 岁的合法继承人，但仍享有雅典广大公众的支持。波卢斯得出结论说，喜欢阿基劳斯的人数就是一种标志，证明他关于专制的理论是正确的。

苏格拉底谦恭地表示，确实要找到喜欢阿基劳斯的人比较容易，而找到支持幸福在于行善这一看法的人较难，他解释说："假如你想找证人，证明我说的话是错的，你可以指望几乎全雅典的人都同意你的观点，不论是土生土长的还是外地来的。"

如果你愿意，尼塞拉特斯之子尼西亚斯连同他的兄弟们都会支持你，他们拥有狄俄尼索斯(酒神)的领地那一整排祭坛。斯凯利尤之子阿里斯托克拉得也会支持你……你要愿意，还可以拜访整个伯里克利家族,或者你选择的任何雅典世家。

但是苏格拉底激烈地否认对波卢斯的论点这种广泛的
支持本身足以证明其正确。

问题在于,波卢斯,你想把人们在诉讼中认为行之有效
的那一套巧辩法用在我身上。在法庭上,人们也以为只要
举出一大批显赫的证人支持他们的观点,而对方只能举出一
名证人,甚至举不出证人,就可以证明对方是错的。但是这
种辩论用之于真理是毫无价值的,因为在法庭上被一大帮不
约而同反对自己的、望之俨然的证人击败是完全可能的。

真正的尊严不是来自多数人的意志,而是来自正当的
说理。我们在制作陶器时,必须听从那些知道如何把釉在
800 度高温下变成 Fe_3O_4 的人的意见;我们造一艘船时,要
在意的是那些造过三层划桨战船的人的判断;我们考虑伦
理问题时——如何做一个幸福、勇敢、正义和善良的人——
不应该被坏思想吓住,尽管它出自修辞学大师、威武的将军
和衣着考究的塞萨利贵族之口。

这听起来像精英主义,的确如此。并不是每个人的话
都值得听。不过苏格拉底的精英主义决无丝毫势利和偏
见。他也许对涉及的观点区别对待,但这种区别的考虑决
不是基于阶级和财富,也不是基于军功或国籍,而是基于理

性——他强调,理性是人人都能获得的功能。

要追随苏格拉底的榜样,我们就该在遇到批评时像训练有素的奥林匹克运动会的运动员一样行动。《古希腊城镇探秘》一书提供了关于体育的进一步情况。

姑且想象我们自己是运动员。教练教给我们一种为掷标枪而锻炼腿力的方法。这需要金鸡独立举起重物。在外人看来这样子很怪,他们嘲弄我们,说我们虚掷了成功的机会。我们在澡堂里听到有人窃窃私语,说我们 ἡμῖν μέλει μᾶλλον τὸ τά σκέλη καλὰ ἐπιδεικνύναι ἢ τὸ βοηθεῖν τῆ πόλει πρὸς τὴν ὀλυμπιονίκην. ① 这话够尖刻的,但是没有什么可惊慌的,只要听听苏格拉底同他的朋友克里托的对话就行了:

苏格拉底:当一个人认真训练时,他应该一视同仁地用心听取所有的赞赏和批评意见,还是只听一位有资格的人的话:医生或教练?

---

① 希腊文,意为"对炫耀小腿的肌肉比对为本市赢得比赛更感兴趣"。——译者

克里托:应该只听一位有资格的人的话。

苏格拉底:那么他就只应该害怕那一位有资格的人的批评,欢迎他的称赞,而不理会来自广大公众的毁誉。

克里托:显然是的。

苏格拉底:他应该按照有专业知识的教练的判断调整自己的行动、练习和饮食,而不是其他大众的意见。

批评的价值取决于批评者的思想程序,而不是人数的多少或是他们所在的阶层。

你难道不认为这是一个良好的原则:并非所有人的意见都应该得到尊重,只应该尊重一部分人的意见,而不是另一部分人的意见……应该尊重好的意见而不是坏的意见……好意见出自对事物有所理解的人,坏意见出自缺乏理解的人……

所以,我亲爱的朋友,即使公众对我们说三道四,我们也不必那么在意,而应重视专家对有关正义与非正义的事物所说的话。

坐在赫里阿斯特法庭长凳上的陪审团成员们不是专家。这些人当中老人和伤兵的人数超常,他们把当陪审员作为一项额外收入的来源。陪审员的酬劳是一天 3 奥波勒斯,少于一个体力劳动者的日工资,不过对一个 63 岁、家居无聊的人来说也不无小补。成为一名陪审员惟一的条件就是雅典公民、思想健全、不负债——不过思想健全并不是根据苏格拉底的标准，而只是能够走一条直线，并在提问时说出自己的名字。陪审员在审讯过程中常常打瞌睡，其中很少人有过类似案例的经验或熟悉相关的法规，也没有人就如何得出判决给过他们任何指导。

审判苏格拉底的陪审员是带着强烈的偏见来的。他们已经受到阿里斯托芬丑化苏格拉底的影响，并且觉得这位哲学家对于曾经辉煌一时的本城邦在世纪末遭受的灾难起了一定的作用。伯罗奔尼撒战争的结局是灾难性的，斯巴达和波斯联盟迫使雅典屈膝投降，城邦遭到封锁，舰队被毁，帝国被支解。贫困地区瘟疫流行，民主受到专制制度的镇压，成千公民死于其罪恶之手。对苏格拉底的敌人说来，许多僭主曾经与这位哲学家有过过从决非偶然。克里底亚①与卡尔米德曾同苏格拉底谈过伦理问题，似乎他们谈话结果所得就是嗜杀的狂热。

雅典如此令人瞩目地盛极而衰的原因是什么？为什么这座希腊最伟大的城邦，75 年前曾在普拉蒂亚陆上和米卡利海上打败过斯巴达，如今却要忍受这一系列的屈辱？那个披着肮脏的大衣在街上闲荡，对明白不过的事发出疑问的人就被当作现成的、但是完全错误的答案。

---

① Critias，雅典诗人和演说家，曾经是苏格拉底的学生，后来是僭主党的领袖，斯巴达人打败雅典人之后为统治雅典的 30 名僭主之一。——译者

苏格拉底明白，他是没有希望胜诉的。他甚至没有时间进行辩护。被告只有几分钟向陪审团讲话的时间，也就是法庭时钟的水从一钵滴满另一钵的光景。

我深信我从未故意错待过别人，但是我不能说服你们相信这一点，因为我们讨论的时间实在太少。如果你们同其他民族一样，不是用一天而是好几天的时间进行重大审判的听证，我想你们也许会被说服，但是在目前情况下，要在短短的时间内开脱这样严重的指控是很不容易的。

雅典的法庭可不是发现真理的讲坛。那只是一群上了年纪或是一条腿的人的匆匆集会，他们从不把自己的意见置于理性的审视之下，而是一心等待着法庭时钟的水从一钵滴满另一钵。

坚持这样想洵非易事。一定需要从成年累月与普通雅典人谈话中所汲取的那种力量，足以做到在某种情况下不理会别人的意见。苏格拉底并非有意如此，他不理会那些意见不是出于愤世嫉俗，那样做就会违反他自己的信念：每个人都有潜在的理性。但是他大半生黎明即起同雅典人谈话，了解他们是如何思想的，看到了一些可惜他们自己通常看不到的东西，尽管他希望有一天他们也能看到。他观察到他们倾向于凭心血来潮决定立场,接受世俗的定论而不加质疑。他在最高权威的反对面前坚持己见并不是出于狂妄。他具有一个理性的人的自信,因为他了解,对手的思维方法常常不正确,尽管他远不是自以为一贯正确。对手的反对就足以置他于死地;不一定需要证明他是错的。

当然,他可以放弃自己的哲学而得到生路。即使被判有罪以后,还可以逃避死刑,但是他的顽强不屈使他错过了这一机会。我们不能从苏格拉底那里学到如何逃避死刑,但是如何在不合逻辑的反对面前维持信心和清醒的立场,他应该是我们至高无上的榜样。

哲学家的演讲曲终奏雅,激情满怀:

> 如果你们处死我,你们将很难再找到我这样的人。事实上,打个玩笑的比方,我是受神灵委派附在这个城邦身上的,这座城就像是一匹良种马,由于身躯太大,容易懒散,需要牛虻蜇一蜇……如果你们听从我的意见,就会让我活下去。但是,我猜想,不久你们就会从瞌睡中醒来,听从阿尼图斯的话,一巴掌把我打死,然后再接着睡。

他没有猜错。当大法官要求第二次,也是最终表决时,陪审团中360人投票赞成把哲学家处死。然后,陪审员回家,死刑犯被带到监狱。

（五）

可以想见,监狱黑暗而封闭,街上传来的声音中免不了有雅典人的讥诮声,他们巴望这个长着妖怪脸的思想者快死。他本来会一判刑立刻处决的,只是这一判决时间恰好与雅典人每年一度的提洛节①巧合,根据传统,在这个时候城邦不能处死任何人。苏格拉底的善良性格赢得了狱卒的同情,狱卒允许他接待来访者,从而减轻他最后日子的痛苦。来探视他的人川流不息:斐多、克里托和儿子克里托布卢什、阿波罗多罗斯、赫莫杰尼斯、厄庇根尼、埃斯基涅斯、安提西尼、克特西普、美涅克赛努、西米斯、克贝、斐多尼得、欧克利德斯以及忒耳西翁。眼看着一个对他人只有巨大的善意和好奇心的人像罪犯一样等待被处死,大家都掩盖不住自己的哀痛。

虽然大卫的画表现苏格拉底为悲痛欲绝的朋友所围绕,但我们不要忘记,他们对苏格拉底的爱是在误解和仇恨的汪洋大海中突显出来的。

---

① Delos,爱琴海小岛,在苏格拉底时代属于雅典,相传为太阳神阿波罗的诞生地,在那里每年举行祭祀阿波罗的节日。——译者

为了与牢房内情景形成反差和追求多样化，可能狄德罗会鼓励有些以饮鸩为题材的画家捕捉其他雅典人对苏格拉底之死的情绪——其结果可能出现这样的画面：例如题为"五名陪审员在法庭度过一天后正在玩牌"，或者"指控者晚饭后正准备就寝"。喜欢煽情的画家可以干脆就把这些场景题作"苏格拉底之死"。

当那一天来到时，只有苏格拉底一人保持平静。他的妻子和三个孩子被带来看他，但是桑娣帕哭得呼天抢地，苏格拉底让人把她带走。他的朋友们比较安静，但也是涕泗滂沱。即使那个见惯了多少人赴死的狱卒也为之动容，尴尬地向他告别：

> "你住在这里的期间，使我认识了你，在所有到这种地方来的人里面，你是最慷慨、最仁慈、最好的人……你知道我是来传什么信的：那么，别了！要来的事不可避免，就请

好自为之吧，"他说完，含着眼泪掉头而去。

然后行刑者来了，手里端着一杯毒药：

苏格拉底见到此人就说："朋友，你是这类事的专家，你
说该怎么做?"他说："就是把它喝下去，然后在屋里走，直到
两腿发沉，然后躺下，它就会自己发作了。"说完，他把杯子递
过去，苏格拉底平静地接过来……手不发抖，面不改色……
他把杯子放到唇边一饮而尽，神色怡然，并不觉得味道苦涩。
到那时为止，我们多数人还能忍住泪(据斐多的叙述)；但是
当我们看着他真的喝下去时，再也忍不住了，眼泪夺眶而出，
不能自已……在我之前，克里托已经控制不住眼泪而走开
了。阿波罗多罗斯早就一直在流泪，此时不禁哭出声来，他
使得每一个在场的人都不能自持，除了苏格拉底本人。

哲学家请求他的伙伴们平静下来——"这像什么样子，
我的怪朋友!"他逗他们说。然后站起来在牢房里走动，让毒
性发作。等他觉得两腿发沉时，就仰卧下来，腿脚开始失去知
觉；毒性向上发展，到达胸口时他逐渐失去意识，呼吸缓慢。
克里托见他的挚友的眼睛定住了，就走过去将它闭上。

这就是我们的同伴的结局(斐多说)……我们能够公平
地说，他是所有我们知道的同时代人中最勇敢、最智慧、最

正直的人。

我自己也情不自禁流下泪来。也许因为据说苏格拉底的脑袋是球状的，两眼距离特别宽，他死去的情景使我想起了我看《象人》录像带时为之哭泣的那个下午。

两个人都遭受了人生最悲惨的命运：行善而被判为恶。

我们也许从来没有因身体缺陷而遭嘲弄，也没有因我们一生的工作而被判死刑。但是那种被误解的场景带有某种普遍性，以上的故事是其最完美的悲剧性的例证。社会生活充满了别人对我们的看法和我们的实情之间的差距。我们谨慎会被指责为愚蠢，我们腼腆会被认为骄傲，我们愿与人同，却被认为谄媚。我们竭力要澄清误解，但是我们口干舌燥，词不达意。我们的死敌占据了有权摆布我们的位置，他们向别人谴责我们。在导致这位无辜哲学家的冤案的仇恨中，我们听出了自己所受到的伤害的回响，是那些不能够或不愿意公平对待我们的人加于我们的伤害。

但是这个故事里也包括报应。哲学家死后不久，公众

的情绪就开始转变。伊索克拉底写道:欧里庇得斯的戏剧
《帕拉米德》上演时,苏格拉底的名字一出现,观众就哭了;
狄奥多罗斯说,指控苏格拉底的人最后被雅典人私刑处死。
普卢塔克告诉我们,雅典人对那些指控者恨之入骨,拒绝与
他们共浴,在社交场合排挤他们,最后他们在绝望中自缢身
亡。第欧根尼·拉尔修的叙述称,苏格拉底死后不久,雅典
城就判处米利图斯死刑,流放了阿尼图斯和莱昂,并斥巨资
为苏格拉底树立了一尊青铜像,是大雕塑家利西波斯制
作的。

　　哲学家预言,雅典人最终会同他一样看问题,的确如
此。这样的报应简直令人难以置信。我们往往忘记,偏见
与妒忌消退是需要时间的。这个故事鼓励我们,在自己与
世不合时不是通过当地陪审团的讥讽的眼神来解释何以
故。苏格拉底被 500 名智力有限的男人审判,他们由于雅典
在伯罗奔尼撒战争中失败而心怀非理性的疑虑,被告的样
子又很怪。但是他仍对更为广大的法庭抱有信心。我们虽
然在某一时间住在某地,但是通过这一范例,可以在想象中
置身于有希望受到更加客观的审判的时代和地域。我们也
许不能及时说服本地的陪审团支持我们,但是我们可以从
后代做出的判决的希望中得到慰藉。

　　但是苏格拉底之死也可能使我们有被误导的危险。它
可能使我们形成一种自我欣赏的信念,在被多数人憎恨与

正确之间建立必然的联系。好像天才和圣人的命运就是先受误解，然后由利西波斯给他们塑铜像。我们可能既非天才又非圣人。我们也可能利用这一范例挑战理性，幼稚地相信，当别人指出我们错了时，我们最正确不过了。

这不是苏格拉底的意图。认为与世不合就是真理的同义词与认为与世不合是错误的同义词一样幼稚。一种思想或行动是否有价值不取决于它广受赞同或广受攻击，而取决于它是否合乎逻辑规则。一个论点不能因为多数人谴责就是错的，但也不能以英雄的姿态总是对抗多数，以为这样就一定正确。

哲学家向我们指出一条路，可以摆脱两种强有力的错觉：应该永远听从舆论，或是决不听从舆论。

如果我们追随他的榜样，努力做到永远听从理性的律令，就会得到最大回报。

第二章

对缺少钱财的慰藉

（一）快乐，一张需求清单

1. 一幢乔治王朝时期风格的新古典式住宅，位于伦敦市中心肯辛顿（坎普顿山路，霍恩顿街）、荷兰公园（奥布里路）、切尔西（马克姆广场，天堂人行道）。外表颇似亚当兄弟设计的皇家艺术学会的正面直立图（1772—1774）。古希腊式棕叶雕花拱顶、外加爱奥尼亚式圆柱的宽大的威尼斯式三套窗，足以捕捉伦敦午后的残阳余晖。

一楼起居室里的天花板和壁炉的图案与罗伯特·亚当①为健伍馆②设计的图书室相似。

2. 一架以法恩伯勒或比金山为基地的喷气飞机（是达索公司的游隼900C，或湾流Ⅳ型飞机），为神经紧张的驾驶员装有航空电子设备、近地警告系统、大气紊流探测雷达及二类自动着陆的自动驾驶仪。在垂直尾翼上，代替标准的条纹形图案的是静物写生名画的片断，例如陈列于普拉多博物馆③的委拉斯开兹④画的鱼，或者桑切斯·科坦⑤的"果蔬画"中的三只柠檬。

3. （意大利）卢卡附近马利亚地方的奥赛蒂别墅。从卧

---

① Robert Adam(1728—1792)，英国著名建筑设计师，其父亲、兄弟都是建筑师。他经常与其兄弟合作进行设计，风格与法国路易十六的相似。——译者
② Kenwood House，伦敦著名新古典主义建筑，位于伦敦北部，1764—1773年由罗伯特·亚当改建，以建筑风格、精致庭园和名画收藏著称。——译者
③ Prado，该博物馆在西班牙马德里，是著名的绘画与雕塑博物馆，特别以陈列西班牙、意大利的名画著称。——译者
④ Diego Rodriguez de Silvay Velázquez(1599—1660)，西班牙著名画家，被认为是17世纪最伟大的画家之一。——译者
⑤ F. Juan Sánchez Cotán(1561—1627)，西班牙著名画家，其水果和蔬菜画形成自己独特的风格。——译者

室可以观水景，可以听喷泉。屋后玉兰花绕墙，冬有阳台，夏有大树遮荫，供嬉戏的草坪绿草如茵。带顶篷的花园呵护着无花果和蜜桃尽情生长。柏树成方，薰衣草与橘树成行，还有一个橄榄园。

4. 一间大书房，一张大书桌，一座壁炉架，窗户面对花园。纸张泛黄、手感粗糙的古版书籍散发出宜人的幽香。书架顶上排列着历代伟大思想家的半身像和占星学用的地球仪。俨然如为荷兰威廉三世国王住宅设计的书房。

5. 与林肯郡贝尔顿馆[①]的餐厅相似的大餐厅,一张 12 个座位的橡木餐桌,常客皆知友,谈笑多雅谑,相互关爱有加。有周到的厨师、无微不至的仆役,麻烦事都有人操心(厨师有几样拿手菜:夏南瓜烙饼、白蘑菇面条、鱼汤、意大利肉汁烩饭、鹌鹑、海鲂,还有烤鸡)。一间小起居室供饭后休憩,用茶和巧克力。

6. 一张卧床正好嵌入壁龛(犹如巴黎的让-佛朗索瓦·布隆代尔[②]设计的那样)。每天一换的床单浆洗挺刮使脸颊

---

① Belton House,英国林肯郡著名乡村俱乐部建筑,始建于 1685—1688 年,后经过名建筑师改建,以园林风景和艺术品、家具、地毯等的陈列著称。——译者
② Jacque-Francois Blondel(1705—1774),原文为"Jean",疑是"Jacque"之误,法国著名建筑家,对路易十六时代的建筑风格有较大影响。——译者

生凉。床极大,脚趾顶不到头,供人在上面纵情翻滚。两间小耳房,一间放饮水和饼干,一间放电视。

7. 一间宽敞无比的浴室,镶贝壳图案的蓝色大理石澡盆安放在室中央隆起的平台上,用脚跟就可开关的水龙头放出宽广而柔和的水。从澡盆可望见天光,石灰岩地板加热供暖,庞培城里伊希斯神庙壁画的复制品悬于四壁。

8. 充足的钱财,靠利息的利息就能生活。

9. 度周末则可在法国"城市之岛"①租一套顶层豪华套间,室内配备着法国最辉煌(也是最孱弱)的路易十六时期的家具:格雷文尼士式半月形五斗柜、绍尼埃式壁架、范德克鲁斯-拉·克鲁瓦式的床头柜②。早晨赖在床上读《巴黎一览》杂志,嚼着盛在塞夫瓷盘中的巧克力面包,同乔瓦尼·贝利尼③的《圣母像》的复制品闲聊生命的意义,间或开开玩笑(那幅画的原作陈列在威尼斯学院的画廊)。画像上

---

① Ile de la Cité,更通常的名称是圣路易岛(Ile de la Saint-Louis),巴黎附近的一个小岛,是巴黎最昂贵的度假地区。——译者
② 以上名字都是18世纪法国和意大利著名家具设计师和品牌。——译者
③ Giovanni Bellini(1430—1516),意大利对威尼斯画派有突出贡献的著名绘画世家之一员。其圣母像为文艺复兴时代的宗教画把神人性化的代表作之一。——译者

忧伤的表情掩盖不住一种冷面幽默和自然流露的天性。完全可以想象她穿着阿涅丝·B或马克斯·玛拉名牌时装在(巴黎)马莱区附近散步。

（二）

有一位哲学家，在那通常厌恶享乐、以艰苦自律的同行中是个异类。他似乎理解这种对享乐的向往，并愿对享乐有所帮助。他写道："如果我把口腹之乐、性爱之欢、悦耳之娱、见窈窕倩影而柔情荡漾，一概摈弃，那我将无法设想善为何物。"

伊壁鸠鲁于公元前341年生于靠近小亚细亚西岸、四季常青的萨摩斯岛。他很早就为哲学所吸引，14岁长途跋涉，去听柏拉图学派的帕非勒和原子论哲学家瑙西芬①的讲课。但是他对他们讲的很多都不同意，于是在不到30岁时决心把他的思想整理成自己的人生哲学。据说他写了300部书，题材无所不包：《论情爱》、《论音乐》、《论公平交易》、《论人生》（共4卷），以及《论自然》（共37卷），不过几个世纪以来由于一连串的灾难，几乎全部散失，结果他的哲学思想只能根据幸存的断篇残帙，加上后来的伊壁鸠鲁信徒的证言重新建立起来。

他的哲学最显著的与众不同之处就是强调感官的快

---

① Nausiphanes，公元前4世纪希腊原子学派哲学家，一般认为他是伊壁鸠鲁第一位导师。——译者

乐:"快乐是幸福生活的起点和目标,"伊壁鸠鲁如是说。他只是肯定了许多人早已有的,而鲜为哲学所接受的想法。这位哲学家承认他酷爱美食:"一切善的根源来自口腹之乐,就是智慧和文化也必须与此相关。"行使得当的哲学相当于快乐指南:

> 如果有人自称对研究哲学尚未准备好,或者已经错过了时候,那就等于说他不是太年轻就是太老,不能享受快乐。

很少有哲学家这样坦率地承认自己爱好享乐的生活方式。许多人为此感到震惊,特别是当他们听说伊壁鸠鲁吸引了一些富人的支持,起初是在达达尼尔海峡的兰普萨库斯,后来是在雅典,并且用他们的钱建立了一所哲学学校来推进快乐。这所学校男女都招收,鼓励他们在一起生活和学习享乐。外人一想到学校里面的所作所为,既让好奇心撩得心头痒痒,又在道德上予以谴责。

经常有心怀不满的伊壁鸠鲁信徒透露出那些在讲课间隙中的活动。伊壁鸠鲁的助手梅特多鲁斯的兄弟蒂莫克拉特散布传言称伊壁鸠鲁一天要呕吐两次,因为他吃得太多了。斯多葛派的狄奥提马做了一件刻薄的事:他发表了 50 封淫荡的信件,硬说是伊壁鸠鲁酒醉之后性欲狂乱时写的。

尽管有这些抨击,伊壁鸠鲁的学说仍然从者甚众。这一学说在地中海地区广为传播;叙利亚、犹地亚、埃及、意大利和高卢都成立了快乐学派;它的影响持续了 500 年,只是在西罗马帝国衰落过程中才逐渐为残暴的野蛮人和基督教徒的敌视所消灭。不过在此之后,伊壁鸠鲁的名字以形容词的形式进入了多种语言,表述他的爱好(牛津英语词典:"伊壁鸠鲁的:致力于追求享乐,引申为:奢侈,肉欲,饕餮")。

这位哲学家去世 2340 年之后,我在伦敦一家报刊发行店中浏览,发现几份名为《伊壁鸠鲁式生活》的杂志,那是一种关于旅馆、游艇和饭店的季刊,印刷的纸张像擦亮的苹果一样光鲜。

伍斯特郡还有一家以伊壁鸠鲁命名的小餐馆,向顾客提供幽静的环境、高背座椅、扇形海贝烤意大利肉汁烩饭配白蘑菇,以此作为对伊壁鸠鲁的爱好的进一步解读。

（三）

从古到今，从斯多葛派的狄奥提马到《伊壁鸠鲁式生活》杂志的编辑，伊壁鸠鲁哲学所引起的联想如此一贯，说明一提起"快乐"，似乎其涵义就不言而喻。"怎样才能快乐？"如果不提钱的话，根本不是个难题。

但是，"怎样才能健康？"就比较难回答。例如我们有时为无名头痛所苦，或者晚饭之后剧烈腹痛。我们知道是有问题，但是难以找到解决办法。

人在痛苦中，往往会想到一些稀奇古怪的治疗法：蚂蟥、放血、荨麻汤、钻孔等等。太阳穴跳得疼痛难忍，好像整个头盖骨都在不断收紧的紧箍中，脑袋随时要爆裂。此时直觉最需要的是在头骨中放进一些空气来。患者要求他的朋友把他的头放在桌上，在脑袋的一侧钻一个小孔。几小时之后，他死于脑出血。

尽管许多候诊室的气氛令人不快,人们一般还是认为有病应该找医生,那是因为一个对人体运行有深刻研究的人总比凭直觉的人能指出更好的健康之道。医学存在的前提,就是外行人对于身体不适的糊涂观念与讲道理的医生所能获得的比较准确的知识之间的差距。医生的作用就是弥补病人对自己身体的无知,有时这种无知可能是致命的。

　　伊壁鸠鲁学说的核心就是:我们凭直觉回答"怎样才能快乐?"同凭直觉回答"怎样才能健康?"一样糟糕。立即出现的答案往往是错。我们灵魂对自身的病痛并不见得比我们身体对病痛陈述得更清楚,我们凭直觉的诊断也不会比对身体的诊断更准确。钻洞疗法象征着我们理解自身有多困难,这一象征意义既适用于肉体也适用于精神。

　　有一个人心中感到很不惬意。早晨懒得起床,对家人

一名铁匠;一名鞋匠;一名鱼贩

闷闷不乐,心不在焉。他直觉地归罪于他选择的职业不好,于是不惜付出高的代价谋求改行。这是我最后一次参考《古希腊城镇探秘》一书。

他急忙认定从事渔业会更快活,于是买了渔网并以高价在市场买了一个摊位。但是他的愁闷并不稍减。

用伊壁鸠鲁派诗人卢克莱修的话说,我们经常"如病人不知病因"。

我们找医生是因为他们对肉体的疾病比我们知道的多。同样的理由,当我们的灵魂不适时,应该去找哲学家,并且用对医生同样的标准来评价他们:

伊壁鸠鲁,前341—前270

正如药不能治病就无用,不能解脱精神的苦难的哲学也是无用的。

伊壁鸠鲁认为,哲学家的任务就是帮助我们解读自己弄不清楚的痛苦和欲望的脉搏,从而使我们免于制定错误的谋求快乐的方案。我们应该停止凭第一直觉行事,而应该先审视我们的欲望是否合乎理性,其方法类似一百年前苏格拉底用以评价伦理定义的诘难法。伊壁鸠鲁答应我们,哲学可以提出有时看来与直觉相反的病因诊断,从而引导我们达到优异的治疗和真正的快乐。

（四）

凡听到过谣传的人一旦发现这位哲学家对快乐的实际爱好,一定会感到意外。并没有华屋美舍,饮食也非常简单。伊壁鸠鲁喝水而不喝酒,一顿饭有面包、蔬菜和一把橄榄就满足了。他对一位朋友说:"送我一罐奶酪,好让我想要的时候饱餐一顿盛筵。"这就是这位把快乐定为人生目标的哲学家的爱好。

他无意欺瞒。他对追求快乐的执着远远超过那些指责他纵欲无度的人的想象。他正是经过理性的分析之后,出语惊人,指出怎样才真正能实现快乐人生——对缺少钱财的人说来很幸运,构成快乐的要素虽然难以捉摸,却似乎不大昂贵。

快乐——伊壁鸠鲁开的需求清单

1. 友谊

伊壁鸠鲁于公元前 306 年,35 岁时回到雅典,他安家的方式不同寻常。他在离雅典市中心几里处,在集市与庇拉尤斯港之间的美立特区找了一所大房子,同一帮朋友一起搬了进去。同他住在一起的有,梅特多鲁斯和他的妹妹、数学家波利埃努、埃马尔库斯、雷奥修及其妻泰米斯塔,还有一名商人,名叫伊多门纽(他不久就和梅特多鲁斯的妹妹结婚)。这所大宅子有足够的房间,朋友们都可以有自己的住房,还有共同就餐和集会、谈话的厅堂。

伊壁鸠鲁说:

> 凡智慧所能够提供的、助人终身幸福的事物之中,友谊远超过一切。

伊壁鸠鲁如此看重融洽的同伴,他建议决不要独自进餐:

> 你在进饮食之前,先好好想一想要与谁同进,而不是吃什么、喝什么;因为没有朋友共餐,生活无异于狮子或野狼。
>
> 伊壁鸠鲁的住宅就像一个大家庭,但毫无阴沉、闭塞之气,有的只是同情和温馨。

除非有人看见我们存在,我们是不存在的;在有人能懂得我们的话之前,我们说什么都没有意义;而经常有朋友围绕身旁,我们才能确认自我;朋友知我、关心我,构成一种力量,让我们不要陷入麻木不仁之中。朋友的许多小小玩笑,透露出他们知道我们的弱点,并且予以容忍,从而认可了我们在世界上占有一席之地。我们可以问他们:"他是不是很可怕?"或者"你有没有感觉到……"这样的问题,能够得到善解人意的回应,而不是那种冷冰冰的不知所云的回答:"不,没特别感到。"——这种回答使人即使在人群中也感到像北极探险者一样孤寂。

真正的朋友不以世俗的标准来衡量我们,他们看重的是我们的本质;就像理想的父母一样,他们对我们的爱不以我们的外表和社会地位为转移,所以我们身穿旧衣服、承认今年没赚多少钱,都不会于心不安。追求财富的欲望不一定单纯出自对奢侈生活的渴望,更重要的动机可能是希望得到别人的赞赏和善待。我们追求发财的最大目的可能就是要获得别人的尊重和关注,否则他人就会对我们视而不见。伊壁鸠鲁分析了我们内心的需要以后,指出:一小群真正的朋友可以给予我们的关爱与尊敬是财富不见得能提供的。

2. 自由

伊壁鸠鲁及其同道还做出了第二项激进的创新。为了避免在自己不喜欢的人手下受其喜怒无常的屈辱,他们辞去了雅典商业界的工作("我们必须从日常事务和政治的牢笼中解放出来"),开始了一种可称之为公社的生活,以简朴换取独立。他们钱少了,但从此不再需要听从那令人厌恶的上级的指示。

于是他们在住宅旁、蒂庇隆老城门边买了一座园子,种了一些供厨房用的蔬菜,可能是 *bliton*①、*krommyon*② 和 *kinara*③ 。他们的食谱既不奢侈,也不丰盛,但是有味道、有营养。正如伊壁鸠鲁向他的朋友门诺休斯所说的,(聪明人)挑选食物不求量多,而求可口。

生活简朴并不妨碍朋友们感到自己是有地位的人,因为他们同雅典世俗的价值观拉开距离,不以物质标准衡量自己。家徒四壁不必汗颜;黄金万两无可炫耀。在城邦的政治经济中心以外,与若干朋友离群索居,就钱财的角度而言,没有什么需要证明自己的。

3. 思想

很少有比思想更好的医治焦虑的良药了。把我们的焦虑写下来,或者在谈话中说出来,其主要内容就显露出来了。了解其实质之后,我们即便不能消除那问题本身,也可以退而求其次,消除它的一些特点:迷茫、错位、惊愕。

在园中思考受到不少鼓舞,因为伊壁鸠鲁的朋友们逐

---

① 拉丁文,意为"卷心菜"。——译者
② 拉丁文,意为"洋葱"。——译者
③ 拉丁文,意为"某种古老的菊芋之类的食物"。——译者

渐为人所知。其中有好几位作家。据第欧根尼·拉尔修称，梅特多鲁斯一人就写了12本书，其中有《智慧之路》和《关于伊壁鸠鲁健康欠佳问题》。可以想见，在那所大宅的厅堂中和菜园里，有着不受干扰的机会同既有智慧又善解人意的人们研究问题。

伊壁鸠鲁特别关切的是同他的朋友们一道分析他们由金钱、疾病、死亡和鬼神引起的焦虑。伊壁鸠鲁的理论是，如果能合乎理性地思考生命有限的问题，就会意识到人一死，物我两忘，复归于无，"要到来时自然到来，为此而预先担忧是庸人自扰"。事先对永远不会经历的境界妄自惊扰是没有意义的：

> 对于真正懂得不活着没有什么可怕的人来说，生命中就没有什么可怕的事了。

清醒的分析使人心神宁静；这样，伊壁鸠鲁的朋友们偶然窥见人生的艰难，也可以免受其扰，而在园外缺乏思考的扰攘尘世中，这种困扰会长期挥之不去。

∞

当然财富总不至于使人愁苦。但是伊壁鸠鲁立论的关键在于，如果我们只有钱而没有朋友、自由以及经过剖析的生活，就决不可能真正快乐。而如果我们有了这些，只缺财富,就决不会不快乐。

为了突出快乐的要素,并指出如果我们因社会不公或经济动荡而不富裕时可以放弃哪些东西而不可惜,伊壁鸠鲁把我们的需求分为三类:

人都有欲望,其中有些是自然而必要的,有些是自然但不必要,有些既不自然又不必要。

快乐的要素和非要素

自然而必要	自然但不必要	既不自然又不必要
朋友	广宅	名望
自由	私人浴室	权势
思想(关于焦虑的	宴饮	
主要原因:贫、病、	仆役	
死、迷信)		
食物、避风雨处、	鱼、肉	
衣服		

对那些不会赚钱而又怕失去钱财的人来说,伊壁鸠鲁的三分法的关键意义是说明,快乐依赖于一些复杂的、与心理有关的事物,而对物质的东西的依赖相对少一些。除了满足温饱和栖身之处所需之外,他为那些把快乐等同于庞大的财务规划、愁苦等同于低收入的人设计了一套发人深思的排行表。

把伊壁鸠鲁设定的快乐与金钱的关系绘制成图表,就可以看出,金钱满足快乐的能力在低收入档内已经存在,收入达到最大值时快乐曲线并不继续上升。开支大了不会使我们不快乐,但是伊壁鸠鲁坚持认为,它不会使快乐超过有限收入已经能达到的水平。

快乐与金钱关系示意图
对拥有朋友、自由等等的人

这一分析是基于一种特定的对快乐的理解。对伊壁鸠鲁说来,只要我们不是处于现行的痛苦之中我们就是快乐的。由于缺衣少食给我们带来现行的痛苦,所以我们必需有足够的钱购买衣食。但是如果我们穿不起开司米毛衣而只能穿一般的毛衫,或者吃不起海鲜而吃三明治,把这叫做痛苦就太过分了。由此而推出以下论断:

在消除了匮乏的痛苦之后,清茶淡饭与丰盛筵席带来的快感是相同的。

我们日常用餐是如右图所示,还是左图所示,对我们的思想状态起不了决定性的作用。

至于吃肉,既不能缓解我们自然的痛苦,也不能摆脱一种如不满足就会痛苦的欲望……吃肉的贡献不在于维持生命,而在于提供多样化的快感,犹如喝味道独特的酒。按我们的本性,没有这一切是完全可以的。

人们很容易把这种对奢华的蔑视归之于古希腊经济不发达,那时富人能得到的产品也很原始。但是在近世,物品的价格与其带来的快乐之不相称,也可以作为这一论据的佐证。

我们如果拥有如左图所示的汽车而没有朋友;有别墅而没有自由;有讲究的亚麻布床单却心事重重难以入睡,不可能感到快乐。

快乐与金钱关系示意图
对没有朋友、自由等等的人

凡不能满足于少量物资的人，永远不会满足

　　为了避免买我们不需要的东西，或为买不起而遗憾，我
们在想要一件昂贵的物品时应该严格地问自己，这样做对
不对。为了衡量我们可能获得的快乐的程度，我们应该进行
一系列的思想实验，在想象中置身于欲望得到满足那一刻：

　　必须把下列诘问法用于一切欲望：
　　如果我们所渴望的得以实现，对我会怎样？ 如果实现
不了，又会怎样？

　　这一方法没有什么实例流传下来，但可以设想至少有5
个步骤，完全可以用说明书或菜谱的语言恰当地表达：

　　1. 设定一项追求快乐的计划

为了假期过得快乐,我必须住在一所别墅里。

2. 设想这一计划可能是错的。寻找设定目标与快乐之间的关联不符的例外情况。有了所想望之物是否仍会感到不快乐?没有它是否可以快乐?

我花钱买了别墅是否仍会感到不快乐?
我不花这么多钱买别墅,假期是否可以过得快乐?

3. 如果能找到例外,那么所想望之物就不是构成快乐的必要和充足条件。

别墅生活可能愁闷无聊,比如说,可能感到孤寂无伴。
在帐篷里很可能过得快乐,假如我是和相知相爱的人在一起。

4. 为准确表述如何获得快乐,就要把例外考虑在内,从而对最初的计划在分寸上进行调整。

在别墅里感到快乐取决于同相知相爱的人在一起。
我不花钱买别墅也能快乐,只要我同相知相爱的人在一起。

5. 现在看来,真正的需要与最初的懵懂的欲望差别很大。

快乐的真谛在于拥有相知的伙伴,而不是华丽的别墅。

（五）

既然昂贵的东西不能带给我们特大的欢乐，为什么对我们还有那么强大的吸引力呢？其原因同那个偏头痛患者在头的一侧钻洞一样，对于我们不理解的需要，昂贵的东西看起来好像是适当的解决办法。我们所需要的精神的东西在物质世界中被仿造。我们需要的是重整自己的思想，却为新的货架所引诱。我们买一件开司米毛衣代替朋友的忠告。

这种思想混乱也不能全怪我们自己。我们周围那些伊壁鸠鲁称之为"无聊的意见"进一步削弱了我们的理解力，这些意见不反映我们自然需要的轻重缓急，一味强调奢华和财富，却很少提到朋友、自由和思想。无聊的意见占上风决非偶然，它符合商业界的利益——歪曲我们所需的轻重缓急以宣扬一种崇尚物质的观念，而贬低那些不能买卖的事物。

他们把多余的物品与我们已经遗忘的需求巧妙地联系起来，从而把我们拴住。

我们可能买了一辆吉普车，而在伊壁鸠鲁看来，我们追求的是自由。

我们可能买了一瓶开胃酒，而在伊壁鸠鲁看来，我们寻找的是朋友。

我们可能买了一件精美的浴衣，而在伊壁鸠鲁看来，能使我们得到安宁的是思想。

为反击奢华形象的吸引力，伊壁鸠鲁的信徒重视宣传广告。

公元 2 世纪 20 年代，在奥诺安达——小亚细亚西南角一座人口 1 万的小城——的集市中心竖起了一块长 80 米高约 4 米的石碑，上面刻着伊壁鸠鲁式的口号，唤起购物者注意。

> 奢华酒食不足以避害，不足以健身。
>
> 超过自然之财富，其无用犹如溢出容器之水。
>
> 真价值不生于剧院、澡堂、香水与油膏，而生于自然科学。

这面墙是奥诺安达的一名富翁第欧根尼出钱建立的，他在伊壁鸠鲁与其同伴在雅典开辟那座园子后 400 年，想要同他的乡亲们分享他从伊壁鸠鲁哲学中发现的快乐的秘诀。他在墙的一角写下如下的话：

> 我已经日薄西山（因年老而即将离开这个世界），在死之前，我要写一篇对美满快乐的颂词，以期对当前春秋正富的人们有所帮助。如果只有一两人，或三四人，或五六人处于困境，我将与他们个别交谈……但是如今大多数人患着

对事物有错觉的通病,如鼠疫般蔓延,人数有增无减(因为他们在互相攀比中互相传染,如羊群的瘟疫一般)……我要用这一柱廊广为宣传治此病的良药,以拯救世人。

那面石墙上刻有25000字,宣传伊壁鸠鲁思想的各个方面,包括友谊的重要性和对焦虑的分析。不厌其详地警告到奥诺安达商店来购物的人们,他们从中得不到多少快乐。

如果我们生性不是那么容易受暗示的影响,广告就不会这样时兴。同样的东西,装潢漂亮地在墙上展示出来,我们就想要;而当它们被打入冷宫,或者听不到对它的好评,我们就失去兴趣。卢克莱修哀叹:人们是凭道听途说,而不是凭自己的见证产生需求的。

不幸的是,奢侈品和昂贵家园的形象到处都是,而关于普通的、个人生活环境的却很少见。朴素的乐趣很少受到鼓励——例如同孩子玩,与朋友聊天,下午晒晒太阳,窗明几净的房间,涂奶酪的新鲜面包("送我一罐奶酪,好让我想要的时候饱餐一顿盛筵")。《伊壁鸠鲁式生活》杂志中推崇的不是这类事。

艺术可能有助于纠正这种偏差。卢克莱修用他的优美的拉丁诗句使我们感受不需付高价而得到的快感，加强了伊壁鸠鲁以理智维护朴素的立论：

"吾身所需兮本无多，	*Ergo corpoream ad naturam pauca videmus*
惟求去痛兮自行乐，	*esse opus omnino，quae demant cumque dolorem.*
率性天然兮无怨尤！	*delicias quoque uti multas substernere possint*
何必铸金童兮擎华烛，	*gratius interdum，neque natura ipsa requirit，*
照绮筵兮中夜饮？	*si non aurea sunt iuvenum simulacra per aedes*
不羡华屋兮金裹银妆，	*lampadas igniferas manibus retinentia dextris，*
画栋雕檐兮风笛悠扬。	*lumina nocturnis epulis ut suppeditentur，*
莫若退隐兮茂林流泉，	*nec domus argento fulget auroque renidet*
绿茵如毡兮良朋为伴，	*nec citharae reboant laqueata aurataque templa，*
身爽神怡兮何用多金。	*cum tamen inter se prostrati in gramine molli*
更逢良辰兮惠风和熙，	*propter aquae rivum sub ramis arboris altae*
繁花点点兮芳草萋萋。	*non magnis opibus iucunde corpora curant，*

乐莫乐兮复何求!"　　　　　*praesertim cum tempestas adridet et anni*

　　　　　　　　　　　　tempora conspergunt viridantis floribus herbas. ①

　　很难衡量卢克莱修的诗对希腊罗马世界的商业活动产生了多少影响;也很难知道奥诺安达的购物者是否因那块巨大的广告牌而发现了自己真正需要什么,从而停止购买不需要的东西。但是可以想见,如果大张旗鼓地进行伊壁鸠鲁学说的宣传运动,很可能导致全球经济崩溃。因为伊壁鸠鲁认为大多数商业活动都是刺激人们不必要的需求,他们不知道自己实际需要什么。那么,提高对朴素的欣赏和自觉,就会破坏消费水平。果真如此,伊壁鸠鲁也将无动于衷:

　　　　以天然的人生目标来衡量,贫穷就是巨大的财富,而无限财富是巨大的贫穷。

　　这一论断使人们必须在下列两种情况中进行选择:一方面是被刺激出来的不必要的欲望导致经济强大的社会;另一方面是伊壁鸠鲁式的社会,提供基本的物质需要,但决不会使生活水平超过维持生存的起码标准。在伊壁鸠鲁的世界里不会有辉煌的纪念碑,不会有技术进步,也极少与远方进行交易的动力。一个需求有限的社会,也将是资源稀

---

　　① 原书这首诗英文与拉丁文并列,中文系从英文译出。——译者

缺的社会。但是——如果相信这位哲学家——这样的社会不会不快乐。卢克莱修已经道出了他的选择：在一个缺少伊壁鸠鲁价值观的世界里：

> 人类将永远是无意义的牺牲品，一生都在无谓的烦恼中度过，因为他们永不满足，不知所止，而不知真正的快乐的增长是有限度的。

而与此同时，

> 正是这种永不满足驱使生活不断向上，远航海外……

我们可以想见伊壁鸠鲁的回答：不论我们觉得海外探险多么了不起，最终衡量其价值的是它引起多少快感：

> 我们最终诉诸快感，用这一感觉来判断一切善。

由于社会财富的增加并不足以保证快乐随之增进，伊壁鸠鲁就会说，昂贵物品所迎合的需求并不能作为快乐的基础。

（六）

快乐，一张需求清单

1. 茅屋一间

2.

3. 避免有上级、受恩赐、勾心斗角

4. 思想

5. 贝利尼的《圣母像》（那幅画的原作陈列在威尼斯学院的画廊）的转世肉身，忧伤的表情掩盖不住冷面幽默和自然流露的天性，身穿普通商店中模特身上的时装。

快乐可能得之不易。不过障碍不在金钱方面。

第三章

对受挫折的慰藉

（一）

雅克-路易·大卫在画《苏格拉底之死》之前13年，曾致力于表现另外一位哲学家，他也是在亲人挚友的嚎啕哭声中平静地迎接生命的终结。

《塞内加之死》作于1773年大卫25岁时，描写的是这位斯多葛派哲学家于公元65年的4月在罗马郊外一所别墅中弥留之际的情景。几小时前，一名罗马军队的百人队队长刚来过这里传达皇帝的旨意，令塞内加立即自裁。刚破获了一桩企图推翻这位28岁的皇帝尼禄的阴谋，暴跳如雷的皇帝以疯狂的滥捕滥杀进行报复。尽管没有任何证据说明塞内加与这一阴谋有关,尽管他担任了 5 年皇帝的导师,10年忠实的副官,尼禄还是下令要他死,只是为了在死亡录上额外再加一名。此时尼禄已杀死了他的异母兄弟不列塔尼库、母亲阿格丽品娜以及妻子屋大维娅;他已经除掉了大批参议员和骑士团骑士,把他们送去喂鳄鱼和狮子。而公元64 年罗马被大火烧为平地时,他躲在安乐窝里。

塞内加的亲友们听说尼禄的命令后都大惊失色,哭了起来。但是,据大卫读到的塔西陀的记载,哲学家不动声色,努力劝他们止泪,重新鼓起勇气:

> 他问他们的哲学哪里去了,多少年来他们互相激励的那种处变不惊的精神哪里去了? 他说:"当然,谁都知道尼禄残暴成性,他弑母杀兄之后,只剩下杀师了。"

他转向他的妻子保丽娜,温柔地拥抱了她(迥异于他哲学上的凛然不可侵犯——塔西陀),要她从他没有虚度的一生中得到慰藉。但是她不能想象没有他的生活,要求割腕自尽,塞内加没有剥夺她的愿望:

> 你树立这样美好的榜样,我将无怨。我们死得同样坚强,不过你的死更加崇高。

但是皇帝不想再加重自己残暴的名声。当卫队看见保丽娜拿刀子割手腕时，强行夺了过去，并把她的手腕包扎好。

她丈夫的自杀不顺利。血从他年迈的身体流出不畅，尽管他连脚腕和膝盖后面的血管都割破了。于是，作为464年前在雅典发生的那次死亡的回响，他要求医生给他一杯毒药。他长久以来一直以苏格拉底为榜样，学习他通过哲学超越外部环境（在尼禄下这道命令的几年前，他在一封信中阐述了仰慕之情）：

> 他在家中备受折磨，妻子粗暴而饶舌，孩子又……他生逢连年战争和暴君统治……但是所有这一切丝毫未改变苏格拉底的心灵，连外表也未改变。这样的奇人、伟人，世间少有！他始终不渝，矢死靡它……命运多舛而不为所扰。

但是塞内加要追随其雅典先辈的愿望还是不能实现。他喝下毒药却不起作用。两次努力无效后，他最后要求把他放进蒸汽浴室，在那里慢慢窒息至死，痛苦万端却仍然镇静自若，命运多舛而不为所扰。

大卫这幅洛可可风格的画并不是描绘这一事件的第一幅画，也不是其中最好的。画上的塞内加更像一名奄奄一息的"帕夏"①,而不是垂死的哲学家。保丽娜挺着袒露的右乳,身上的服装更像是为大歌剧院而不是为罗马帝国准备的。不过,这位罗马人处变不惊的精神为后人景仰,持久不衰,大卫对这一场景的处理,尽管略嫌笨拙,却正好纳入这一历史长河。

虽然塞内加事与愿违,厄运来得如此突然,如此激烈,他却没有被常人的软弱所击倒,而在这晴天霹雳的现实面

卢瓦塞·利德特,1462 年

鲁本斯,1608 年

里贝拉,1632 年

焦尔达诺,1680 年

---

① Pasha,土耳其高级官员的称谓。——译者

前保持了尊严。通过他的死,他与其他斯多葛派的同道们共同创造出一种持久的关联:提起"哲学的"一词就联想到对待灾难镇静自若的态度。他首先把哲学视为一种纪律,帮助人克服主观愿望和客观现实之间的冲突。如塔西陀所述,塞内加对他的同伴们的哭泣的反应,是问他们的**哲学**哪里去了,他们处变不惊的决心哪里去了,好像二者就是一回事。

塞内加一生经历过,也见证过诸多非常的劫难。庞培城在大地震中化为瓦砾;罗马与卢登努姆被一场大火夷为平地;罗马的人民和帝国臣服于尼禄皇帝的淫威,在他之前还有卡利古拉这个苏顿尼斯确切地称之为"凶神恶煞"的暴君,此人曾经在暴怒中吼道:"我希望你们罗马人只有一条脖子!"

塞内加本人也遭受过挫折。他受的培养是准备从政的,但是20岁出头就得了肺结核,缠绵病榻6年之久,精神极度悒郁,几乎自杀。由此而延缓了他的事业。等他进入政界,正逢卡利古拉权势越来越大时。即便这位国王被刺杀之后,塞内加的地位也一直是岌岌可危的。梅萨利纳女王的一场阴谋使完全无辜的塞内加遭到贬黜,流亡科西嘉岛8年。终于被召回罗马,却要他违心地接受一个罗马宫廷中最险恶的职务——阿格丽品娜的12岁的儿子卢西乌斯·多米提乌斯·阿赫诺巴布斯的导师,此人在15年后下令要他在妻子和全家面前自杀。

塞内加知道自己为什么能克服焦虑不安：

是"哲学"给了我生命，而这是我对它最起码的回报。

他的经历是一系列挫折的综合词典，而他的智慧就是对挫折的一系列回应。长年哲学的积累使他做好准备，能泰然面对尼禄皇帝的百人队队长扣响别墅之门时带来的灾难。

塞内加和苏格拉底的双头石雕

（二）塞内加挫折词典

序言

　　挫折的范围虽然很广——从脚趾头绊了一下到死亡都能算——而每一种挫折的核心却都有着同样的基本构成，那就是主观愿望与严酷的现实之间的冲突。这种冲突从我们襁褓中就开始：发现自己够不着能满足欲望的东西，发现不能指望这个世界总能如己之愿。而对塞内加来说，我们能够达到的智慧，就是要学习如何避免用我们对挫折的反应来加剧这个世界的顽固性，这种反应包括盛怒、自怜、焦虑、怨恨、自以为是和偏执狂。

　　在他的著作中贯穿始终的一个思想就是：我们对有准备的、理解了的挫折承受力最强，而准备最少、不能预测的挫折对我们伤害最严重。哲学教给我们顺应全方位的现实，从而使我们纵使不能免遭挫折，也至少能免于因情绪激动而遭受挫折带来的全部毒害。

　　哲学的任务是教会我们在愿望碰到现实的顽固之壁时，以最软的方式着陆。

现实

愿望

愤怒

这是最幼稚的冲突。我们找不到遥控器或钥匙、道路堵塞、饭店客满,于是我们摔门,拔花草,大吼大叫。

1. 哲学家认为这是一种疯狂:

> 这是滑向精神错乱最快速的捷径。许多(盛怒的)人……咒他们的孩子不得好死,自己受苦受穷,家门败落,却不承认自己是在盛怒之下,就像疯子不承认自己精神错乱一样。……他们会同最好的朋友反目成仇……无视法律……一切都用暴力解决……他们已经重病缠身,比其他一切坏事都严重。

2. 他们在心平气和时,可能道歉,解释说他们刚才为一种自己控制不了的强大力量所左右,也就是说,强于理智的力量。"他们"——意即理性的他们——本意并不要骂人,并为大喊大叫而后悔;"他们"控制不了内在的阴暗力量。发怒的人通过这样的解释诉诸一种占统治地位的、对思想的看法:把理性功能,也就是本真所在,描绘成常常会受到狂热的激情的袭击,理智对此既不能分辨,也不能负责。

这种说法与塞内加对思想的看法截然对立。他认为愤怒不是来自失控的感情爆发,而是来自理智本身的根本性的

(但是可以纠正的)错误。他承认，我们的行动并不总是在理智的控制之下：如果在身上泼冷水，就会情不自禁地打战；如果手指掠过眼睛，我们一定眨眼。但是愤怒不属于这类不自禁的生理动作，它只能在我们理性地持有的某些思想的基础上发作；只要我们改变了思想，我们就可以改变发怒的倾向。

3. 根据塞内加的看法，促使我们发怒的原因是我们对世界和对他人持有过分乐观的观念，这种乐观达到危险的程度。

4. 我们对挫折反应不当的程度取决于我们认为怎样算是正常。可能下雨违反我们的意愿，但是我们已经见惯暴风雨，不大可能因下雨而发怒。由于我们理解对这个世界能期待什么，由于我们的经验告诉我们希望什么是正常的，我们的挫折感就得到缓解。我们并不是每当想要的东西得不到就怒不可遏，只有我们认为有权得到时才这样。我们的盛怒来自那些侵犯了我们认为是生存的基本规则的事物。

5. 有了钱就可以指望在古罗马过相当舒适的生活。塞内加的许多朋友都在城里有大房子，乡间有别墅。里面有浴室、带廊柱的花园、喷泉、拼花装饰、壁画和镶金的躺椅。有成群的奴隶做饭、看孩子、整理花园。

6. 然而，在那些享有特权的人中间似乎总是有一种异乎寻常的怒气。塞内加的那些富朋友们整天围着他怒气冲冲，埋怨生活不像他们所希望的那样，他观察他们之后写道："富裕培养坏脾气。"

塞内加认识一个名叫维第乌斯·波利奥的富人，他是奥古斯丁国王的朋友。他的奴隶有一次在宴会上打碎了一只玻璃盘，维第乌斯特别讨厌打碎玻璃的声音，因而勃然大怒，竟下令把那个奴隶扔进鳄鱼池。

7. 这种怒气从来不是无法解释的。可以找到维第乌斯·波利奥愤怒的理由：因为他所信奉的世界里，宴会上是不打碎玻璃的。我们找不到遥控器就大喊大叫，因为我们所信奉的世界里，遥控器是不会乱放的。怒气来自一种信念，认为某种挫折没有写进生活的契约中，这种信念发源于近乎喜剧性的乐观，但其后果却是悲剧性的。

8. 我们应该慎言慎行。塞内加设法调整我们的期望值,使我们遇到以下不如意的事时不至于咆哮:

当晚饭迟开了几分钟:
有什么必要把桌子踢翻,把酒杯摔碎?
把自己往柱子上撞?
当周围有嗡嗡声:
为什么一只别人懒得赶走的苍蝇,或是一只挡道的狗,或是仆人不小心把钥匙掉在地上,会让你这样怒不可遏?
当饭厅的静谧受到了干扰:
何必中止用餐去拿鞭子,就因为奴隶们在聊天?

生活必不可能十全十美,我们必须顺应之。

恶人做恶事有什么奇怪?仇人害你,朋友惹恼你,儿子有过失,仆人行为不端,难道这些都是前所未有之事?

我们若是不抱那么大的希望,就不会那么愤怒。

震惊

一架瑞士航空公司的飞机载着229名乘客按正常班次从纽约飞向日内瓦。离开肯尼迪机场50分钟后,正当航空小姐推着服务车走在这架麦道11(MD-11)飞机的过道上时,机长报告称机舱内出现烟雾。10分钟后,飞机在雷达屏幕上消失。这架机翼有52米长的庞然大物坠入了沿(加拿大)新斯科舍省哈利法克斯风平浪静的大海中,机上的人无一生还。几小时前还是各有计划的活生生的人,如今救援人员已无法辨认。只见手提包在海上漂浮。

1. 假如说,我们不仔细考虑突发灾难的危险,从而为我们的天真付出代价,那是因为现实包含着两种令人糊涂的残酷的特性:一方面是世世代代的延续性和可靠性;一方面是无法预料的灾难。我们处在夹缝之中,一边是合理的召唤,让我们假设明天还会和今天一样;另一边是大难临头的可能性,从此生活再不能恢复原样。由于我们忽视后者的倾向十分强烈,塞内加请出了一尊女神。

2. 很多罗马钱币背面都刻有这位女神像,一手握山羊角,一手握舵桨。她貌美,经常身着薄衫,面带羞涩的微笑。她的名字叫"命运",原来是司丰饶之神,是朱庇特的长女,每年5月25日全意大利的神庙都要祭祀她,无子女的和求雨的农夫都来朝拜她。但是她的辖区逐渐扩大,同财富、升迁、爱情和健康联系在了一起。羊角象征着她赐福予人的权力,舵桨则象征着她改变命运的更为凶险的权力。她可以广施恩惠,然后以吓人的速度改变舵桨的方向,脸上依然挂着不可捉摸的笑容,眼看着我们吞鱼骨而窒息至死,或者在一次泥石塌方中消失。

3. 由于我们受伤害最大的多半是意外事故,而我们不可能什么都预料到("命运"女神没有不敢做的事),所以塞内加建议我们时刻心存灾难的可能性。任何人乘车出行、走下楼梯,或向朋友道别时,都要随时意识到发生致命意外的可能性,塞内加希望这种意识使事态既不可怕,也不突然。

4. 若要证明多么轻易地可以让我们复归于无,只需举起手腕凝视片刻那流在脆弱的青绿色血管里的鲜血:

我们应该对什么都不感到意外。我们的思想应该事先准备迎接所有的问题,我们应该考虑的不是惯常发生的事,而是有可能发生的事。

人是什么？就是那轻轻一碰就会破裂的血管……一具脆弱的、赤条条、生来没有防护的身体，有赖于别人的帮助，任凭命运的作弄。

5. 卢登努姆曾经是高卢最繁华的罗马居民区。它位于阿拉尔河与罗讷河的汇合处，得天独厚，正好是贸易和军事的十字路口。城里有雅致的浴室和剧院，还有一家政府的铸币厂。公元64年的8月里，一颗火星失控，酿成大火，迅速在狭窄的街道蔓延开去，惊慌失措的居民纷纷跳窗逃命。火苗扫过一家又一家，到太阳升起的时候，整个卢登努姆从郊区到集市，从浴室到庙宇，都已化为灰烬。幸存者们披着沾满黑炭的衣服站在他们已经烧得面目全非的豪宅前。火势如此迅猛，噩耗还来不及到达罗马，城市已成焦土。

你说："我没有想到此事会发生。"当你知道这是有可能发生的，当你见到它已经发生，你难道还认为有什么事是不会发生的吗？

6. 公元62年2月5日，同样的灾祸袭击坎帕尼亚省。大地震动，庞培的大部分倒塌了。随后几个月中，许多居民决定离开坎帕尼亚，移居半岛其他地方。他们的行动向塞内加表明，他们认为地上存在着完全安全的、命运之神达不到的地方，例如他们可能要去的利古里亚或卡拉布里亚。于是他提

出以下的论点（很有说服力,尽管在地理学上有些站不住）:

> 谁向他们许诺过,这片或那片土地更为坚实可靠? 所有地方条件都是一样的,如果还没有发生地震,以后也会有震动的。也许今晚,也许等不到晚上,就在今天,你稳稳站立的脚下那块土地就会裂开。你怎么知道那些地方今后情况会好些,命运之神已经耗尽了力气,对它无能为力? 或者,那些在废墟上重建的地方从此会好起来? 如果我们相信世界上有任何地方是安全的,可以免于灾难,那我们就错了……造物从来没有创造过一成不变的东西。

7. 在卡利古拉登上王位之时,罗马有一个远离政治的家庭中母亲失去了爱子。美蒂琉斯是一名前途远大的青年,还没有过 25 岁生日,他的死使他母亲痛不欲生。她退出一切社交活动,日夜沉湎在哀痛之中。她的朋友们关切地看着她,希望她能恢复常态,但是她没有。一年、两年、三年过去了,她还没有丝毫节哀的迹象。三年以后她还是和在她儿子葬礼上一样以泪洗面。于是塞内加给她写了一封信。他先表示深切的同情,然后委婉地说道:"我们之间对问题有不同看法,就是悲痛是否应该这样深而无止境。"马尔恰是在对抗一件看起来可怕而罕见的事情——惟其罕见,就更加可怕。她周围的母亲的儿子都还在,那些刚刚出道的年轻人,在军队服役,或开始从政。为什么单单把她的孩子抢走?

8. 死亡的确不寻常,并且可怕,但是——塞内加大着胆子说——并非不正常。如果马尔恰把眼光从一个狭隘的圈子放开去,就可以发现一张长长的令人哀痛的名单,都是命运之神杀死的人之子。屋大维娅失去了她的儿子,还有利维娅、科涅利亚、色诺芬、保卢斯、卢修斯·庇布勒斯、卢修斯·苏拉、奥古斯都以及西庇阿,都失去了儿子。马尔恰避免把目光向过去扫视,于是就把这些事排除在她认为是正常的范围之外,这是可以理解的,但是危险的:

> 我们从不在恶事真正出现之前就已预料……多少葬礼从我们门前经过,但我们从不认真思考死亡。多少夭折发生过,但我们仍为自己的婴儿作长远打算:他们如何穿上托加①,如何在军队服役,然后继承父亲的财产。

孩子可能活下去,但是认为他们一定能够活到成年,甚至活到晚餐时刻,那就太天真了:

> 没有人给今夜打保票,不,我给的喘息时间太长了,甚至没有人给这一个钟头打保票。

----

① toga,古罗马儿童到 14 岁时穿的成人服装。——译者

把对未来的期望建立在或然率的基础上是危险的天真。只要是人类曾经遭遇过的意外,不论多么罕见,间隔的时间多么长,都是一种可能性,我们应该有所准备。

9. 正因为命运女神长时期的发慈悲有麻痹我们的危险,塞内加要求我们每天花一点时间想想她。我们不知道下一步会发生什么事,我们必须做一些预料。每天清晨,我们应该进行塞内加所谓的"预想",把所有这位女神可能加于我们身心的痛苦思考一遍:

塞内加预想录

(智者)一日之计始于如下思考……

命运之神所赐无一物归我所有。

世事无常,公私皆然。

命运如旋风,城廓与人皆如此。

经过长年维护、辛勤劳动、托庇神佑而筑成之任何建筑,旦夕之间化为瓦砾。否,旦夕太长,灾祸来临如迅雷。帝国顷覆在一时、顷刻之间。

亚细亚、阿卡亚,多少城廓在一次地震中夷为平地? 叙利亚、马其顿,多少市镇为大地吞噬? 塞浦路斯又有多少次灾难造成颓垣败壁?

吾等生存其中,而周围事物皆必有一死。

汝生而终有一死,汝所生者亦终有一死。

一切都应在考虑之内，一切都应在预料之中。

10. 同样的思想当然可以用另外的方式表达。比如可以用更加冷静的哲学语言说：主体的能动作用只是其生命过程中决定事物的因素之一。但是塞内加还是愿意用一系列的夸张语法来表述：（这一段结尾原文更加铿锵有力）

"每当有人在你身旁或身后倒下时，你要大声喊道：'命运之神，你欺骗不了我，你要乘我不备扑到我身上。我知道你的计划。诚然，你打击了别人，但我知道你的目标是我。'"	*Quotiens aliquis ad latus aut pone tergum ceciderit, exclama*：'*Non decipies me, fortuna, nec securum aut neglegentem opprimes. Scio quid pares; alium quidem percussisti, sed me petisti.*'①

11. 多数哲学家不这样写作，因为他们相信，只要论点是合乎逻辑的，向读者表达的文风对效果起不了决定性作用。塞内加却对人的思维有不同看法。他认为论点如鳗鱼：不论多么合乎逻辑，除非用形象和恰当的文风固定在人

---

① 即左文的拉丁原文。——译者

的思想中,它还是能从抓得不紧的头脑中溜走。我们需要用隐喻来引申一种看不见摸不着的意思,否则我们就会把它丢在脑后。

命运之神的根源尽管非哲学而是宗教,她却是最完美的形象,可以使我们总是心存遭遇意外事故的可能,把一系列对我们安全的威胁合成为一个可怕的拟人化的仇敌。

不公正感

这是一种感觉,感到公正的规则被侵犯了。这种规则规定,如果我们正直,就应当得到好报,如果我们是坏人,就应得到惩罚——这种公正的观念灌输在儿童最早的教育中,也见于多数宗教典籍中,例如在《旧约·申命记》中就说,义人"他要像一棵树栽在溪水旁……凡他所作的尽都顺利。恶人并不是这样,乃像糠秕被风吹散"①。

善→善报

恶→惩罚

当一个人行为正确而仍然遭遇祸事,就惑然不解,无法把这件事纳入公正的框架中。世界看来很荒唐。于是这个人就会在两种可能中徘徊:或觉得自己终归还是坏人,所以才受到惩罚;或觉得自己实在不坏,因此一定是对公正的管理发生了灾难性的失误,自己是它的牺牲品。对不公正抱怨的本身

---

① 此处引文出自《圣经·诗篇》。——译者

就暗含着一种信念:坚持认为这个世界基本上是公正的。

1. 公正的意识对马尔恰并无帮助。

2. 这一意识迫使她摇摆于两种感情之间:一种是虚弱的感觉,认为儿子美蒂琉斯被夺走是因为自己坏;另一种是对全世界强烈的愤慨,认为自己本质上一直是好人,而儿子却死了。

3. 但是我们的命运并不总能用我们的道德价值来解释;我们可能受诅咒,或受祝福,其后面并没有什么公正。并非我们所有的遭遇都与我们的为人有关。

美蒂琉斯之死并不是因为他母亲坏,他母亲是好人,但他还是死了。也不能因此说这个世界不公。用塞内加的形象来说,他的死就是命运之神所为,而这位女神并不是道德裁判员。她并不像《申命记》①里的上帝那样评估她的牺牲品,然后论功行赏。她在加害于人时在道德上是盲目的,就像龙卷风一样。

---

① 如前,此处《申命记》应为《诗篇》。——译者

4. 塞内加知道自己体内也存在着强有力的冲动,要按照一种误导的公正的模式来解释失败。公元41年年初克劳狄登基时,梅萨利纳皇后想要除去卡利古拉的姐妹尤里安·列维拉,塞内加成了这桩阴谋中的一个卒子。皇后指控尤里安与人通奸,并诬陷塞内加为其情人。顷刻间,他失去了家庭、钱财、朋友、名誉,政治生涯也从此断送,并被流放到科西嘉岛,那是广袤的罗马帝国中最荒凉的部分。

他可能会经历这个阶段:时而自责自艾,时而满腔怨恨。他也可能自己后悔看错了梅萨利纳的政治立场,对自己的忠诚和才干受到克劳狄如此回报十分怨恨。

这两种情绪都是基于一幅道德宇宙的图景,在那里,外部环境反映内部品质。他想起了命运之神,就从这种惩罚性的模式中解脱了出来:

我不允许命运之神对我作出判决。

塞内加政治上的失败不必解释为对自己罪孽的报应,这并非洞察一切的上帝坐在天庭上审查所有证据后发布的理性的惩罚。这只不过是一位心怀怨恨的皇后的阴谋的副产品,残酷而道德上毫无意义。这样,塞内加不但自己与贬黜拉开距离,而且他曾一度拥有的皇室大臣的身份也配不上他的功劳。

命运之神的干预,不论是仁慈还是凶恶,使人的命途无常。

焦虑

这是一种对于情况不能确定的焦躁不安的状态,我们希望情况好转又担心它恶化。这种情绪最典型的后果是使人不能享受本应是快乐的事:文化的、性爱的,或是社交的。

即使在壮丽的景色中,还会因私下担心其覆灭而焦虑不安,可能宁愿独自呆在一间屋子里。

1. 传统的安慰的方式就是说宽心话。告诉焦虑的人他过虑了,事情一定会如愿的。

2. 但是这种宽慰可能是对焦虑最残酷的解药。我们所描绘的美好图景有双重作用:既使焦虑的人对最坏的情况毫无准备,又无意间暗示果真最坏的情况出现,将是大祸临头。塞内加的做法比较明智,他要我们想到坏事大概是会发生的,但又说其实这些坏事也未必像我们担心的那么坏。

3. 公元63年2月间,塞内加的一位在西西里当公务员的朋友卢西琉听说有一桩告他的案子,可能危及他的事业,永远玷污他的名声。他写信告诉塞内加此事。

哲学家回信道:"你可能期待我劝你想象一个喜人的结局,安心在希望中等待。但是我要领着你通过另一条道达到心灵的平安。"——以下就是他的劝告:

如果你想消除一切担心,那么请设想你所害怕的一切都会发生。

塞内加担保,一旦我们理性地看待事与愿违的情况,我们一定会发现它实际包含的问题比所引起的焦虑要轻得多。卢西琉有理由难受,但用不着为之发狂:

> 如果你官司打输了,充其量不就是流放或入狱吧?……"我可能沦为穷人",那么我就是芸芸众生中的一员;"我可能被流放",那我就把我要去的地方看做是我本来的出生地。"他们可能给我上镣铐。"那又怎样?我现在难道就丝毫不受束缚吗?

囹圄之苦和流放固然是坏事,但是——这是立论的关键——再坏也坏不过绝望的卢西琉在对其焦虑作冷静的分析之前所担心发生之事。

4. 由此推论,对于担心会失去财富的富人,千万不要拿大概他们不会破产这类话去宽慰他们。应该让他们在一间不避风雨的房间里住几天,只靠清汤和不新鲜的面包充饥。塞内加听从一位他最喜爱的哲学家的告诫:

伟大的享乐主义导师伊壁鸠鲁常常在某一个时期过一段极端艰啬、刚够果腹的生活,目的是看看是否值得费那么大劲去弥补亏空。

塞内加预言,那些富人将会有重大发现:

"这真的是我所害怕的情况吗?"……每一次忍受三四天(这种贫困生活),有时还可以多几天……我敢说……你们将理解,一个人心灵的平静并不靠财富。

5. 许多罗马人发现宣传这种理论的塞内加自己过着相当奢侈的生活,感到惊讶,甚至可笑。塞内加在40岁出头时通过他的政治生涯已经积累了足够的财富,可以购置别墅和农场。他吃得很好,而且养成了对昂贵家具的喜好,特别是带象牙腿的香橼木桌子。

他讨厌人家说他的行为有点非哲学:

不要阻止哲学家致富;没有人判定智慧必然贫穷。

接下去是动人的实用主义:

我鄙视财富领域中的一切,但是让我选择的话,我将选择其中比较好的那一半。

6. 这不是伪善。斯多葛主义并不提倡贫穷;它提倡的是我们既不害怕也不鄙视贫穷。它认为财富——用技术名词来说——是一种优先产品,既不是必不可少的,也不是罪恶。斯多葛派人士可能接受命运女神的恩赐和愚人一样多。他们的房屋也可以一样大,家具一样漂亮。而确定他们的智慧的只有一点:如何应付突如其来的贫穷。他们会泰然离开他们的华屋和奴仆,没有愤怒,没有绝望。

7. 智者应该能够泰然离开命运女神一切恩赐,这是斯多葛派最极端而奇特的要求,因为命运女神所赐不仅是房子和钱财,还有朋友、家庭,甚至我们的身体。

> 智者什么也不会失去。万物皆备于他一身。
> 智者是自足的……如果他因疾病或战争而失去一只手,或者某种意外事故使他失去一目或双目,他会满足于剩给他的那些。

这似乎有些荒唐,除非我们对塞内加所谓的"满足"一词的理解加以提炼。我们失去一只眼睛不会感到高兴,但是即使失去眼睛,生活也还能过下去。有正常数目的眼睛和手是优先产品。举两个例子:

智者不会因为自己身材矮小而妄自菲薄，但是他还是宁愿长得高大。

　　智者可以没有朋友而生活下去，在这个意义上他是自足的，但这不等于他愿意没有朋友。

　　8. 塞内加的智慧不仅是理论上的。他被流放到科西嘉岛时发现他的一切奢华生活丧失于一旦。那个岛从公元前238年起就属于罗马，但是没有得文明之利。岛上少数的罗马人活动范围不出东端的两块居住地：阿莱里亚和马里亚纳，塞内加不大可能会被允许住到那里面去，因为他曾诉说在当时耳之所闻莫非"蛮语"。而且他的名字还与岛北端的一座凶宅相联系，那建筑自古以来就有"塞内加之塔"之称。

　　可以想见，那里的生活条件与罗马成痛苦的对比。但是这位前罗马的富有的政治家在一封给母亲的信中说，他已努力适应了这里的环境，那要归功于他多年来每天早晨的静思和定期的只进清汤的节食生活：

　　　　我从来没有信任过命运女神，即使在她似乎愿意和平相处之时也没有。我把她所赐予我的一切——金钱、官位、权势——都搁置在一个地方，可以让她随时拿回去而不干扰我。我同那些东西之间保持很宽的距离，这样，她只是把它们取走，而不是从我身上强行剥走。

受嘲弄感

　　（i）来自无生命的物体

　　一支铅笔从桌上落地，或者抽屉柜打不开，都使人感到自己的愿望被有意挫败。这种无生物所带来的挫折感还参杂着受蔑视的感觉。那物件好像在表示对本人自以为拥有，并为周围的人所认同的聪明才智和地位并不买账。

　　（ii）来自于有生命的物体

　　印象中他人在默默地嘲笑自己，因而感到十分痛苦。

　　我来到一家瑞典的旅馆，一名工作人员送我到房间时主动要帮我拿行李，他笑着说，"这对你这样的男人实在太重了"，他特别对"男人"一词加重语气，暗示相反的意思。他长了一头北欧人的金发（也许是滑雪运动员或者猎鹿人，若在古代就是一名武士），表情坚决。"先生（Monsieur）①会喜欢这房间的，"他说。我不清楚他为什么称我为"Monsieur"，明明知道我是从伦敦来的。他还用"会"字，带有命令的味道。等我发现这房间外面车声喧哗，不堪其扰，淋浴器不灵，电视机又坏了，他这种说法就更加不符事实，明显是阴谋。

　　平时腼腆、文静的人如果感觉到被人狡猾地嘲弄了，会怒火中烧而暴跳如雷，做出残忍之事——甚至杀人。

　　1. 当我们受到伤害时，很容易认为这种伤害是故意造

---

　　① Monsieur 为法文，意为"先生"。——译者

成的。我们很容易把两个本来是以连接词"并且"联起来的短语变成用目的词"为了"联起来。本来是"铅笔从桌上落地,并且我很恼火",变成了认为"铅笔从桌上落地是为了要使我恼火"。

2. 塞内加收集了一些这类自以为受无生命的物体迫害的例子。希罗多德的《历史》提供了一例:波斯王居鲁士,这位伟大的帝国缔造者,有一匹漂亮的白马,他经常骑着上战场。公元前539年春天,居鲁士王希望扩张他的领土,向亚述人宣战,并派出一支庞大的军队直奔其位于幼发拉底河岸的首都巴比伦。行军一直很顺利,直到他们来到格底斯河边。这条河从马蒂恩山上流下来,注入底格里斯河,是有名的险流,夏天也是如此。而此刻,河水是褐色的,浪花飞舞,正因冬雨而暴涨。国王的将军们建议暂缓进行,但是居鲁士不为所动,下令立即过河。但是正当人们在准备船只时,居鲁士的马乘人不备跑开,想要游过河去。它为激流翻倒,冲到下游,死了。

居鲁士脸色煞白。这条河竟敢夺走他的神圣的白马!这匹武士之马曾经把克劳苏斯夷为平地,令希腊人闻风丧胆。他咆哮如雷,指天发咒,在暴怒中决定报复这条大胆妄为的格底斯河。他发誓要惩罚这条河,把它削弱到连妇女也能蹚过去而不湿膝盖。

于是居鲁士王把扩张帝国的计划放在一边,把军队分成两大队,在河的两岸各划出180条流向不同的小河道,下令士兵挖掘。他们挖了整整一个夏天,士气全消,迅速战败亚述人的希望破灭了。工程完毕后,格底斯河变成了360条小溪,水流迟缓,惊讶不已的当地妇女果真都能穿过,连裙子都不必提起。波斯王的怒气平息了,于是下令他的筋疲力尽的军队继续向巴比伦进军。

3. 塞内加也收集了类似的自以为受有生命的物体迫害的例子。其中之一是关于叙利亚的罗马总督皮索的。他是一位勇敢的将军,但是有着烦躁的心灵。有一次,一名士兵休假回来,与他同行的朋友没有一起回来,他说不知道朋友哪里去了。皮索就认定这名士兵是在说谎;他一定是杀了他的朋友,为此应该偿命。

被判死刑的士兵发誓说他没有杀任何人,并哀求给一点时间进行调查,但是皮索自以为高明,下令立即行刑。

但是,正当负责此事的百人队队长准备砍掉那士兵的头时,那失踪的伙伴到达了军营门口。整个军队自发地欢呼起来,百人队队长松了一口气,下令取消行刑。

皮索却对这一消息不那么高兴。他听到欢呼声,认为那是嘲笑他的判断力。他怒气冲冲,脸涨得通红。盛怒之下,竟下令把两个士兵都杀了,而这两个士兵一个并没有杀人,一个没有被杀。还因为此时他感到自己受到迫害,迁怒于百人队队长,下令把他也处死了。

4. 叙利亚总督立即把士兵的欢呼看做想要破坏他的权威,质疑他的判断力。居鲁士立即把河水淹死他的马看做是故意谋杀。

塞内加对此类错误判断有一种解释;那是由于像居鲁士和皮索这样的人的精神中存在着某种卑下的品质。他们总是预料要受辱,其背后实际是担心自己有理由受到嘲弄。当我们怀疑自己是伤害的恰当的目标时,那就很容易相信确实有人或有东西在设法伤害我们。

    "某人今天没有同我谈话,可是他同别人谈话了";"他傲慢地拒绝同我谈话,或者公开取笑我的话";"他没有让我坐在贵宾席,还让我坐末座"。

所有这些可能都出于完全无心的原因。他今天没有同我谈话,因为他想下星期见我。他看来在取笑我,其实只不过脸上有点发痒。但是一个精神卑下的人首先想到的不是这样的解释。

5. 所以,我们必须设法为我们的第一印象加一层防火罩,拒绝根据这一假设贸然行动。我们一定要自问:别人不回信,是否必然是为了惹恼我们而故意怠慢;钥匙不见了,是否必然是被偷了:

（智者）不把错误的解释强加于一切事物。

6. 关于他们为什么能做到这一点，塞内加在给卢西琉的一封信中作了间接的解释，那天他读到哲学家赫卡通的著作中的一段话：

> 我要告诉你我今天（在他的著作中）喜爱的一段话："你问我有哪些进步？我开始成为我自己的朋友。"这真是极大的好事……你可以肯定，这样的人一定是全人类的朋友。

7. 有一个简便的法子衡量一个人内心卑下，或是对自己友善的程度：可以检验一下我们对噪音的反应。塞内加住在一座体育馆附近，墙很薄，吵嚷声不断。他向卢西琉这样描述他的烦恼：

> 想象一下，我耳边有多少种噪音在回响！……例如，有一位身强力壮的先生在练习掷铅球，当他用劲，或假装用劲时，我可以听到他的吼声；每当他松口气时，我可以听见他那高频率的咝咝喘气声。我再把注意力转向一名不在活动而在享受普通的、廉价的按摩时，我可以听到手掌拍打他的肩膀的声音。除此之外，还有间或出现的流浪汉或小偷被抓住的声音，喜欢在洗澡时欣赏自己声音的人的引吭高叫……拔

头发人的刺耳尖叫……还有糕点小贩的各种叫卖声,卖香肠的,卖糖果的,人人都争相叫喊以吸引伙食房的注意。

8. 对自己不友善的人很难想象小贩高声叫喊就是为了卖糕点。罗马一家旅店的底层的建筑工人可能是假装在修一堵墙(1),其真实意图是故意招惹楼上那位正在读书的人(2)。

> 卑下的解释:建筑工人敲打是为了要让我恼火。
> 友善的解释:建筑工人在敲打,同时我感到恼火。

9. 为了使自己处闹市而心静,我们必须相信,那些吵闹的人对我们全然不识。我们应该在外界噪声和内心的应受惩罚感之间筑起一道防火墙。我们不应把对他人的动机的悲观的解释注入到本来与他们无关的场景之中。这样做了之后,噪音仍然使人不愉快,但是不必激怒我们。

但求室内安然无扰,任凭室外疯狂世界。

（三）

当然，如果我们对一切挫折逆来顺受的话，人类伟大的成就就不多了。我们的聪明的动力在于经常提问："现存的是否必然如此？"于是而产生政治改革、科学进步、改善关系以及优秀的著作。罗马人最长于不认输。他们讨厌冬天的寒冷，就建了地下取暖系统。他们不愿走泥地，就铺路。公元1世纪中期，住在普罗旺斯尼姆城的罗马居民决定要得到比自然赐予他们的更多的水，于是花了1亿塞斯特斯建立起一项工程，成为人类反抗现状的出色的象征。罗马工程师们在尼姆的北部乌采斯附近找到了足以供应他们城市的浴室和喷泉的水源,于是制定引水规划,筑高架水渠、铺地下管道,让水穿过山岭、峡谷,经50英里到达本市。当工程师们遇到加尔河的深谷时,他们没有在自然的障碍前气馁,而是筑起了一条庞大的三层渠道,360米长,48米高,日引水量达35000立方米。这样,尼姆的居民就永久摆脱了浅水沐浴之苦。

可惜,那些孜孜以求,探索变革的心理官能很难知所止。即便在没有希望改变现实时,它们仍不断在心目中展开变革的场景。为了促发足以鞭策我们去行动的能量,就用一阵阵的难受——焦虑、痛苦、愤慨、受刺激——来提醒我们现实很不如意。但是如果我们随后不能实行改良,如果我们失去了平静却不能改变河道,那这一阵阵的难受就毫无意义。所以,塞内加的智慧就在于正确地区分何处能够凭己意重塑现状,何处是不可改变的现实,必须泰然接受。

斯多葛派还用另一种形象来比喻我们的生存状态;有时能实行一些变革,但永远必须服从外在的必然。我们就像拴在一辆不可捉摸的车子上的狗。绳子的长度足以让我们有一定的活动余地,但是决不允许随意到处跑。

这一比喻是斯多葛派哲学家芝诺和克里西波斯创造,罗马主教希波吕托斯报道的:

当一条狗拴在一辆车上时,如果它愿意跟着走,它就被拉着,同时跟着走,这样它自发的行动与"必然"巧合。但是如果它不想跟着走,反正它也得被迫跟着走。人也是一样:即使他们不愿意,他们也得被迫跟着命定的道路走。

狗当然希望随意到处跑。但是,如芝诺和克里西波斯的比喻所暗示的:如果它不能,那么不如乖乖地在车后面跟着跑,而不要被车子硬拽着以至于绞死。

如塞内加所说:

牲口跟缰绳较劲,只会越抽越紧……任何缰绳都是顺着它伤害少,而越逆着它挣扎伤害越大。对压顶而来的恶事惟一的缓解剂就是逆来顺受,向必然低头。

为减少我们对违背我们意愿的事物反抗的激烈程度,我们应该想想,我们的脖子上也从来是套着绳索的。智者知道什么是必然,立即顺从它,而不徒耗精力去抗议。一位智者听说他的行李在转运中遗失了,他几秒钟之内就放弃了。塞内加讲述了斯多葛派对丧失财产的反应:

当芝诺收到一次海难的消息,知道他的全部行李都丢失了时,他说"命运之神要我做一个负担轻一些的哲学家"。

　　这看起来像是一副消极无为的药方,鼓励人向一切挫折低头,而其中有些是有可能克服的。它可能让我们连一座小型水坝也无心去建,例如像加尔桥北几公里处波耳内日那样的水坝,只有 17 米长,4 米高。

　　但是塞内加的论点比这深刻。把并非必然的事当做必然接受下来同对必然的事进行反抗一样不合理。我们可能误把非必然当做必然而拒绝可能之事,我们也可能拒绝承认必然而妄想不可能之事。对二者作正确的区分,就需要理性。

　　不论我们与绳索拴住的狗有多少相似之处,我们有一点比狗优越,那就是我们有理性,而狗没有。所以狗一开始并不知道它是让绳子拴着,也不理解车子的移动和它脖子痛之间的关系。方向的变换使它糊涂,它很难捉摸出车子走的路径,因此只能不断忍受阵阵的疼痛。但是理性能使我们用理论准确地推算出车子的路径,这样,我们就有机会通过与必然之间保持适当的松弛而增加自由感,这种机会在所有的生物中唯我们所独有。理性使我们能够决定,什么时候我们的愿望与现实的冲突是无法调和的,于是命令我们甘心情愿地,而不是怨恨满怀地接受必然。我们可能无力改变某些事态,但还是有自由决定对待它们的态度。正是从自发地接受必然之中,我们找到了明白无误的自由。

公元 62 年 2 月里,塞内加碰到了一个不可更改的现实。尼禄不再听这位老导师的话,他躲避他,鼓励宫廷中对他的毁谤,而且任命了一名嗜血成性的行政长官提格林努斯帮他任着性子滥杀无辜和进行性虐待。在罗马大街上把处女抢到皇帝的寝宫中。元老院议员的夫人们被迫参加祭神狂欢仪式,目睹她们的丈夫被杀死。尼禄夜间微服上街游逛,在偏僻街道上割断普通行人的喉管。他爱上了一名男孩,希望他是女孩,就阉割了他,然后进行一场玩笑的婚礼。罗马人讥讽说,如果尼禄的父亲多米提乌斯当年同那样的"女人"结婚的话,现在罗马人的日子会好过些。塞内加意识到自己处于极端危险之中,就企图退出宫廷,住到罗马郊外的别墅中去过平静的日子。他两次提出辞职,尼禄两次拒绝,热情地拥抱他,发誓说他宁死也不离开他亲爱的导师。塞内加的阅历中没有任何事足以使他相信这种许诺。

于是他求助于哲学。他不能逃脱尼禄,既然他不能改变,理性就叫他接受。在那几年难以忍受的日子里,他致力于研究自然,开始写一本关于大地和星球的书。他仰望苍穹和天上的星座,研究无边的大海和高山峻岭。他观察闪电,探索其成因:

闪电是一团压缩的火猛烈甩出来的。有时我们双手捧起水,然后合掌把水挤出,起到水泵的作用。假设类似的现象发生在云端。由于空间狭窄而挤压云层,挤出了云层间的空气,强大的压力点着了空气,并像弹弓一样给射了出来。

他研究地震,认为是被压在底层内的空气找出路的结果,是一种地质的胀气。

在证明地震是由于空气移动的结果的诸多论据中,你们应特别提出以下这一条:当一次大地震发泄了对城市和国家的怒气之后,紧跟着不会有同样大的震动。在大震之后,通常只有较轻的余震,因为第一次激烈的震动已经给挣扎的空气打开了出口。

塞内加的科学理论有误,这不重要;更加有意义的是,一个生命随时都可能被一名喜怒无常、嗜杀成性的皇帝结束的人似乎从观察大自然的现象中得到极大的宽慰——也许正是强有力的自然现象提醒我们认识到一切我们无力改变的、必须接受的事物。冰川、火山、地震、龙卷风都是令人敬畏的、超人的象征。在人类世界,我们相信总能改变自己的命运,从而有希望,有忧虑。而海涛兀自拍岸,彗星兀自划过夜空,显然说明存在着完全漠视我们愿望的力量。这种漠视非独自然界为然,人也能向他的同类施以同样盲目的力量,不过自然界能够以最优雅的方式教训我们必须服从必然。

  隆冬带来严寒,我们必须颤栗。夏天带着溽暑回来,我们必须出汗。气候反常损害健康,我们必须生病。在某些地方我们可能遭遇野兽,或者比野兽危害更大的人……我们无法改变事物的秩序……我们根据这一自然规律调整自己的灵魂,使它们顺应它,服从它……凡是你不能改变的,最好忍受下来。

  塞内加第一次向尼禄递了辞呈之后就开始写关于自然的书。他获得了 3 年时间。然后,公元 65 年 4 月间皮索反对皇帝的阴谋败露了,一名百人队队长受命来到哲学家的别墅。他对此是有准备的。上身袒露的保丽娜和她的侍女们可能泣不成声,但是塞内加已经学会顺从地跟着车子走,没有抗议就割了手腕。正如他在马尔恰痛失爱子时劝过她的:

何必为
部分生活而哭泣?
君不见
全部人生都催人
泪下。

第四章

对缺陷的慰藉

（一）

古希腊和罗马的智慧被冷落了几百年,有时还遭敌视,文献散失、被焚,幸存下来的残卷保存在寺院的阁楼和图书馆中,到16世纪又重新得意成为显学。在欧洲的知识精英中涌现出一种共识:到那时为止,世界最优秀的思想存在于从帕台农神庙建成到罗马陷落那段时期的希腊城邦和意大利半岛上极少数天才的头脑中,方今读书人的当务之急就是熟悉这些著作的丰富的内容。于是包括柏拉图、卢克莱修、塞内加、亚里士多德、卡图卢斯①、隆基努斯②与西塞罗等的主要著作,以及一些经典作品的选段——如伊拉斯谟③的《警句》与《名言录》、斯多布斯的《观点》、安东尼奥·德·格瓦拉④的

---

① Caius Valerius Catullus(前87—前54),古罗马著名拉丁诗人,以田园抒情诗著称。——译者
② Cassius Longinus(213—273),希腊新柏拉图派哲学家及修辞学家,为罗马人处死。——译者
③ Desiderius Erasmus(1469—1536),生于荷兰,16世纪著名人文主义神学家。——译者
④ Antonio de Guevara(1481—1545),西班牙宫廷教士,历史学家,曾为查理第五的忏悔神父,《金色信札》又称《王公赞》,提出理想的国王。——译者

《金色信札》以及彼得罗斯·克里尼托斯的《尊贵的学问》——都重新出版,遍布欧洲各国的图书馆。

在法国西南部,波尔多以东 30 英里处一座郁郁葱葱的山头,坐落着一幢华丽的城堡式巨宅,黄色石墙上覆盖着深红屋顶。

那是一位中年贵族同他的妻子弗朗索瓦丝、女儿莱奥诺以及仆从和牲畜(鸡、羊、犬、马)的住家。这所房产是米歇尔·德·蒙田的祖父用家族从事渔业的收入于 1477 年置下的,到父亲一辈又加盖了两翼,并扩大了耕地。蒙田本人从 35 岁起就接管了这片产业,不过他对理家毫无兴趣,而且对农业一窍不通("我连卷心菜和莴苣都分不清")。

他宁愿在城堡一角那座塔楼的三层楼上圆形书斋中度光阴:"我一生中的多数日子,每一日的多数钟点都是在那里度过的。"

书房有三扇窗(按照蒙田的说法,毫无遮拦地把美景尽收眼底),桌一张、椅一把、书千卷——哲学、历史、诗歌和宗教——排放在半圆形的五层书架上。蒙田就是在这里从由马尔西里奥·菲奇诺翻译成拉丁文的柏拉图文本读了苏格拉底（"古往今来第一智者"）向不耐烦的雅典陪审团所作的坚定不移的讲话；在这里，他通过第欧根尼·拉尔修的《生平》和1563年德尼斯·朗班编辑的卢克莱修的《自然颂》读到了伊壁鸠鲁的快乐观；也是在这里，他一再地读1557年巴塞尔新版的塞内加作品集（这位作者"特别对我脾气"）。

他自幼就是以古典著作开蒙的，拉丁文是他的第一语言。七八岁时已经学了奥维德①的《变形记》。16岁以前，他买了一套维吉尔②的著作，熟读《埃涅阿斯记》，还有泰伦斯③、普劳图斯④的作品以及恺撒的《评论集》。他嗜书如命，所以任波尔多市议员13年之后，决心引退，以便完全献身于书。读书是他生活的慰藉：

> 它在我退隐中慰我良多，令我摆脱百无聊赖之苦，随时助我从烦人的应酬中脱身。它能磨钝痛苦的刀锋——只要

---

① Publius Ovidius Naso（前43—前17），古罗马著名拉丁文诗人，风格多样，为当时上流社会的宠儿。《变形记》（Metamorphoses）为15卷神话长诗。——译者
② Virgile（前70—前19），最有名的拉丁文诗人，对后来整个欧洲文学界都有极大影响。《埃涅阿斯记》（Aeneid）史诗是其著名代表作之一。——译者
③ Terence，拉丁名Publius Terentius Afer（前190—前159），迦太基喜剧诗人。原为非洲奴隶，为元老院泰伦斯所解放，并使其接受自由派教育。他的作品以刻画普通人的心理见长。——译者
④ Titus Maccius Plautus（前254—前184），古罗马诙谐诗人。——译者

不是那无法抵御的剧痛。无以解忧，唯有读书。

但是书斋的书架及其所包含的对智力活动的无限敬仰并不是事情的全部。只要站在房间的中央，仰望天花板留心观察，就可以看见木梁上的 57 条语录，那是蒙田在 16 世纪 70 年代中期从《圣经》和经典著作中摘录出来让人刻上去的，这些语录表现了对有思想的益处的深刻保留：

人生至乐在于绝智。——索福克勒斯

你可曾见自作聪明的人？疯子可能比他略胜一筹。——谚语

最确定不过之事唯有不确定，最可悲而最骄傲者莫过于人。——普林尼

万事令人厌烦，人不能说尽。——《圣经·传道书》

古代哲人相信我们的理性力量足以赋予我们其他生物

所得不到的幸福和伟大。理性使我们能控制情欲，纠正本能造成的错觉。理性能缓和我们身体的原始欲望，引导我们与自己的食欲和性欲之间保持平衡的关系。理性是成熟的，几乎是神奇的工具，帮我们把握世界、把握自己。

西塞罗在《图斯库卢姆谈话录》（书斋中有一本）中对智力工作大加赞赏：

> 没有比做学问更美妙的职业了；做学问就是使我们在今世了解物质的无限，了解自然界、天、地、海洋的无比伟大；做学问教给我们虔诚、克己、心胸宽大，它把我们的灵魂从黑暗中拉出来，让它见识万物——最高的、最低的、最先的、最后的，以及所有在两端中间的；做学问给我们以过美好幸福生活的手段，它教给我们如何无怨无惑地度一生。

尽管蒙田家藏千卷书，而且得益于良好的古典教育，这段赞辞却使他愤怒填膺。这段话与刻在梁上的语录的精神截然相反。他一反平时的性格，以这样激烈的言词表达他的愤慨：

> 人其实是很可怜的……听他吹牛……这家伙是不是在描述全能而不朽的上帝！实际上，成千上万的村妇在自己村子里过着比他（西塞罗）更宁静、平和、有恒的生活。

这位罗马哲学家傲然无视这样的事实:大多数学者的遭遇都是极端不幸的;在天地万物中唯独人被选中去承受骇人听闻的苦难,以至于在黑暗的深渊中我们常恨自己生而为人,还不如蚂蚁和乌龟。

或者山羊也好。我在离蒙田的城堡几公里外,高舍地方的小村庄中一家农场院子里看见它。

它从来没有读过西塞罗的《图斯库卢姆谈话录》,也没有读过他的《论法律》。但是它很满足,嚼着莴苣叶,时或像一位老妇人表示不满那样摇摇头。这种生存状态未尝不值得羡慕。

蒙田自己被这一想法所打动并加以发挥:像动物一般生活强似拥有巨大书斋的理性的人的生活。动物生了病本能地知道如何照顾自己:山羊受了伤,能从几千种植物中找出白鲜草来,乌龟让毒蛇咬了自动就去寻找牛至,鹳鸟能给自己用盐水灌肠。相反的,人只能依赖昂贵而误人的医生(药箱里装满了怪诞的配方:"蜥蜴尿、大象粪、鼹鼠肝、从白鸽的右翼下抽出的血,还有,给阵发性急腹痛患者用的研成粉末的耗子屎")。

动物毋需长期学习也能理解复杂的思想。金枪鱼是自发的天文学专家。据蒙田称,"不论它们在哪里遇到冬至,就留在那里直到下一次春分。"它们也懂几何和算术,因为它们结队而游,成完美的立方形:"你只要数其中一行,就可得出整队的数目,因为长、宽、高的数目都是一样的。"狗有一种内在的对辩证逻辑的理解。蒙田讲述有一只狗找他的主人,

来到了三岔路口。它先望望一条路,然后再望望另一条,最后决定沿第三条路跑下去,因为它肯定主人一定选择了这条路:

> 这是纯粹的辩证法:那条狗用的是析取和连结命题法,穷举命题的各个部分。它是完全自学来的还是从特拉布宗的乔治的《辩证法》那里学来的,这有关系吗?

动物在恋爱问题上也占上风。蒙田怀着羡慕之情读一头大象爱上亚历山德里亚的一名卖花女的故事。当这头大象被牵着走过市场时,它懂得如何把皱皱的象鼻子滑进她的领口,以任何人类达不到的灵巧手法摩挲她的乳房。

没有经过试验,最低等的农场牲畜也能胜过古代顶尖智者的超然物外的修养。希腊哲学家皮朗①有一次乘船旅行遇到了大风暴。所有的乘客都惊惶失措,害怕那脆弱的船不堪汹涌怒潮一击。只有一名乘客没有失态,静静地坐在一角,表情泰然自若。那是一头猪。

> 我们还敢说拥有理性的好处是为了缓解我们的苦难吗?(我们把理性抬得那么高,并且据此认为自己可以君临万物之上。)如果有了知识,我们失去了没有它反倒能够享

---

① Pyrrho 或 Pyrrhon 或 Purrhôn(前365—前275),古希腊怀疑学派哲学家。——译者

受的宁静,有了知识,我们的生活状态还不如皮朗故事里的猪,那要知识做什么呢?

思想是否给了我们任何值得感谢的东西,是大可质疑的。

> 我们获得了反复无常、犹疑不决、怀疑、痛苦、迷信、焦虑(为可能发生的事,即使是死后)、野心、贪婪、妒忌、艳羡、桀骜不驯、疯狂、食欲难填、战争、谎言、不忠、背后中伤和猎奇。我们以公平、善于推理的理性以及判断和认知的能力而自豪,但是我们为此付出的代价之过分也异乎寻常。

果真可以选择的话,蒙田大约最终也不会选择像山羊一样生活——那只是极而言之。西塞罗描绘了一幅理性的仁慈的图景。过了16个世纪之后,由蒙田来提出其反面:

> 自知说了或做了蠢事,那不算什么,我们必须吸取的更加充分而重要的教训是:我们都是大笨蛋。

最大的笨蛋就是西塞罗这样的哲学家,因为他们根本想象不到自己竟会是笨蛋。对理性的错误自信就是产生白痴的源泉——同时,间接地,也产生缺陷。

蒙田坐在他的画栋雕梁下勾画出了一种新的哲学：承认我们离古代大多数思想家以为的那种理性的、宁静的生物有多远。我们的心灵多半是歇斯底里、胡言乱语、粗鲁而躁动，相比之下，动物在许多方面显得是健康和美德的模范——对这一不幸的现实，哲学家是有责任反思的，而他们很少这样做。

我们的生活部分是疯狂，部分是智慧。但是凡描写生活的人总是恭敬地对其中一大部分讳莫如深。

然而，如果我们承认自己的弱点，不再以自己并不掌握的本事自诩，那么——根据蒙田慷慨的救赎哲学——我们以自己特有的半是聪明、半是笨蛋的方式，终究还能达到差强人意的程度。

（二）性缺陷

既有肉体又有思想实在成问题，因为前者与后者的庄重和聪明形成诡异的反差。我们的肉体发出气味、感觉疼痛、萎缩、跳动、抽搐、衰老。它迫使我们放屁、打嗝，放弃明智的计划去和人上床，出着汗，发出急吼吼的呻吟，那声音就像美洲的野狼隔着旷野互相召唤的嚎叫。我们的思想受制于肉体任性的或者有规律的起伏。我们整个生活观可以因一次午餐过量造成消化不良而改变。"我在饭后与饭前判若两人"，蒙田说：

> 当我身体健康，又逢阳光明媚时，我是个和善的人；只要有一个长进肉里的脚趾甲，我就会变得暴躁，脾气坏得谁也惹不起。

最伟大的哲学家也不能免于受肉体之辱。蒙田说："试设想柏拉图患了癫痫或中风，然后将他的军，要他求助于他灵魂中所有美妙而高贵的功能。"或者设想在一场研讨会中，柏拉图忽然要放屁：

主管我们排泄的括约肌有自己收放的规律,完全独立于我们的意愿,甚至违反我们的意愿。

蒙田认识一个人能做到随自己的意愿控制放屁,而且曾经伴着诵诗的节奏放过一连串的屁。不过这个人的本事并不足以改变蒙田总的看法,那就是我们的肉体压倒我们的思想,括约肌是"最冒失,最没规矩的"。蒙田还听说过一件悲惨的事:有一个人的屁股"特别暴躁难缠,逼得它的主人不断地放屁,连续 40 年,终于要了他的命"。

难怪我们总想否认与这些令人难堪和屈辱的器官共存。蒙田遇到过一位女士,她强烈地意识到自己的消化器官有多讨厌,就想在生活中只当它们不存在:

> 这位女士(是最了不起的妇女之一)……认同这种意见:咀嚼会使面部变形,严重损害女人的优雅、美丽;所以每当肚子饿时就避免公开露面。我还认识一位男士,他不能忍受看他人吃东西,或是人家看他吃东西,结果他填饱肚子时必须避开一切人,比他出空肚子时还要紧。

蒙田还知道有的人为自己的性欲所折磨,终于自阉。还有一些人把搅拌雪与醋的压缩器施于自己的过分活跃的睾丸,以此来压制性欲。马克西米连皇帝意识到王者之气和肉体不相容,下令任何人不得见到他的裸体,特别是腰以下。他特意在遗嘱里规定,安葬他时必须穿着整套内裤。蒙田说,"其实他还应该加一条附录:给他穿裤子的人必须蒙上眼睛。"

不论这种激烈的做法对我们有多大吸引力,蒙田的哲学却是调和的哲学:"最愚蠢的自讨苦吃就是蔑视自己的身体。"不要企图把自己切为两半,我们应该停止同自己令人尴尬的皮囊打内战,而要接受它,承认它是我们存在的不可更改的事实,既不可怕也不丢脸。

1993 年夏,L. 和我一起到葡萄牙北部度假。我们沿着米尼奥的村落行驶,然后在维亚纳堡的南部住了几天。就在这里,在假期的最后一天,在一家俯瞰大海的小旅馆里,我发现——毫无先兆——我已经不能做爱了。要不是我去葡萄牙之前几个月恰好读到蒙田《随笔集》的第 1 卷第 21 章,那我简直无法挨过这一关,更不用说提起这件事了。

在那里面,作者讲述他一位朋友听说一个人正当要进入一个女人身体时突然阳物不举。这一预萎的尴尬局面对蒙田这位朋友造成的印象太强烈了,以至于他下一次同女人上床时这一图景在脑海中挥之不去。他十分害怕同样的灾难又会降临到自己的头上,结果为这一恐惧所征服,果真阴茎硬不起来了。从此以后,不论他多么想要女人,他就是无法勃起,每一次失败的羞耻的记忆又变本加厉地嘲笑他、折磨他。

蒙田的朋友认为能够坚定不移地、理性地操纵自己的阴茎是正常的男性特征,他在这件事上失败之后就成了性无能。蒙田认为错不在阴茎:"除非是真正的性无能,只要你做成了一次,你就再也不会无能。"自以为能用精神来完全控制自己的肉体,认为这才是常规,害怕背离它变成不正常,正是受这种观点的压迫,那位朋友才会失败。解决的办法是把图像重新画过:只有接受在做爱时对阴茎失控是一种无害的可能性,才能预防这种事的发生——那位受打击的朋友后来发现了这一点。他同一个女人上床时,学会了:

事先承认他有这方面弱点,并且公开说出来,从而心理放松,不再紧张。把病态看做是预料中的,就会少一些受压制感,心理负担也就不那么沉重。

蒙田的坦率使我这个读者的心灵也得到解放。对突然出现的阳萎摆脱了暗室中不可言说的羞耻感,而用这位决不厌弃肉体的哲学家见怪不怪、世事洞明的眼光重新对待之,对蒙田描述的下述现象的个人负疚感得到了缓解:

这个器官（普遍的）不听话，我们不要时它不知趣地勃起，我们最需要时它却又不配合。

一个跟情人失败后只会嗫嚅着道歉的男人其实可以再振雄风的，他应该宽慰他所爱，承认他的无能属于范围广阔的性事失败的一种，既不罕见，也不特别。蒙田曾认识一位加斯科地方的贵族，他同一位女士在一起时出现了阳萎后，逃回家去，把自己的生殖器割下来，给那位女士送去"以补过"。蒙田建议他应该换一种做法：

> 如果（两人）没有准备好，就不该急于行事。最好……等待合适的时机，而不要第一次不成功就绝望，使自己陷入永久的愁苦境地……一个男人如果第一次不成功，可以先做一些温柔的试探表达迸发的激情，而不要顽固地证明自己的缺陷就此到底了。

这是倾诉我们性生活中最孤寂的时刻的一种新的语言，亲切而不张扬。蒙田开辟了一条通向寝室的私密忧愁的道路，抽掉其羞耻感，自始至终努力使我们与自己的肉体和解。他把人们私下都经历过而极少听到的事勇敢地说出来，拓宽了我们敢于向爱人和向自己表达的范围——蒙田的勇气基于他的信念：凡是能发生在人身上的事就没有不人道的，"每一个人的形体都承载着全部人的状况"，这状况

就包括——我们不必为之脸红和自怨——有时阴茎不听话
而出现阳痿的风险。

　　蒙田认为我们之所以跟自己的肉体有那么多麻烦,部
分要归咎于在体面的社会中缺乏坦诚的探讨。有代表性的
小说或图像中从来不把女性的优雅与她对做爱的强烈兴趣
相联系,提到权威人士也从不提他们的括约肌或生殖器。
国王和贵妇人的肖像画从不鼓励我们去想象这些显赫灵魂
会放屁或做爱。蒙田用唐突而优美的法文填补了这种图画:

Au Plus eslevé throne du monde si ne Sommes assis que sus
nostre clu. ①

Les Roys et les philosophes fientent, et les dames aussi. ②

　　他原可以换个说法,不说"屁股"而说"臀部",不用"拉
屎"而说"如厕"。1611 年伦敦出版的兰德尔·高格拉夫的
《法语与英语词典》(有意进一步提高法文的年轻人和所有
最想达到对法语最准确的把握的人都可参考)解释"拉屎
(fienter)"一词专指虫豸、走兽的排泄物。蒙田之所以用这
样强烈的语言,那是为纠正哲学著作和上流客厅里同样强
烈的对肉体的否定。认为贵妇人从来不用上厕所,国王没
有屁股,这种流行的看法使蒙田觉得该是提醒世人他们既

---

① 法文,意为"登上至高无上的御座,仍只能坐在屁股上"。——译者
② 法文,意为"国王与哲学家皆拉屎,贵妇人亦然"。——译者

亨利三世

卡特林·德·梅迪奇

拉屎又有屁股的时候了。

　　人类的生殖活动十分自然,十分必要,十分正确,它们
究竟做了什么使我们觉得尴尬而难以启齿,把它们排除在
严肃的、规矩的谈话之外? 我们不怕说出"杀戮"、"偷盗"
或"背叛"这样的词,但是另外那些词我们却只敢悄悄地在
牙缝里嘀咕。

　　蒙田的城堡的邻近地带有几片山毛榉树林,一片在北
边接近卡斯蒂永-拉巴塔耶村,另一片在东边接近圣维维
安。蒙田的女儿莱奥诺一定对那树林的静谧和壮观很熟
悉。但是树名却不让她知道,因为法文中山毛榉树"fouteau"与"foutre"相似,而后者是同女人性交的意思。

"我只有这么一个女儿,感情充沛一点的女孩子像她这么大已经到了法律允许结婚的年龄了,"蒙田这样谈起她女儿,接着谈她14岁时的情况:

> 她苗条而文静;一直独处闺中由母亲一手带大,所以看起来比实际年龄小一些,刚刚开始脱去童稚之气。她在我面前读一本法文书,刚读到"fouteau"这个字,那位照顾她的保姆就急忙打断,粗鲁地拽着她,让她跳过这一令人尴尬的沟壑。

蒙田苦着脸说:20个粗野的男仆也没有这道叫她一遇这个字就跳远的严厉命令更能让莱奥诺意会到"fouteau"一词下面隐藏的内容。但是在那保姆——她主人称之为"老丑婆"——看来,这个字非跳过去不可,因为一位年轻女士的尊严决不能同她几年之后和一个男人在寝室中必然会了解的事联系起来。

蒙田指责我们通常对自己的描述漏掉了许多本色的东西。部分是为了纠正这一点,他才写自己的书的。他38岁退下来时就准备从事著述,但是不能决定写什么题材。要写一部惊世骇俗的书,同那半圆形的书架上千卷书中任何一种都截然不同,这一想法是逐渐在脑子里形成的。他抛开了千年来写作中的忸怩,毅然写他自己。他下决心明明白白地写自己的思想和肉体，1580年两卷《随笔集》在波尔多出版，8年以后第三卷在巴黎出版。他在序言中宣称：

> 如果我处在那些仍然享受着美妙的造化天工的自由民族中间，我保证一定会心甘情愿将自己完整的、赤裸裸的肖像呈现在你们面前。

迄今还没有任何作者愿意在读者面前一丝不挂。有的是关于圣人、教皇、罗马皇帝和希腊政治家的正式的、衣冠楚楚的肖像。甚至蒙田也有一幅托马斯·德·勒（1562—1620）画的肖像，穿着市长的长袍，戴着1571年查理九世赐给他的项链形圣米歇尔骑士勋章，神情俨然，深不可测。

但是这位身着长袍的西塞罗式的人物并不是蒙田的《随笔集》所要披露的自己。他着意要表现一个完整的人，塑造一个与多数肖像所造成的印象迥异的人的形象。所以他的书里包括他的膳食、生殖器、粪便、性征服和放屁——这些细节过去很少见于严肃的著作，对以理性动物自居的人的自画像来说是尖锐的讽刺。

蒙田告诉他的读者：

> 他的生殖器是组成他自我的不可或缺的部分。

我之所以为我，每一样器官都同样的重要，而没有任何器官比这一件更造就我为真正的男人。我有义务向公众展现自己完整的形象。

> 他觉得性事都是嘈杂而凌乱的。

在任何别的领域你都能保持某种体面；任何其他活动都接受礼仪规则，而就是这件事只能当做是杂乱无章的，或是可笑的。你倒试试看想出一个聪明、规矩的法子来做这件事！

> 他坐马桶时喜欢安静。

在所有自然的活动中，这件事是我最不能容忍打扰的。

> 而且他上厕所很规律。

我的大便和我从不失约，每天一起床必到（除非受到急事或疾病干扰）。

我们之所以重视周围那类肖像，是由于我们把它作为生活的榜样，别人自称如何，与我们自己某些方面正好相符，我们就接受下来；人家身上可以表现出来的地方，我们也善待自己身上的，人家避而不谈的，我们也视而不见，或者有所体验也感到羞耻。

> 当我设想男人反应最灵敏和最明智的（性交）姿势时，

同时又觉得一个人竟敢自以为在这件事上反应灵敏和明智简直是厚颜无耻。

并不是说明智是不可能的,而是蒙田要细致地界定明智的定义。真正的明智必须与我们的基本自我相适应,不过分高估智力和高度文化修养在生活中的作用,并理解我们肉身凡胎有时会有急迫的、极不光彩的欲求。伊壁鸠鲁和斯多葛派哲学主张我们可以控制自己的肉体,决不让自己的生理和情感方面占上风。这一主张很高尚,来自我们最崇高的愿望,但同时也是做不到的,因而起适得其反的效果。

> 巍峨的哲学巅峰如果没有人能呆在上面,规则如果超过我们的实践和能力,又有何用?

按照另类物种的标准来规定人的责任,是很不明智的。

肉体是既不能否定也不能战胜的。但是,正如蒙田希望提醒那"老丑婆"的,至少不必逼人在尊严和对山毛榉(fouteau)这个字的兴趣之间作选择。

> 可不可以这样说? 在这个世俗的囚牢里,我们身上既不是纯肉体的,也不是纯精神的,硬把一个活人撕成两半适足以害人。

（三）文化的缺陷

另一个造成缺陷感的原因是人们急忙、傲慢地把世界分为两大阵营：**正常**的和**反常**的。我们的经历和信仰常常遇到不屑一顾的态度：一句略表惊讶的问话："真的？多怪！"伴随着耸耸眉毛，就轻易地把我们的合法性和人性给否定了。

1580 年夏，蒙田完成他毕生的心愿，第一次离开法国去旅行，骑马出发经德国、奥地利和瑞士到罗马。与他同行的有 4 名青年贵族，包括他的弟弟贝特朗·德·马特库隆，还有十几名仆人。他们的计划是离家 17 个月，行程 3000 英里，骑马经过的城市包括巴塞尔、巴登、沙夫豪森、奥格斯堡、因斯布鲁克、维罗纳、威尼斯、帕多瓦、博洛尼亚、佛罗伦萨和锡耶纳，最后于 1580 年 11 月的最后一天傍晚时分抵达罗马。

一行人一路走过去，蒙田发现每到一省，人们对"正常"的观念就有变化。在瑞士小镇的旅店里认为正常的是床高出地面许多，需要台阶上去，周围有漂亮的帐子，旅客应该有单独的房间。而几英里以外的德国，正常的是床贴着地，没有帐子，旅客四人一间房。那里的店主人提供羽毛被，和法国旅店的被单迥异。在巴塞尔，酒里是不掺水的，一顿饭有六七道菜,而在巴登,星期三只吃鱼。瑞士最小的村庄也至少有两名警察守卫,德国人每一刻钟打一次钟,在有的地方甚至一分钟打一次。在林道,端上来的汤是椴榉叶做的,肉菜在汤之前上,面包是茴香做的。

法国旅客最不能入乡随俗。他们在旅馆里对那些摆着陌生食品的柜子敬而远之,要求供应他们在家乡习惯的"正常"菜肴。他们避免同任何不会说法语的人说话,认为他们不会说就是犯错。挑剔地啄着那茴香面包。蒙田从自己餐桌上望着他们:

> 他们一离开自己的村庄就好像鱼离开了水。无论到哪里,都紧抱着自己的生活方式,对外国的方式骂个不休。遇到一个同胞……就当作喜事来庆贺……他们郁郁寡欢、小

心翼翼地旅行,把自己紧紧裹在大衣中,保护自己免受那陌生地域的感染。

15 世纪中叶,德国南部各省出现了一种新的家庭取暖设施:卡斯登炉。那是一种可移动的铁盒子,用长方形的铁片焊接而成,里面烧煤或木柴。在漫长的冬日里,有很大优越性。封闭的炉子比明火壁炉产热量大 4 倍,而且还节约燃料,还不用打扫壁炉。热能被铁壳吸收,然后逐渐均匀地散发到空中。炉子周围装有管子,既可通风又可晾衣服,一家人可以把炉子周围作为冬天的起居室。

但是法国人对此不感兴趣。他们认为制作明火壁炉更省钱;他们嫌德国炉子不提供亮光,而且吸收太多室内的水分,使气氛压抑。

这个题目竟造成地区隔阂。1580 年 10 月间,蒙田在奥格斯堡遇到一个德国人,他作了长篇发言,批评法国人用明火壁炉取暖,然后描述铁炉的优越性。他听说蒙田只逗留几天(15 号到达,19 号离开),对他表示同情,列举离开奥格斯堡的种种不便之处,其中包括回到明火壁炉时会感到头昏——这头昏正好是法国人责怪铁炉引起的。

蒙田进一步考察这一问题。在巴登，他分到一间烧铁炉的房间，在习惯了炉子发出的某种气味后，他一夜睡得很舒服。他发现有了这炉子，他起床穿衣时就不用先披上毛皮晨衣。几个月后他来到意大利，在一个寒冷的冬夜表示十分想念那小旅店的铁炉。

他回家以后，衡量了两种取暖方式的利弊：

> 的确，那炉子的热气使人有压抑感，它的材料还散发一种气味，不习惯的人会感到头痛……另一方面，由于它散热是均匀的、有恒的、达到整个房间，不像我们的壁炉那样制造看得见的火焰、烟尘和干燥，这些条件使它足以与我们的炉子相抗衡。

使蒙田感到恼火的是那位奥格斯堡的先生和法国人都不假思索地坚信自己的取暖方式优于他人的。假如蒙田从德国归来后在自己的藏书楼中安上一个奥格斯堡的铁炉，他的同胞们就会以他们对待任何新鲜事物的怀疑态度对待之。

每一个民族都有许多风俗习惯,不但不为另一民族所知,而且被认为野蛮、怪异。

当然,铁炉或者壁炉都没有任何野蛮或怪异之处。任何社会自己确定的关于正常的定义似乎都只有部分的合理性,总是不公平地排斥大片实践的领域,视之为异端。蒙田向那位奥格斯堡的先生和加斯科的邻居指出,铁炉和明火壁炉在可以接受的取暖方式的广阔天地中都有其合法的一席之地,他这样做的目的是想拓宽读者对何谓正常的狭隘的地域观念,而追随他最喜爱的那位哲学家的脚步:

人们问苏格拉底为何方人士,他不说"雅典",而说"世界"。

这个世界最近出现的奇事出乎任何欧洲人的想象。1492 年 10 月 12 日星期五,蒙田出生前 41 年,哥伦布到达佛罗里达湾的巴哈马群岛中的一个岛,接触到了关纳哈尼印第安人,他们从未听到过耶稣的名字,赤身裸体到处走动。

蒙田对此事产生强烈兴趣。圆形藏书楼中有好几册关于美洲印第安部落的书,其中包括弗朗西斯科·洛佩斯·德·戈马拉的《印第安部落通史》、吉罗拉莫·本佐尼的《新世界纪事》和让·德·莱利的《巴西游记》。他从中读到:南美洲人喜欢吃蜘蛛、蚱蜢、蚂蚁、蜥蜴和蝙蝠,"他们把这些东西煮熟了浇上各种汁吃"。有些美洲部落的处女公开展示她们的私处,新娘在婚礼日可以纵欲狂欢,男人可以同男人结婚,死人给煮熟,踩成酱用酒拌了,在祭神的集会上由他的亲属吃下去。有的国家女人站着而男人蹲着小便。有的国家男人让前身的汗毛生长而剃去背上的毛。有的国家男人行割礼,而另一些国家的人特别害怕龟头见光,"小心地把包皮拉下来盖上,用绳子扎好"。有的国家见人打招呼是把身子转过去,背对他,当国王吐痰时,宠臣伸手去接,当他大便时,"侍卫们把他的粪便用细麻布包起来"。每一个国家似乎都有自己独特的审美观:

> 在秘鲁,大耳朵是美丽的:她们用人工尽量拉长耳朵。有一个还活着的人说他在东方见过一个国家特别推崇把耳朵拉长,坠以各种珠宝,以至于他常常遇到可以让他连衣服带胳膊穿过耳朵眼的妇女。别处有整个民族都讨厌白牙,刻意把牙染成黑的。还有别的地方是染成红色……墨西哥妇女认为低额头是美的表现,所以她们把身体别处的毛都拔掉,单单让前额的头发长得浓密,而且还用人工突出这一点。她们如此崇拜大乳房,故意把它翻过肩膀喂孩子奶。

从让·德·莱利的书上,蒙田知道巴西的图比族人赤身裸体如在伊甸园,一点不感到羞耻(当欧洲人送给那里的女人衣服时,她们咯咯笑着拒绝了,她们觉得奇怪,为什么有人要把这么不舒服的东西来加重她们的负担)。

给德·莱利的书作版画的人（他在巴西呆了8年）特意要纠正欧洲流行的图比族人和野兽一样浑身是毛的说法(de Léry: 'Ils ne sont point naturellement poilus que nous ne sommes en ce pays')①。图比族男人剃光头，女人留长发，扎漂亮的红辫子。图比印第安人喜欢洗澡，一看见河就跳下去互相擦洗。有时一天可以洗到12次。

他们睡在长条的仓库式的房子里，可容200人。床是棉织的，像吊床一样拴在柱子之间（图比人打猎时带着床走，午后把它吊在树间睡午觉）。每6个月整个村子搬一个新地方，因为居民认为换换景色对他们有好处('Ils n'ont d'autre réponse, sinon de dire que changeant l'air, ils se portent mieux' —de Léry)②。图比人的生活十分有规律，常常活到100岁，老年

男人和女人都像刚从娘胎里出来时一样一丝不挂。
——让·德·莱利，
《巴西游记》(1578)

---

① 法文，意为"德·莱利：'他们生来并不比我国人多毛'"。——译者
② 法文，意为"'他们没有别的答复，只说换换空气会更健康'——德·莱利"。——译者

147

也没有灰发或白发。他们还非常好客。每当村里新来一个人时,妇女都要掩面哭喊道:"你好吗?你大老远的来看我们,辛苦了!"马上就请客人喝图比人最爱喝的饮料,是用一种植物的根做的,颜色像红葡萄酒,味道很辣,但是对肠胃有好处。

图比族的男人可以娶不止一个妻子,据说对她们都很钟爱。蒙田讲述称:"他们整个道德观只有两点:作战坚定和对所有妻子的爱。"妻子们显然对这种安排很快乐,没有表现出任何妒忌心(性关系是很松的,惟一的禁忌是不得与近亲同床)。蒙田尽情地描绘细节,而他的妻子就在城堡楼下:

> 他们的婚姻有一个美好的特点值得一提:一如我们的妻子竭力打掉我们对别的女人的柔情,他们的妻子以同样的热情替自己的丈夫争取其他女人的爱情。她们对丈夫的名誉比什么都关心,因此不惜下功夫争取自己的同行——妻子,越多越好,因为这可以表明丈夫的价值。

无可否认,这一切都十分奇特,但是蒙田并不认为有什么不正常。

蒙田属于少数。哥伦布发现新大陆后不久,西班牙和葡萄牙殖民者就从欧洲到那里进行探险。他们得出结论,土人比畜生好不了多少。天主教骑士比列加格农把他们称作"长着人脸的野兽";加尔文派牧师里切尔认为他们根本没有道德观念,分不清善恶;罗朗·儒贝医生检查了5名妇女之后就肯定她们是没有月经的,因此干脆不属于人类。

把他们排除在人类之外后,西班牙人就开始像杀野兽一样屠杀他们。到1534年,即哥伦布到达后42年,阿兹特克和印加帝国就遭毁灭,人民不是被杀就是变成奴隶。蒙田在巴托洛梅·拉斯·卡萨斯的《西印度群岛的毁灭》一书中读到这一野蛮行为。(这本书是1552年在塞维利亚出版,1580年由雅克·德·米格罗德翻译成法文,题为《西班牙人在西印度群岛,即所谓新大陆,犯下的残酷暴行》。)印第安人是毁于他们自己的好客和他们的武器太弱。他们向西班牙人开放他们的村庄和城市,而他们的客人却完全出其不意地袭击了他们。他们的原始武器当然敌不过西班牙人的大炮和剑,征服者对俘虏没有丝毫仁慈。他们杀戮儿童,挑开孕妇的肚子,挖人眼,把整个家庭活活烧死,夜里放火烧村庄。

他们训练猎犬追捕逃到森林中去的印第安人,把他们撕成碎片。

用铁链把男人锁在一起,送到金矿、银矿里去劳动。一个人死后就把他的尸体从锁链上砍下来,而锁链那一边的同伴还继续劳动。多数印第安人在矿里都活不到3星期。妇女则当着她们丈夫的面被强奸后毁容。

最常用的肉刑是割下巴和鼻子。拉斯·卡萨斯叙述有一个女人看见西班牙人和他们的狗来了,就和她的孩子一起上吊死了。一名士兵走到他们跟前,用刺刀把孩子劈成两半,一半喂了他的狗,然后找来一名修道士给孩子的另一半行安葬礼,以保证那孩子在基督的天堂有一席之地。

被强迫男女分居、处于孤寂焦虑之中的印第安人大量自杀。从蒙田出生的1533年到他的《随笔集》第三卷出版的1588年之间,据估计"新大陆"的土著居民从8000万下降至1000万。

西班牙人如此心安理得地屠杀印第安人是因为他们自信知道一个正常人应该是什么样的。根据他们的理性认识,穿马裤、有一个妻子、不吃蜘蛛、睡在床上的才是正常人:

他们的话我们一句也听不懂;他们的举止,乃至长相、衣着都跟我们的大不相同。我们有谁不把他们当野人和走兽?有谁不认为他们的沉默是由于愚笨和兽类的无知?反正……他们对我们的吻手礼和复杂的、深深的鞠躬完全不理会。

他们也许外表像人类:"啊!可是他们不穿裤子……"

在这种屠杀背后是混乱的推理:把正常和不正常区别开来的逻辑出自典型的演绎法,我们从几个特例推出普遍规律(正如逻辑学家所提出的:我们观察到 A_1 是 ø,A_2 是 ø,A_3 是 ø,所以得出结论,所有的 A 都是 ø)。要判断某人是否聪明,就去找我们迄今为止所遇到过的每一个聪明人的共同特征。如果我们遇到第一个聪明人看来像图 1,另一个

1.

2.

3.

4.

1.

2.

3

像图 2，另一个像图 3，我们多半会得出结论：聪明人一定读很多书，穿黑衣服，表情严肃。再看到图 4 那样的人，我们很可能认为他愚笨而不屑一顾，甚至以后把他杀了。

　　法国旅客对卧室里的德国炉子惊恐而反感，他们肯定在来德国之前在本国见过许多好的壁炉。或许其中有的像图 1，有的像图 2，有的像图 3。以此推理，他们得出结论，优良的取暖设备的要素在于明火壁炉。

　　蒙田为这种心智的傲慢而叹息。南美洲的确存在野蛮人；但不是那些吃蜘蛛的人：

　　　　人人都把他们不习惯的事物称作野蛮；除了本国的舆论和风俗，我们没有其他标准来衡量真理和正确的理性。我们总是认为本国的宗教和政治制度十全十美；一切行事处世的方式都是既深刻又完美！

　　他并不是想要取消野蛮和文明的区别；各个国家的风

俗习惯的价值是有所不同的(文化相对主义与民族主义一样的原始)。他只是要纠正我们作出这种区别的方法。我们国家可能有许多美德,但是其依据不是由于它是**我国**的。一个域外国家可能有许多缺点,但不能简单以它的风俗不寻常来认定缺点。以国籍和熟悉与否作为区别好坏的标准是荒谬的。

法国的礼俗规定,如果鼻通道有障碍物,必须擤到手帕里。但是蒙田有一位朋友对此作了思考之后,认为可能直接用手指擤鼻涕更好些:

> 他为自己的观点辩护……问我那脏鼻涕凭什么有特权让我们必须准备细麻布手绢来包起它,然后小心翼翼地带在身上……我想他说的也不是毫无道理,但是囿于习惯势力,我连这一点奇怪之处也发现不了,而我们对他国的类似的奇怪风俗却如此深恶痛绝。

以小心说理取代偏见,这是衡量一种行为的正确方法,令蒙田感到沮丧的是那种轻率武断的态度,把自己不熟悉的等同于缺陷,全然无视古代最伟大的哲学家关于心智谦逊的基本教导:

> 问彼何所知,答曰所知惟一事,即我无所知,是为古往

今来上上智。

∽

那么,假如我们遇到含蓄的指我们为不正常的表示:用一句略表惊讶的问话:"真的? 多怪!"同时耸耸眉毛,就轻易地把我们的合法性和人性给否定了,该怎样呢? 蒙田的朋友在加斯科涅用手指擤鼻涕就遇到了这种反应,这种态度走向极端就会灭绝南美洲的部落。

也许我们应该记住,对于不正常的指责在很大程度上是有历史的和地域的基础的。要摆脱它的束缚,只需多了解超越时间空间的风俗习惯。在特定的时间为某一群人认为不正常的事物不一定永远如此。我们可以在自己的思想中超越边界。

蒙田的书房里摆满了帮助他超越偏见的局限的书。有历史书、旅行日记、传教士和船长的报告、异域的文学,还有穿着奇装异服的部族吃着不知名的鱼的图画集。通过这些书,蒙田能够为自己身上那些在当地罕见的特点找到合法性——罗马性、希腊性,更接近墨西哥人和图比人而不是加斯科涅人的一些方面:宁愿有 6 个妻子,或剃光背上的毛,或一天洗 12 次澡;他只需求助于塔西陀的《编年史》、冈萨雷斯·德·门多萨的中国历史、戈拉特的《葡萄牙史》、勒贝尔

何处认为何事为反常

德国
用壁炉，吃没有茴香
的面包，睡床单。

法国
用铁炉，吃茴香面
包，有三个妻子。

巴黎

阿尔卑斯山区
钟不常敲，警察很
少，房子不油漆。

塞田的城堡

至罗马

斯基的《波斯史》、利奥·阿弗里卡纳斯的《非洲游记》、卢西
尼亚诺的《塞浦路斯史》、波斯特尔的"土耳其与东方历史丛
书"、明斯特的《宇宙志》（其中还有关于"稀有动物"的图
片），就能稍慰自己这些方面带来的孤寂之感。

　　当别人自称掌握普遍真理使他感到压抑时，他可以依
法将所有古代伟大哲学家关于宇宙的理论罗列出来，然后
证明，尽管每一位都自以为掌握了全部真理，他们之间的分
歧还是达到了可笑的程度。经过一番比较之后，蒙田讽刺
地表示他完全不知道是接受：

　　　　柏拉图的"理想"，伊壁鸠鲁的原子说，留基伯和德谟
　　克利特的充实与真空说，泰勒斯的水说，阿那克西曼德的
　　自然界无限说，或是第欧根尼的以太说，毕达哥拉斯的数

和对称说,巴门尼德的无限说,穆赛乌的一体说,阿波罗多罗斯的火与水说,安那克萨哥拉的同质粒子说,恩培多克勒的物活论,赫拉克利特的火说,还是其他任何一种从我们精致的人类理性的无限混乱的判断中推导出的,肯定而明晰的观点。

新世界的发现和古代文献一起形成强大的力量,摧毁了蒙田称之为"完全只信自己的、令人痛苦的好斗的傲慢"。

任何人只要动脑筋收集出于人类智慧的荒唐蠢事,就可以讲出许多新奇的故事……当我们发现那些曾大大提高人类智慧的重要人物犯下如此明显的巨大错误时,我们就可以作出判断,知道对于人以及他的全部智能和理性该怎么看了。

在马背上周游欧洲 17 个月对蒙田帮助很大。见证了其他国家的生活方式有助于缓解他在本土感受的压抑气氛。一个社会认为奇怪的事物可能在另一个社会受到欢迎,认为合理而正常。

异国他乡可能使我们恢复被本土狭隘的傲慢踏灭了的信心和希望;可能鼓励我们变得让自己更满意。任何一个特定的地域关于正常的观念——不论是雅典、奥格斯堡、库斯科、墨西哥、罗马、塞维利亚还是加斯科涅——都只能容纳我们天性的一部分而不公平地把其余部分都归入野蛮和怪异的范畴。每一个人都可能体现人的全部特性,但是看来没有一个单个的国家能容忍这种人性的全部复杂性。

在蒙田刻在木梁上的 57 条语录中有一条是泰伦斯的:

Homo sum, humani a me nihil alienum puto. ①

蒙田骑马周游列国,同时发挥想象力,他建议我们摒弃地域偏见和自我分界,而代之以局限性较少的世界公民的观念。

当我们被指责为不正常时,还有一种慰藉是友谊。朋友总是能善待我们,把我们看做比一般人心目中更为正常的人。我们可以向朋友倾诉一些不足与外人道的看法,通常这些看法会被指责为太刻薄、张扬性欲、让人绝望、狡猾、软弱——友谊是一种小小的阴谋,用来对付一般人所谓的合理的事物。

蒙田和伊壁鸠鲁一样,认为友谊是幸福的组成部分:

> 在我看来,情投意合的伙伴之亲切友爱为无价之宝。啊!朋友!信哉古人言:有朋常来,其味甘于水,其不可或缺甚于火。

他曾经有幸有这样的朋友为伴。他在 25 岁时经人介绍

---

① 拉丁文,意为"我是人,凡属于人的于我都非异类"。——译者

认识了一位 28 岁的作家、波尔多市议会议员艾蒂安·德·拉·博埃西。这是一见如故的友谊:

> 我们见面之前已经在互相寻觅,因为久闻其名……一听到对方的名字就拥抱起来。第一次见面是在人群拥挤的全镇节日聚会上,我们一见如故,互相倾心难分难舍,从那一刻起,我们就亲密无间,任何关系无可比拟。

蒙田认为那种友谊 300 年才出现一次;同平时经常被称作友谊的那种不痛不痒的交往没有共同之处:

> 我们通常称作朋友或友谊的只不过是机缘相投,在精神上互相支持的熟人或比较亲密的交往。而我所说的友谊是两个灵魂融合在一起,达到天衣无缝、难分彼此的程度。

如果蒙田没有遇到那么多令他失望、对他们只能说三分话的人,这份友谊也不会那么珍贵了。他对拉·博埃西如此深情正说明他与别人交往时往往掩盖庐山真面目,以避免对方猜疑和惊讶的表情。多年以后,蒙田这样解析他对拉·博埃西的感情的源泉:

Luy seul jouyssoit de ma vraye image. ①

———————————

① 拉丁文,意为"能欣赏我真面目者惟此君"。——译者

这就是说，在蒙田所有的熟人中，拉·博埃西是惟一真正理解他的。他可以让他回归本真，凭着他的心理的敏锐，帮助蒙田做到了这一点。他挖掘出蒙田性格中宝贵的，然而一直被忽视的方面——这说明我们择友不仅是为了他们对我们好，在一起过得愉快，而且，可能更重要的是，因为他们是真正的知己。

然而好景不长。第一次见面4年之后，1563年8月，拉·博埃西得了急腹症，几天后就去世了。蒙田终其身笼罩在失友之痛之中：

> 说真的，与同这样一个人为伴的4年美妙时光相比，我的余生不过是灰烬与烟雾，是难耐的漫漫黑夜。自我失去他那一天起，我只是无精打采地苟活下去。

《随笔集》中贯穿着一种渴望，要找到一位堪与死去的挚友相比的精神伴侣。拉·博埃西逝世18年之后，蒙田还常常悲从中来。1581年5月间，蒙田到卢卡附近的别墅去做水疗期间，在旅行日记中写到他一整天都浸沉在思念德·拉·博埃西先生的悲痛中。"我长期陷于其中不能自拔，对我身体损害甚多。"

他从此在交友中再未有这样的福气，但是他发现了最精美的补偿。他通过《随笔集》创造了另一种形式的手段来表现拉·博埃西所欣赏的自我。他在纸上就像同挚友在一起时那样回归本真。

他写作是出于对周围的失望,但同时也受希望的激励:别的地方可能有人会理解。他的书向一切人诉说,没有特定的个人。他意识到把自己内心深处向书店中的陌生人展示的悖论:

> 我把许多不愿告诉任何个人的事告诉了公众;如果有忠实的朋友要了解我最私密的想法,我请他们到书商的书架上去。

我们倒是应该感谢这种自相矛盾的做法。书商是孤独者最好的归宿,有那么多书都是由于作者找不到人倾诉而写的。

蒙田也许是为了排解自己的孤寂而开始写作的,而他的书多少对我们的孤寂之感也能有所排解。一个人坦率的、毫无遮掩的自述——他谈到了自己的性无能和放屁,谈到了他的亡友,还谈到他坐马桶时需要不受打扰——使我们感到自己有些方面不那么古怪了,那是我们在平常的交往中难以启齿的、却是我们身上真实的一部分。

（四）智力的缺陷

关于怎样才算一个聪明人,有一些主流的设定:

聪明人须知

其中之一,反映在中小学和大学的课程上,聪明人应该能回答以下问题:

1) 求下图中 x 边长与 x 角之值

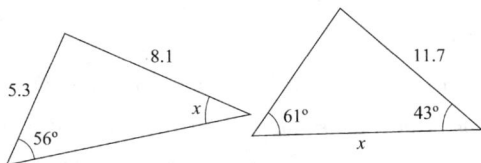

2. 以下诸句中哪些是主语、谓语、系词、量词(如果有的话):狗是人类最好的朋友;卢西琉是恶毒的;所有蝙蝠都属于啮齿类;屋里没有绿的东西?

3. 托马斯·阿奎那的第一动因的论据是什么?

4. 翻译:

Πᾶσα τέχνη καὶ πᾶσα μέθοδος, ὁμοίως δὲ πρᾶξίς τε καὶ προαίρεσις, ἀγαθοῦ τινὸς ἐφίεσθαι δοκεῖ· διὸ καλῶς ἀπεφήναντο τἀγαθὸν οὗ πάντ' ἐφίεται. (διαφορὰ δέ τις φαίνεται τῶν τελῶν· τὰ μὲν γάρ εἰσιν ἐνέργειαι, τὰ δὲ παρ' αὐτὰς ἔργα τινά· ὧν δ' εἰσὶ τέλη τινὰ παρὰ τὰς πράξεις, ἐν τούτοις βελτίω πέφυκε τῶν ἐνεργειῶν τὰ ἔργα.) πολλῶν δὲ πράξεών οὐσῶν καὶ τεχνῶν καὶ ἐπιστημῶν πολλὰ γίνεται καὶ τὰ τέλη· ἰατρικῆς μὲν γὰρ ὑγίεια, ναυπηγικῆς δὲ πλοῖον, στρατηγικῆς δὲ νίκη, οἰκονομικῆς δὲ πλοῦτος.[1]

亚里士多德,《尼各马科伦理学》,第 1 卷第 i—iv 页

5. 翻译:

In capitis mei levitatem iocatus est et in oculorum valitudinem et in crurum gracilitatem et in staturam. Quae contumelia est quod apparet audire? Coram uno aliquid dictum ridemus, coram pluribus indignamur, et eorum

---

[1] 希腊文,意为"一切技艺、一切探询,乃至一切行动和选择,都号称是追求善;因此,善被宣称为一切事物的目标。但是还可以发现,各种目的之间是有所区别的;有些是活动,有些是与生产它们的活动相分离的产品。当目的与活动分离时,其产品从本质上就优于活动。既然行动、技艺与科学是多种多样的,它们的结果也是多种多样的:医学的目的是健康,造船业的目的是船只,战略的目的是胜利,经济学的目的是财富"。——译者

aliis libertatem non relinquimus, *quae ipsi in nos dicere adsuevimus*; *iocis temperatis delectamur*, *immodicis irascimur.* ①

塞内加,《论恒心》第 16 卷第 4 节

蒙田曾面对许多这类问题,并都回答得很好。他就读于当时法国最优秀的学府,波尔多的吉耶讷学校。该校建于 1533 年以取代古老的比较差的艺术学校,在米歇尔(蒙田)6 岁被送到那里时已经是全国赫赫有名的一座教育中心。教职员中包括一位开明的校长安德列·德·戈维亚、著名的希腊学者尼古拉·德·格鲁齐、亚里士多德学派学者纪尧姆·盖朗特,还有苏格兰诗人乔治·布坎南。

如果要对支撑吉耶讷学校的教育思想做一番界定——事实上,在它之前和之后的多数学府也都差不多,大致可以说,其理论的出发点是:学生对世界(历史、科学、文学)的知识越多越好。但是蒙田在这所学校规规矩矩从头学到毕业之后,提出了一条非常重要的补充命题:

---

① 拉丁文,意为"有些人拿我的秃顶开玩笑,还取笑我眼睛昏花,腿太细,身材不好。都是实话,为什么听来却感觉受了侮辱? 同样一件事情,一个人面前说说,我们当做笑话;但如果好几个人在场,我们就要生气。明明是我们经常用来自嘲的话,却不愿意别人随便乱说。开玩笑有个分寸是趣事;过了头,便是冒犯"。——译者

一个人如果有大智，就会用是否有用和是否适合于自己的生活这把标尺来衡量一切事物的真价值。

只有能使我们感觉更好的东西才值得学习。

有两名古代思想家在吉耶讷学校的课程中大概占据显要地位，而且作为智力高超的榜样。学生大概必须学习亚里士多德的"前提与后续推理法"，在那里，这位希腊哲学家是逻辑学的先驱。他提出：如果 A 是所有 B 的谓项，而 B 是所有 C 的谓项，那么 A 就是所有 C 的谓项。亚里士多德的理论是：如果一项命题肯定或否定 P 是 S，那么 S 与 P 就是这一命题的"项"，P 是谓项，S 是主项。他还说，所有命题不是普遍的就是个别的，或是肯定，或是否定 P 是 S 的全部或是一部分。另外一位就是罗马学者马尔库斯·特伦提厄斯·瓦罗①，他为恺撒大帝建立起整个图书馆，自己写了 600 本书，包括一部关于文科的百科全书和 25 册关于字源学和语言学的著作。

蒙田对此并非无动于衷。写出一整书架的关于文字起源的书，并发现普遍的肯定词，的确是丰功伟绩。但是如果我们发现有此成就的人并不比从来没有听说过哲学逻辑的人更快活，甚至略微不快活一些，就可能提出疑问了。蒙田

---

① Marcus Terentius Varro（前116—前27），古罗马学者。先服役于庞培军中，后归顺恺撒，为凯撒建立最早的公共图书馆，以学识渊博、著述丰繁而载入史册。——译者

研究了亚里士多德和瓦罗的生平以后,提出一个问题:

> 瓦罗和亚里士多德的渊博对他们有什么好处呢?帮他
> 们摆脱疾病之苦?解脱他们可能与一个普通门房同样遭遇
> 的不幸?逻辑能安抚他们的痛风吗……?

为理解这两个人为什么都那么渊博而又都那么不快
活,蒙田把知识分为两大类:学问与智慧。在学问栏目下他
罗列的题目包括逻辑学、字源学、语法、拉丁文和希腊文。
在智慧的栏目下,他列出的是远为广阔而更难捉摸、更有价
值的知识,包括一切足以使人生活得更好的——蒙田的意
思是生活得快活而合乎道德——的知识。

吉耶讷学校的问题在于,尽管有这样的校长和教师,它
在传授学问上成绩优异而在传授智慧方面完全失败——实
际上是在学校的层面上重复那些损害了瓦罗和亚里士多德
的生活的错误:

> 我很愿意回到我们的教育之荒谬这个题目上来:这种
> 教育的目的不是要我们变得更好、更智慧,而是更有学问。
> 它成功了。它没有教给我们去追求美德,吸纳智慧,却使我
> 们慑服于其派生词和字源学……
> 我们很容易问:"他会希腊文或拉丁文吗?""他能写诗
> 或散文吗?"而我们应该做的是,看谁懂得最好,而不是谁懂

得最多。我们只是为填满记忆而用功，却给理解力和是非观留下一片空白。

他从来不擅长体育："对于跳舞、网球、摔跤，我从来没有学会过哪怕一点点粗浅的技巧；对游泳、击剑、跳高、跳远，我也一窍不通。"然而他对多数教员在课堂所教的缺乏智慧强烈反感之余，断然为法国课堂上的青少年提出了截然不同的另一种方案：

如果我们的灵魂不能更好地运转，如果我们没有更健康的判断力，那么我宁可我们的学生把时间花在打网球上。

他当然更愿意学生去上学，但是要上那种不是教字源学而是传授智慧的，能够纠正长期对抽象事物的偏见的学校。小亚细亚米利都地方的泰勒斯就是这种偏见的早期体现者。此公以在6世纪时试图丈量天有多高，并用同样的三角理论算出埃及金字塔的高度而名垂千古。后者无疑是极为复杂

而辉煌的业绩,但蒙田并不希望这些来占领他的课程表。他更同情泰勒斯认识的一名冒失的年轻人的教育思想:

> 我一直感激那位米利都的女青年,她见这位本乡的哲学家……总是两眼朝上,望苍穹而沉思,就过去不客气地告诉他:等他把脚底下所有的事物都解决了,再考虑云端的事也不迟……对任何研究哲学的人你都可以像那女子责备泰勒斯一样,告诉他,他忽视了脚下的事物。

蒙田注意到在其他领域内也存在同样的重特殊而轻平实但并非不重要的事物的倾向。他也像那个米利都的女子一样,要把我们拉回到地上来。

> 攻城陷阵、领导大使馆、治理国家,固然是光辉的事业。而吵架、欢笑、买、卖、爱、恨、与亲人——还有自己——和气、正当地相处,不偷懒,不自欺,却是更了不起,更难能可贵的。不论人家说什么,在退隐的生活中以这样的方式所承担的责任,其艰难和紧张决不亚于另一种生活。

那么,蒙田希望学生在学校学什么呢? 什么样的考试能测试出他心目中的智慧——那与不幸的亚里士多德和瓦罗的智力技能相去如此远的智慧?

这种考试要提出涉及日常生活的问题:爱、性、病、死、孩子、金钱与野心。

蒙田式的智慧的试卷

1. 大约七八年前，在6英里地外有一个村民，现在还活着。他的妻子妒忌成性，长期以来折磨得他头脑不堪其扰；一天，他回到家里，妻子又像往常那样以没完没了的唠叨来迎接他。他忍无可忍，气急之下，忽然拿起还在手里的镰刀，把那撩起他妻子如此狂热的器官割了下来，甩到她脸上。（《随笔集》Ⅱ,29）

a）应该怎样解决家庭争吵？

b）那妻子是在唠叨还是在表达情爱？

2. 考虑以下两句话：

愿死亡降临于我正在种卷心菜之时，我就可以既不为死，也不为未完成的种植而发愁。

我连卷心菜和莴苣都分不清。（《随笔集》Ⅱ,17）

什么是对待死亡的明智的态度？

3. 让女人早些了解生活的现实（阴茎的大小）比让她们凭热烈的想象力去猜，可能是更加贞洁、更加有效的做法。她们可能根据自己的希望和欲求把我们那个器官想象成比现实大3倍……那些男孩子在我们王宫的走廊和楼梯上到处乱涂乱画的硕大的生殖器造成多大的危害！这些画造成了对我们实际能力的残酷的误解。（《随笔集》Ⅲ,5）

一个身上"活生生的现实"长得比较小的男人应该用什么办法提起这个话题?

4. 我认识一位绅士,在他的大厅里宴请了一群体面的客人。四五天之后,他开玩笑说(完全不是真的)他请客人吃了猫肉饼。有一位在座年轻女士大惊失色,立即犯严重胃病而发高烧,终于不治。

分析这件事的道义责任所在。

5. 如果自言自语不显得是神经病,每天都会有人听到我骂自己:"你这个大笨蛋!"(《随笔集》Ⅰ,38)

最不足取的自寻烦恼就是自轻自贱。(《随笔集》Ⅲ,13)

一个人应该给自己多少爱?

发出测试智慧而不是学问的考卷,其结果很可能是立刻对智力重新排队——出现令人惊讶的新精英阶层。那些不入流的人现在要被认为比那些久负盛誉而其实难副的传统候选人更聪明,一想到这种前景,蒙田就无比欣喜。

聪明人应有怎样的神情和外表
通常我们读书读不懂时就以为那本书有高超的智慧。深奥的思想当然不能用儿童的语言来表达。但是——这样我一生中见过成百个工匠和农民比大学校长更有智慧,更快活。

说也许不太厚道——把艰涩与深刻联系起来是感情生活中常见的悖谬在文人圈中的反映,神秘莫测的人能够在简单的头脑中引起崇敬,却不能打动坚实可靠、清晰的头脑。

蒙田心安理得地坦率承认他不喜欢那些神秘的书。他写道:"这些书我读不了多长时间,我只爱读好看、易懂、引起我兴趣的书。"

我不想为任何事情伤脑筋,即使为做学问也不,不论这多么宝贵……我所求于书的就是以一种高尚的消遣办法自娱……我在阅读中遇到难懂的段落时,决不为此咬断指甲,作了一两次努力之后就让它过去了……一本书看腻了,就换一本。

一个家藏千卷书,博学如希腊、拉丁哲学的百科全书的人说这种话只能当做胡言乱语或是开个玩笑。如果蒙田以一位喜作严肃的哲学讲话的枯燥无味的绅士面貌出现,那是装腔作势。他一再强调自己懒散是一种策略,用以打破那种对聪明和好文章的陈腐观念。

蒙田要表明的意思是,关于人文的书没有理由要写得艰涩而枯燥;表达智慧并不需要特殊的语汇和句型,读者也不会从厌倦中得到好处。如果运用得当,乏味感可以作为判断一本书的价值的一种指标。但是这永远不会成为充足的判断指标(低级的乏味感也可以下滑为有意的漠视和不耐烦),某种适当的乏味感可以抵消我们对浅薄的废话的容忍度。那些在读书过程中不注意自己已经感到乏味的人,就像不关心自己的疼痛感一样,很可能不必要地加剧自己的苦恼。有时觉得所读之书索然无味可能是错的,但不论犯这种错误的危险有多大,从来不让自己对所读之书不耐烦可能陷阱更多。

每当我们遇到一本难懂的书时,我们都可以选择:是认为作者无能,表达不清楚;还是我们自己愚钝,抓不住它的意思。蒙田鼓励我们去责怪作者。一种难懂的文风多半是出于懒惰而不是聪明;晓畅的文章很少这样写的。还有一种可能就是这种文章掩盖了内容的空虚;让人看不懂是对空洞无物再好不过的掩护。

艰涩难懂好比是一枚钱币,学者祭起它来当法宝以掩盖学问的空虚;而蠢人则在付款时急于接受它。

哲学家没有理由非要用与市井语言格格不入的词语。

正如以奇装异服来吸引人注意是小家子气一样，言词也是一样；寻求新奇的说法或生僻的字眼是出于幼稚的小学教员式的虚荣心。但愿我的写作能做到只限于巴黎中央菜市场的词汇。

但是朴素的写作是需要勇气的，因为那些顽固地认定读不下去的文章是智力的标志的人很可能会不屑一顾，认为它是头脑简单的产物。这种偏见极为顽强，蒙田甚至怀疑，大多数大学里那些自称最崇拜苏格拉底的学者，如果在自己家乡见到这位哲学家，脱掉柏拉图的《对话》中的俨然形象，披着脏兮兮的斗篷走过来用简单的话同他们对话时，他们是否还会欣赏他：

苏格拉底的追随者传下来的关于他的对话的图像使我们肃然起敬，只是因为我们已经被普遍的赞扬镇住了。这不是出于我们自己的了解；因为它不符合我们现在的行事处世。如果今天再出现类似的情况，很少人会高评他。不经过人工重彩浓墨予以突出和夸大的优雅，我们已经不会欣赏了。我们的眼光已经如此粗糙，那种朴素天真、自然流露的优雅根本引不起我们的注意……对我们来说，天真不就是属于头脑简单之流，是该否定的特质吗？苏格拉底让他的灵魂随普通百姓而动：某农民如是说；某妇人如是说……他的推理和类比都是从最普通的、尽人皆知的人类活动中来；任何人都能理解他的话。在这样一种平常的形式下，我们今天绝对不会看出他惊人的理念之崇高和辉煌；我们把任何没有以博学的形式吹大的事物都视为卑下和平庸；除了大肆炫耀的浮华之外，我们看不到其他的财富。

这是一种呼吁，要我们对那些明白晓畅并不唬人的书也要认真去读，引申下去，我们如果因为财力或教育中有缺陷而穿着朴素的外衣，说话的词汇超不过巴黎中央菜市场的摊贩，也不必认为自己是傻瓜。

聪明人须知

他们应该知道事实，假如他们不知道，而且还傻到从书本中获得了错误的事实，那么他们就不要怪学者对他们不留情，把他们一巴掌打倒，傲慢而彬彬有礼地指出，有个年代错了，引文有误，一段话断章取义，或是重要的资料来源遗漏了。

但是蒙田设计的聪明的要素是：一本书的重要性在于它对生活有用和适宜；准确地复述柏拉图或伊壁鸠鲁的话不如判断他们所说是否有兴味，并能早日帮我们克服焦虑和寂寞来得有价值。人文领域的作者的责任不是表现出

"类科学"的准确性，而是带来幸福和健康。蒙田对那些拒绝这一观点的人发牢骚：

> 那些专注于评判书本的学者除学问外不承认其他价值，除了钻研学问使自己知识渊博外不承认其他智力活动。把这西庇阿错当成那西庇阿①，那你就再没有值得说的了，难道还有吗！在他们看来，不了解亚里士多德，就没法了解你自己。

《随笔集》本身就经常出现引语错误，出处不对，论据不合逻辑以及用词缺乏定义。作者丝毫不以为意：

> 我是在乡间家里写作，无人可求助或为我纠错，我通常来往的人也没有会拉丁文祷词的，更不用说正确的法文了。

当然书里有错误（"我书里充满错误"，他夸口说），但是这不会使《随笔集》一败涂地，正如准确无误不见得保证其价值。写一些无益于智慧的书，比混淆西庇阿·埃米利亚努斯（前185—前129）与西庇阿·阿非里加努斯（前236—前183）罪过更大。

---

① Scipio，古罗马高乃依族常用的名字，出过不止一个以此为名的历史名人，因此有弄错人之说。——译者

聪明人的思想从何处来

从比他们更聪明的人那里来。他们应该花时间在引用和评论那些占据知识之树的高枝的权威的作品上。他们应该就柏拉图的道德观或是西塞罗的伦理学撰写论文。

蒙田颇得力于这一想法。《随笔集》中经常出现评论的段落,还有数百处引语,因为蒙田觉得这些作者一语中的,能比他自己更优雅而精辟地表达出来。他引了柏拉图128次,卢克莱修149次,塞内加130次。

当别的作者以我们达不到的明晰和心理准确性表达了先得我心的思想时,我自然会情不自禁地直接引用他们。他们比我们自己还了解我们。我们尚欲言又止,说不清楚的想法,他们已说得那么清晰,遣辞那么优美。我们在他们写的书上划的铅笔道和作的眉批,以及借用的话,都标明我们是在何处找到了一小块自己,或是找到用自己思想的原料构成的句子——如果这些话写于穿托加袍、用动物作牺牲的古代,竟然与今天的我们不谋而合,那就更加了不起。我们把这些话引进自己的著作,表示对他们的敬意,也提醒自己有自知之明。

但是伟大的著作除了照亮我们的经验,激励我们自己去发现之外,也会构成麻烦的阴影。它们可能使我们对自己生活的一部分弃置不顾,就因为关于这方面还没有足以

证明的文字。它们不但没有扩大我们的视野,反而错误地划定了界限。蒙田认识一个人,他似乎为自己的引证狂付出了太高的代价:

> 每当我向这位熟人问起他对某个问题知道什么时,他就要给我看一本书。甚至他要告诉我自己屁股上长了癣,都得先查字典找到"屁股"和"癣"的含义之后才敢说。

其尽信书而不愿信自己也如此!假如书能表达我们所有的潜能,连我们长癣都知道,那我们也就无可抱怨。然而如蒙田认识到的,伟大的书本对那么多题目都避而不谈,所以我们如果听任它们来划定我们好奇心的界限,就会阻碍我们思想的发展。在意大利的一次聚会集中体现出这个问题:

> 我在比萨遇到一位举止得体的先生,他是亚里士多德的信徒,到了这样的程度,以至于他的基本理论是:考验一切良好的思想和每一项真理的试金石和度量计就是看它是否符合亚里士多德的教导。除此之外,一切都是无意义的、虚妄的:一切的一切,亚里士多德都已经见到了、做到了。

当然他见到了、做到了很多事。在所有古代思想家中间,可能亚里士多德是最全面的,他的著作覆盖了广阔的知识面(生物的生成与腐化、天、气象学、灵魂、动物的器官、动物的行动、诡辩术、与尼各马可谈伦理学、物理学、政治学）。

但是亚里士多德的成就的规模本身就给后代留下了问题。有的作者太聪明，对我们并没有好处。他们说得太多，好像对所有的事物都有最后发言权。他们的天才禁止其后代有任何心怀不敬，而这正是创造性的工作所必不可少的。亚里士多德的悖论在于他恰恰阻止了那些最崇敬他的人学习他的榜样。他是由于怀疑其前人已经建立的知识而成就其伟大的。他并不拒绝学习柏拉图和赫拉克利特的著作，但是在赞赏他们的力量的基础上，对他们的弱点提出了尖锐的批判。要真的做一个名副其实的亚里士多德的信徒，就意味着允许凭自己的思考与成就最伟大的权威也能有所分歧，这是蒙田认识到，而那位比萨的先生没有认识到的。

不过，宁愿引用和评论别人的话，而不愿自己思考、说自己的话，这也是可以理解的。评论一本别人写的书，虽然在技术上很费力，需要花很多时间去研究、注释，但是可以避免受到新创作的作品常会经受的那种残酷的攻击。人家可能指责评论者没有正确反映伟大作者的思想，但是不会要评论者为那些思想负责。这也是蒙田《随笔集》中有那么多引语和评论的原因：

> 我有时让别人说我要说的话是因为我自己的语言修养不足，有时是由于我的智力不逮……而有的时候是为了

制服那些轻薄之徒，他们对一切写作，特别是活着的人的近作，都急急忙忙地进行批判……我需要以别人的盛名来掩护我的软弱。

人往往在死后几百年受到比生前更多的重视，这种现象实在令人震惊。同样的说法，出于古人笔下就被接受，而由当代人说出来就会招来嘲笑。评论家不会拜倒在他大学同学的豪言壮语面前。这些人是不允许俨然像古代哲学家那样说话的。塞内加写道："任何人都逃不掉因出生而受惩罚"。但是，后人也有类似的想法时却最好不要这样说，除非他有自取其辱的偏好。蒙田没有这种偏好，于是就寻找庇护。《随笔集》结尾有一段自白，流露出感人的脆弱无奈之情：

> 如果我有信心做我真正想做的事，我就会不顾一切，彻底地自说自话。

他之所以没有信心，是因为时间、空间离得越近，他的思想就越难受到像塞内加和柏拉图的思想那样的待遇：

> 在我家乡加斯科涅的氛围中，人们见我印出来的文字感到滑稽。我的名声所到之处，离我家越远，评价越高。

他的家人和随从听到过他打鼾，见过他换床单，在对待他的态度中绝没有他在巴黎所受到的敬意,更不用与他死后相比了。

> 一个人可能在世人面前奇妙非凡;然而他的妻子和随身仆人看不出他有什么过人之处。几乎没有人在家里被当做奇人。

这句话可以从两方面来理解:本来就没有人真的是奇妙非凡的,但只有家人和随从能从近处看到令人失望的真相。或者,有人的确很有意思,但是他的年龄和居处都离我们太近,我们往往不当回事,因为人有一种奇怪的排斥身边事物的倾向。

蒙田并不是在自怜自艾;他只是以一些对当代陈义较高的作品的批评为例,说明一种有害的症状:本能地认为真理总是在远离我们的地方,在另一种气候中,在古代图书馆,在很久以前的人写的书中。问题是,真正有价值的东西是否为生于巴特农神殿落成和罗马陷落之间这段时期的极少数天才所专有,还是如蒙田大胆提出的,它也向你我开放。

他指出了一种极为奇特的智慧来源,比皮朗的那头航海的猪、图比印第安人或是加斯科的农夫还要奇特,那就是读者。如果我们对自己的经历给予适当的关注,学会把我们自己当作可能参与智力生活的一员,那么,蒙田认为,我们大家都可以达到不亚于古代巨著中的真知灼见。

如此想法洵非易事。我们所受的教育就是以遵循书本权威为美德，而不是遵循我们自己凭感官每天在内心记录而成的大书。蒙田努力要我们回归自我：

> 我们会说："西塞罗如是说"；"这是柏拉图的道德观"；"这是亚里士多德的 *ipsissima verba*①"。但是我们自己要说什么呢？我们作出了什么判断？我们在做什么？鹦鹉学舌也不比我们差。

用鹦鹉学舌来形容写评论可不是学术语言。可以提出一连串的论据说明注解柏拉图的思想或是西塞罗的伦理学多么有价值。而蒙田却偏要强调这种学术活动的怯懦和沉闷。进行二手创作要求不高（原创性的发明比引用他人的话所需要的条件不知高多少），这种工作的困难仅仅是技术性的，耐心加一间安静的图书馆足矣。再者，学术界的传统鼓励我们去学舌的许多著作本身并没多大意思。它们之所以被放在教学课程的中心地位只是因为出于名家之手，而许多同样的、甚至更有价值的课题无人过问，就因为从来没有大学者阐述过。艺术与现实的关系早就被认

---

① 拉丁文，意为"原话"。——译者

为是严肃的哲学课题,因为是柏拉图首先提出来的;而腘
腆与个人外表的关系却不算,因为古代哲学家没有注意到
这个问题。

鉴于这种对传统的违反常情的崇拜,蒙田认为值得向
读者承认,实际上他认为柏拉图有局限性而且有时很乏味。

> 我认为(柏拉图的)《对话》太拖沓,扼杀了实质问题;
> 我还哀叹,这样一个原该有许多更有价值的话可说的人却
> 把时间花在这些冗长而无用的预备性讨论上,不知我们时
> 代的规范能否原谅我这样狂妄亵渎先贤?

(一位显要的著作家暂时让另一作家私心窃有所疑,蒙
田对此于心有所不安。)至于西塞罗,就直接加以抨击,不必
有任何歉意:

> 他的引言、定义、分节和字源学吞噬了他的大部分著
> 作……如果我用一个钟头(那在我是很多了)读他的书,然后
> 再回想我从中得到了什么精髓,多半如一阵风,空无一物。

蒙田暗示,学者之所以如此重视经典,是出于一种虚
荣心,想以攀附显赫的名字来让别人以为自己聪明。其结果
就是广大的读众要面对堆积如山的有学问而无智慧的书:

关于书的书比关于任何其他题目的书都要多：我们所做的就是互相上光。只见一窝蜂地都在评论别人，而原创的作者园地却是一片荒芜。

但是在每个人的生活中都能找到有意思的思想，蒙田坚持认为，不论我们的生平多么微不足道，从自己身上得出的洞见还是胜过从所有的古书中得出的：

假如我是一名优秀的学者，我就能从自己的经历中找到足够的令自己聪明的源泉。任何人只要回想自己上一次怒火发作的情况……就能比亚里士多德对这种感情的丑恶之处看得更清楚。只要回想自己生过的病，那些威胁生命的病和促成身体逐渐变化的一件件小事，任何人都会对以后的变化有所准备，并检查自己的身体状况。即便是恺撒的生平也不如我们自己的足以为范例；不论是皇帝还是平民，影响其一生的种种遭遇总不外乎在人身上所能发生之事。

只有那故意唬人的学术思想才使我们不这样想：

我们每一个人都比自以为的更富有。

我们大家都能获致智慧的思想，只要我们不再妄自菲薄，以为我们没有 2000 岁，对柏拉图的《对话》不感兴趣，静静地生活在乡间,就与此事无缘。

　　全部道德哲学都能附属于一个人平凡的私生活,并不亚于其他更丰富的生活。

也许是为了大力强调这一观点,蒙田给我们讲了那么多他自己的生活有多平凡、多私人化,因此他告诉我们:

　　他不喜欢苹果:
　　除了西瓜之外……我对任何水果都无特殊好感。
　　他跟萝卜有一段复杂的关系:
　　起初我觉得萝卜挺适合我,后来发现不是;现在又好了。
　　他实施最先进的牙齿卫生:
　　我的牙齿一直都特别好……从儿时起我就学会用餐巾擦牙,一起床和饭前饭后都擦。
　　他吃饭太快:
　　我吃得太急,常常咬了舌头,有时还咬了手指。
　　还喜欢擦嘴:
　　我吃饭没有台布没关系,但是如果没有干净的餐巾就会很不舒服……很遗憾,我们没有沿着国王们开创的风俗继续下去:像换碟子一样,每一道菜换一次餐巾。

也许都是婆婆妈妈的小事,但是它有象征意义,提醒我

西塞罗，前106—前43

们这部书后面有一个思想者"我"，从一个平凡的不爱吃水果的灵魂提出了一种道德哲学——以后还可能继续提出。

即使我们外表与过去的思想者没有共同之处，也不必灰心。

根据蒙田重新画过的够格的、半理性的人的肖像，不会希腊文、有时放屁、一顿饭后就改变主意，对书本感到乏味，对古代哲学家一无所知，常常混淆这西庇阿与那西庇阿，都是可以的。

善良而平凡的生活，努力寻求智慧而从未远离愚蠢，有此成就足矣。

第五章

对伤心的慰藉

（一）

就悲情而言,可能他是哲学家中感情最细腻的。

1788 年,阿瑟·叔本华生于但泽。后来他以遗憾的心情看待自己的出生:"我的一生可视为一段无用之插页,是对我长眠于'无'之极乐境界的干扰。"他进一步阐明:"人的存在是一种错误,可以说今天很坏,一天比一天坏,直到最坏的事出现。"叔本华的父亲亨利希是一名富

生平(1788—1860)

商,母亲约翰娜比父亲小 20 岁,是风头很健的交际花,对儿子关心很少,结果他成为历史上最大的悲观主义哲学家:"我还是 6 岁的时候,一天晚上父母从外面散步回来,发现我深陷于绝望之中。"

1803—1805 年,叔本华 17 岁时父亲去世(看来是自杀的,尸体被发现漂浮在他家仓库旁的小河沟里),留给他一

亨利希·叔本华　　　　　约翰娜·叔本华

笔遗产，保证他终身不必工作。这并不能带给他安逸。他后来回顾道："17岁上，我还没有受到多少正规教育，像青年释迦牟尼看到病、苦、老、死一样，痛感人生的苦难。真相是……此岸世界不是爱众生者所造，而是魔鬼的作品，它把众生带到世上就是为看着他们受苦受难而取乐；所有的资料都证实这一点，这也是占主流的观点。"

叔本华被送到伦敦，在温布尔登的伊戈尔寄宿学校学习英语。他的一位朋友罗伦斯·梅耶收到他的信后回信说："我很难过，你在英国的经历引得你恨整个这个国家。"恨归恨，他对英语的掌握却臻于完美，在谈话中常被当作英国人。

叔本华周游法国，访问了尼姆城，一千八百年前罗马工程师们曾在那里修建输水管，把水引过辉煌的加尔桥，保证市民总是有足够的水沐浴。这一罗马古迹并不能打动叔本华:"这些遗迹使人想起千百万人的遗骸早已化为腐草。"

叔本华的母亲抱怨她的儿子热衷于"思考人间苦难"。

温布尔登,伊戈尔寄宿学校

1809—1811年,叔本华进入哥廷根大学,决心成为哲学家:"人生殊可悲,我决定以毕生思考它。"

在一次郊游中,有一位朋友建议去会会女人。叔本华打掉了这个计划,他的理由是"人生苦短,倏忽不定,不值得费这个力气"。

1813年,他到魏玛去看母亲。约翰娜·叔本华与当地最有名的公民约翰·沃尔夫冈·冯·歌德结为好友。歌德常到她家去（以同她的女仆苏菲和叔本华的妹妹阿黛尔聊天为乐事）。叔本华与歌德初次相见后，形容他"安详、平易近人、友好，愿他的名字永世受到赞誉"！歌德写道："年轻的叔本华看来是一名奇特而有意思的青年。"阿瑟对这位作家的好感始终没有得到回报，哲学家离开魏玛时，歌德送给他两句诗：

青年叔本华像

Willst du dich des Lebens freuen,
So musst der Welt du werth verleihen. ①

叔本华不为所动，他在笔记本里歌德的诗句旁附了一段尚弗②的话："Il vaut mieux laisser les hommes pour ce qu'ils sont, que les prendre pour ce qu'ils ne sont pas."③

1814—1815 年，叔本华移居德累斯顿，写了一篇论文（《论充足理由律的四重根》）。他朋友很少，与人交谈也不

---

① 德文，意为"欲求人生乐趣，必先珍惜此世"。——译者
② Nicolas de Chamfort(1741—1794)，法国 18 世纪道德伦理学家，一度同情法国大革命，但不满其恐怖手段，最后自杀。他对当时社会持愤世嫉俗的批判态度。——译者
③ 法文，意为"与其把人认作实非其人，不如听其保持本来面目。"——译者

期待回应:"有时我同男人或女人谈话就像小女孩同她的玩偶说话一样。她当然知道娃娃听不懂她的话,但是她有意自欺来创造一种交流之乐。"他成为一家意大利小酒馆的常客,那里可以吃到他最爱吃的菜——威尼斯萨拉米香肠、夹菌小肠和帕尔马火腿。

1818年,他写完《作为意志和表象的世界》,自知是一篇杰作。那篇文章里解释他为何缺少朋友:"一个天才是很难合群的,因为除了他的独白之外还有什么对话能如此智慧而有趣呢?"

1818—1819年,叔本华到意大利去庆祝他作品的完成。他欣赏那里的艺术、自然风光和气候,不过身体还是很虚弱:"我们应该经常意识到,没有人能远离这样的境地——恨不得用剑和毒药结束自己生命;谓予不信,只要遇到一次意外、生病、或命运和天气的不测风云,就会很容易转而信服。"他访问了佛罗伦萨、罗马、那不勒斯和威尼斯,在招待会邂逅了不少迷人的女性:"我很喜欢她们——只要她们愿意要我。"受到拒绝促使他得出这样的看法:"只有男性的智慧为性冲动所蒙蔽时才会以佳人来称呼那些矮身材、窄肩膀、宽胯骨、短腿的性别。"

1819年,《作为意志和表象的世界》出版。售出230册。"任何人生的历史都是苦难的历史";"但愿我能驱除把一代蚂蟥和青蛙视为同类的幻觉,那就太好了"。

1820年,叔本华在柏林谋求到一个在大学教哲学的教职。他开讲座,讲"哲学的整体:即世界与人的思想之精华的理论"。只有 5 名学生来听。而在旁边一座楼里,可以听到他的对手黑格尔正对着 300 名听众讲学。叔本华这样评价黑格尔的哲学:"其基本思想是最荒谬的幻想,一个颠倒过来的世界,是哲学的插科打诨……其内容是傻瓜喜爱的最空洞无意义的词语展示;他的表述……是最讨厌的胡言乱语的废话,使人想起疯子的呓语。"他开始不再对学术界抱有幻想:"作为通例,还不曾有人认真对待哲学,讲哲学的人尤其不,正如作为通例,没有人比教皇对基督教义更少信仰。"

1821 年,叔本华与一名 19 岁的歌手卡罗琳·梅东坠入情网。他们的关系断断续续维持了 10 年,但叔本华无意把这一关系正式化:"结婚意味着尽量做使对方讨厌之事。"但是他向往一夫多妻制:"一夫多妻制的许多好处之一是:做丈夫的不必与妻子的娘家亲戚们关系如此密切,方今就是对这点的恐惧阻止了许多婚姻。与其要一个丈母娘不如要十个!"

1822 年,二度访问意大利(米兰、佛罗伦萨、威尼斯)。启程之前,他要他的朋友弗雷德里克·奥桑查一查"书报杂志中提到我的情况",这一任务没有费奥桑多少时间。

1825 年,在学术界失败之后,叔本华想做翻译家。但是他提出把康德译成英文和把《项狄传》①译成德文,均遭出版

---

① *Tristram Shandy*,18 世纪英国小说家劳伦斯·斯特恩的著名长篇小说,全名为:*The Life and Opinions of Tristram Shandy*,共 9 卷。——译者

社拒绝。他在一封信中提到"在布尔乔亚社会中占一席之地"的凄惨愿望，却从未实现。"如果这个世界是上帝创造的，那么我不愿做那个上帝；世上的悲苦令我心碎。"幸好他在最阴郁的时刻可以靠对自己估价得到慰藉，"我还要提醒自己多少回……我的精神和思想对日常生活而言……就如把天文望远镜放在歌剧院中，或是用大炮猎兔子？"

1828 年，40 岁。他安慰自己："任何有出息的男人过了40 岁……难免有一点愤世嫉俗。"

1831 年，现在 43 岁，住在柏林，叔本华再次想到结婚。他瞩意于一名 17 岁的活泼美丽的姑娘弗罗拉·魏斯。在一次游船的聚会上，他向她献殷勤，对她微笑，递给她一串白葡萄。弗罗拉在日记中写道："我并不想要这串葡萄，因为老叔本华接触过它，我感到恶心，就悄悄地在身后让它滑到水里了。"叔本华匆匆离开了柏林："生命本质上没有任何价值，只是靠需要和幻觉保持运动。"

1833 年，他在美因河畔法兰克福一套简朴的公寓中定居，那是一座有五万居民的城市。他这样形容这一大陆欧洲的金融中心："一个小而僵化、内里粗俗、靠浮华的建筑撑起来的城市，是夜郎自大的阿布代①农民之乡，我才不爱理睬他们。"

---

① Abdera，古希腊地名，那里的居民被认为以闭塞愚昧为特点，此处借用以形容法兰克福的居民。——译者

此时与他关系最亲密的是一只接一只的卷毛狗,他感到它们有着人类所缺乏的温柔和谦卑:"一看到任何动物,我就开心。"他对那些卷毛狗关爱备至,以"先生"称呼他们,并对动物福利产生浓厚兴趣:"有高度智慧的狗,人类最忠实的朋友,竟被人拴上锁链!每当我看到这样的狗总是深感同情,并对它的主人无比愤慨。我每想起几年前《泰晤士报》的一则报道就备感欣慰:某勋爵有一只大狗,用锁链拴起。一天他走过院子,心血来潮,走过去拍拍那条狗,不料那狗把他整条胳臂从上到下撕了一个大口子。真是活该!它这样做的意思是说:'你不是我的主人,而是把我短暂的一生变成地狱的魔鬼!'我希望所有用锁链拴狗的人都遭遇这样的事。"

这位哲学家每天生活规律十分严格。早晨写作 3 小时,吹长笛(罗西尼的曲子)1 小时,然后戴上白领结到玫瑰市场英国馆子吃午餐。他胃口极大,一幅巨大的餐巾塞在领子里。他用餐时拒绝同其他食客打招呼,不过在喝咖啡时间或与人交谈。其中有一个人描述他"牢骚满腹得有点滑稽,说话虽然生硬,实际脾气挺好,并不伤人"。

还有一个人描述他经常吹嘘他牙齿好,说明他比常人优越,或者用他的话来说,比那些"庸碌的两脚动物"优越。

午餐以后,叔本华就钻到他的俱乐部——附近的卡西诺协会——的图书馆去看《泰晤士报》,他认为这是报道世上悲苦之事的最好的报纸。下午他牵狗在美因河畔散步 2

小时,口中喃喃自语。晚上到歌剧院或戏院,对迟到者的杂音、脚步声、咳嗽声都愤怒不已,并写信给当局要求采取严格措施予以禁止。他虽然熟读并仰慕塞内加,但对这位罗马哲学家对噪音的说法却不予苟同:"我一向认为,一个人能安然容忍的噪音量与他的精神力量成反比……一个习惯于摔门而不是用手关门的人不仅是举止失仪,而且是粗鲁而思想狭隘……只有……当觉悟到任何人都无权以吹口哨、大喊大叫、抡锤子、甩鞭子……等等来打断他人的沉思时,我们才达到了相当的文明程度。"

1840年,他有了一只新的白卷毛狗,以婆罗门教的世界灵魂阿特曼命名。此时他热衷于东方宗教,特别是婆罗门教(每天夜里读几页《奥义书》)。他称婆罗门人为"最高贵、古老的人种",而且威胁要开除他的女佣玛格丽特·施内普,因为她违背了不许给书房的佛像掸灰尘的命令。

他独处的时间越来越多。他母亲很为他担心:"连续两个月独居一室不见任何人,这对你不好,我的儿子,也让我难过,一个人不能与世隔绝到这样地步。"他经常白天长睡:"如果生活是一种享受,那么人人都会不情愿进入无知觉的睡眠状态,而会欣然再醒过来。但是事实正相反,人人都愿长睡不愿醒。"他把自己与两位他最喜欢的思想家相比,以此来为自己嗜睡辩护:"人的头脑越发达……思想越活跃,需要的睡眠就越多。蒙田说过自己一向睡得很熟,一生中很大部分时间都花在睡眠上;他到老年时还每天在一张榻上睡 8 至 9 小时。据说笛卡儿也爱睡觉。"

1843 年，叔本华搬进法兰克福一幢新房子，美景街 17 号，位于市中心美因河附近。他在这条街上度过余生，不过在 1859 年为了他的狗与房东吵架之后，搬到了 16 号。

1844 年，他的《作为意志和表象的世界》出第二版，并又加写了一卷。他在"前言"中写道："我不把现已完成的著作献给我的同代人或同胞，而是献给全人类，因为我确信它对人类不会没有价值，尽管对它的承认将姗姗来迟，这是任何形式的善不可避免的命运。"这一版销售量还不到 300 册。"吾人最大乐事莫过于受到仰慕；但是仰慕者有种种原因不愿表达其仰慕之情。因此，能以不论何种方式衷心自我仰慕者是最快乐的人。"

1850 年，阿特曼去世。他买了一只棕色卷毛狗，起名布兹，成为他的爱犬。据说，有一次一列军乐队经过他家门口，他中断了正在进行的谈话，去搬一张凳子放在窗口，好让布兹能凭窗眺望。邻居的孩子们都管那畜生叫"小叔本华"。

1851 年，他出版了一部随笔和格言的选集《杂文与笔记》，出乎作者意料的是这本书成为畅销书。

1853 年，他享誉全欧洲（他称之为"名誉的喜剧"）。波恩、布雷斯劳和耶拿的大学都请他去讲学。他收到许多崇拜者来信。一位西里西亚的女士给他寄来一首含情脉脉的长诗。一位波希米亚的男士写信告诉他，他每天在他的肖像上放一圈花环。他的反应是："一个人长期处于微不足道、备受冷落之后，人们终于敲锣打鼓地来了，还把这当回事！"不过他也从中得到一些满足："如果一个具有伟大思想的人把捉摸不定的舆论当作指北星，他还能实现他的目标，坚持常年创作吗？"那些有哲学头脑的法兰克福人以买卷毛狗来向他表示敬意。

1859 年，盛名之下，他受到了女性的关注，他对她们的看法也有所缓和。原来他认为她们"适合做幼儿的保姆和教师，正是因为她们自己幼稚、愚蠢和见识短"，现在的看法是：她们能做到无私和有洞察力。有一位名叫伊丽莎白·奈伊（拿破仑手下一位元帅的后裔）的漂亮女雕塑家是他的崇拜者，10 月里来到法兰克福，在他的公寓里住了 1 个月，为他塑了一座半身像。

　　"她在我的住处整天工作。我午餐后回到家里，我们一起用咖啡，一起坐在沙发上，我感觉好像结婚了一样。"

　　1860 年，健康日益恶化，看来离终点不远了："想到不久以后我的身体将为虫豸吃光，我还能忍受；但是想到那些哲学教授们蚕食我的哲学，使我不寒而栗。"9 月底，他在美因河畔散步回家，感到喘不过气来，就此溘然长逝，始终坚信"人的存在是一种错误"。

∞

　　这就是可能给人的心灵提供无与伦比的帮助的哲学家的一生。

（二）一则当代的爱情故事
加叔本华式的注释

一个男人坐在从爱丁堡驶向伦敦的火车里，打算做些工作。那是一个和暖的春日午后。

他面前桌上放着纸张、一本日记，椅子扶手上有一本摊开的书。但是自打车驶过纽卡斯尔，一位女士上车坐在隔走廊与他并排的座位上之后，他就无法集中思想。那位女士随便向窗外望了一会儿之后，就转向一堆杂志。从火车走过达灵顿开始，她一直在看《时装》杂志。她使那个男人想起克里斯滕·柯克画的赫格-古尔贝尔夫人像（不过这两个名字他都想不起来了），那幅画是他几年前在丹麦一家博物馆见到的，曾为之怅然良久。

不过这位女士与赫格-古尔贝尔夫人不同，她是棕色短发，穿牛仔裤、运动鞋，T恤衫上套一件米黄色V字领毛衣。他注意到她白皙而布满雀斑的手腕上戴着一块大得不相称的体育用电子表。他想象自己的手穿过她的栗色头发，抚摸她的后脖颈，然后通过袖子滑进毛衣里面，看着她在他身旁熟睡，嘴微微张着。他还想象同她一起住在伦敦南部樱桃树夹道的街上一所房子里。他猜想她可能是大提琴手，或是图案设计师，或者是专事基因研究的医生。他在脑子里设计开始同她交谈的方案：向她问时间，借铅笔，问去洗手间的方向，谈天气，找她借本杂志看。他渴望火车出事故，把他们这节车厢甩到正在经过的广阔的麦田里。在混乱中，他将领着她安全逃离出去，同她一起在一间急救站搭起的帐篷中休息，喝着那里提供的温吞茶水，四目对视，脉脉无语。多年以后，他们再相逢时提到曾经在爱丁堡快车的不幸车祸中相遇，兴味盎然。但是火车看来不像要出轨，于是他尽管知道这样做无聊而荒唐，还是禁不住清清喉咙，凑过去问那位天使有没有一支多余的圆珠笔。这举动像是从一座高桥上往下跳。

1. 这个故事吸引不了传统的哲学家：这种爱情的心潮起伏太幼稚，不值得研究，这个题目应该留给诗人或疯子。琢磨牵手和洒香水的情书不是哲学家的事。叔本华对这种淡漠感到不解：

> 这样一件在一般人的生活中占如此重要地位的事，哲学家们迄今为止几乎完全不屑一顾，现在竟作为未经处理的原料摆在我们面前，真是咄咄怪事。

对此事的忽视,可能是由于生活的这一方面违反人的理性所塑造的自己的形象,因而断然予以否认。叔本华坚持还原这一令人尴尬的本来面目。

> 爱情……随时都可打断严肃的工作,有时最伟大的头脑也会一时为之所惑。它无所顾忌地……干扰政治家的谈判、学问家的研究。它甚至能将情书或者小卷头发塞进部长的卷宗或是哲学家的手稿中……它有时会要求人牺牲健康,有时是牺牲财富、地位和幸福。

2. 叔本华同比他早生 255 年的那位加斯科随笔作家一样,关心被公认为所有生物中最理性的人类身上不太理性的因素。在他美景街的住房的书房中有一套蒙田的著作。叔本华从中读到一个屁、一顿丰盛的午餐、一个长到肉里的脚趾甲都足以颠覆人的理性,他同意蒙田的看法:我们的思想是从属于肉体的,尽管我们高傲地持相反的观点。

3. 但是叔本华还要进一步。他不满足于颠覆理性的松散的例证,而是给我们内里的那种他认为先于理性,强大得足以歪曲一切理性的计划和判断的力量起了一个名字,叫作"生命意志"——其定义是人类与生俱来的求生存和繁殖的本能。这一"生命意志"可以使已经毫无生趣的人在遇到海难或重病时为生存而斗争。它能使头脑最冷静,事业心最强的人为咿呀学语的婴儿逗得心动。即使当时无动于衷，随后也会想要自己生一个，在孩子出世时爱得发狂。也正是"生命意志"使人在长途火车上遇到隔座一位漂亮的旅客就昏了头。

4. 叔本华大概为爱情受挫而心怀怨恨（向女学生献葡萄洵非易事）；但他不认为这有什么过分或反常。这种心情本是与爱情的作用相称的：

> 有什么可大惊小怪的？何必这样急切、喧哗、悲痛、费力？……何必把这样一件小事看得那么重要？……问题是，这并非小事一桩，相反，此事的重要性与为之付出的渴望、热情和孜孜以求的努力是相适应的。一切爱情的最终目的……比人的一生中任何目标都重要，所以人人都这样认真去追求是值得的。

那么，最终目的是什么呢？既不是沟通感情也不是发泄性欲，既不为求知音，也不为求欢愉。爱情在生活中占统治地位，因为：

> 它对缔造下一代……对未来人类的存续和特有的体质起决定性作用。

正是因为爱情如此强有力地指引我们走向"生命意志"

的两大律令之一,所以叔本华认为它是我们为之着迷的事情中最不可避免的,最可以理解的。

5. 诚然,我们问对方要电话号码时心目中并未想到传宗接代,但这也不足以否定上述理论。按照叔本华的说法,我们自身分裂为意识和潜意识两半,潜意识受"生命意志"所控制,意识服从于潜意识,却不能了解它所有的计划。意识不是一个自主的实体,而是只有部分视力的仆人,服从于一心想要生儿育女的"生命意志"。

> (智力)不能闯入意志决定的秘密工作室。当然它是意志的一个亲信,但不是知晓一切的亲信。

智力所理解的只不过是促进繁殖所必需的那一点——也就是很少一点点:

> (它)始终……被排斥在意志的真正决心和秘密决定之外。

这种排斥可以解释为什么我们意识到的只是自己热切地希望再见到某人,而下意识地却是受到旨在繁殖下一代的力量的驱使。

为什么需要这样的自欺欺人呢?因为,据叔本华说,我们如果不是先昏了头,就不见得会同意进行繁衍子孙。

6. 这一分析当然违反我们理性的自我形象,但是至少足以对抗那种说法:认为浪漫的爱情是可以避免的,是对更加严肃的任务的背离;对于闲得发慌的少年来说,神迷于月下,啜泣于枕边是可以原谅的;而年事更长的人就因为在火车里惊鸿一瞥就不顾自己的工作,那是完全不必要的癫狂之举。叔本华的意志论把爱情视为生物学上不可避免之物,是物种延续的关键,使我们对因爱情而产生的怪异行为采取比较谅解的态度。

在伦敦北区的一家希腊餐馆里,一男一女在一张靠窗的桌旁相对而坐。两人中间放着一碗橄榄,但是谁也想不出如何以雅致、高贵的姿态去嗑,于是橄榄没人碰。

她没有带圆珠笔,但是给他一支铅笔。停顿片刻之后,她说她多么厌烦坐火车长途旅行,这是多余的废话,不过给了他一丝所需要的鼓励。她既不是大提琴手,也不是图案设计师,而是一家律师事务所的公司金融专业的律师。她原是纽卡斯尔人,但在伦敦已经住了8年。等火车抵达伦敦尤斯顿车站时,他已经得到电话号码,以及共进晚餐的首肯。

服务员过来问点菜,她点了沙拉和箭鱼。她是下了班直接来的,穿一身浅灰套装,戴着原来那块表。

他们开始谈话。她说她周末最喜欢的活动是爬山。从学生时代就开始了,以后遍游法国、西班牙、加拿大。她描述在几百米高处俯瞰山谷,以及在高山上露营,早晨帐篷顶上挂下冰柱的乐趣。而与她共餐的伙伴上二层楼就要头晕。她另一项爱好是跳舞,她喜欢那种精力充沛和自由放任的感觉。她还常常熬通宵,而他通常上床的时间是11点半。他们谈工作。她现在正接手一桩关于专利权的案子。一名茶壶设计人诉一家英国公司侵犯知识产权。该公司根据1977年专利法的60-1-a条款应予赔偿。

还有关于一个即将接手的案子的冗长的叙述,他就听不懂了。但是他深信她智力高超,他们两人十分般配。

1. 爱情最莫测的一个奥秘是“为什么是他”? 和“为什么是她”? 为什么在众多可选的人中我们单单钟情于这一个? 他们在餐桌上的谈话不见得总是有所教益,双方的习惯也不那么合得来,为什么就互相珍惜胜过他人? 为什么其他某些人尽管客观上更迷人,也许更好相处,而我们纵使满怀好意,也产生不了激情?

2. 叔本华认为这种挑选并不足奇。我们不能自由地同随便哪一个谈恋爱,因为我们不是同任何人都能生育生命意志的健康儿女。我们受生命意志驱使而去接近的人,都是能增加生育美丽聪慧的后代的机会的,而我们厌弃的是减少这一机会的人。生命意志发现了可以共同为人父母的理想伴侣,爱情只不过是这一发现的有意识的表现,如此而已,岂有他哉?

一旦两情相悦——英语最贴切的说法是互相迷恋——

实际上就应看做是一个新人从此刻开始形成。

交往初期,在平淡的谈话下面的潜意识里,双方实际上是在互相忖度,将来两人能否生出一个健康的孩子:

> 一对异性青年初次会面时相互从头到脚仔细打量,在那潜意识的极度认真之中有一种特殊的东西。那是物种的守护神在对两人可能产生的个体进行考察。

3. 那么生命意志通过这一审视在探索什么呢?在找健康的孩子的证据。生命意志必需保证下一代在心理上和生理上都适于在一个祸福无常的世界上生存,所以它所谋求的孩子是四肢匀称(不太矮,不太高,不太胖,不太瘦),思想稳定(既不谨小慎微,又不浮躁莽撞,既不冷酷无情,又不感情冲动,等等)。

由于我们的父母在求偶中犯错误,我们就不大可能达到理想的平衡。我们常常生而太高,太刚,或太柔;我们的鼻子太大,下巴太小。如果这种不平衡现象任其继续发展,人类不久就将在怪异中挣扎。因此,生命意志就必须把我们推向那些能以其缺陷平衡我之缺陷的人(大鼻子与纽扣鼻子相结合可以产生完美的鼻子),从而使下一代能恢复生理和心理的平衡。

人人都企图通过另一人来抵消自己的弱点、缺陷和变异之处，以免延及子孙，演变成完全的畸形。

这一相互对消理论使本华信心满怀地预言相互吸引的路径。矮个子女人容易爱上高个子男人，而高个子男人很少爱上高个子女人（他们下意识地害怕生出一个巨人来）。女里女气不喜欢体育的男人往往被短发（还戴大手表）、假小子式的女人所吸引：

两个个体相互抵消的条件是……他的阳刚的程度刚好同她的阴柔的程度相符，这样，各人的片面性正好相互抵消。

4. 可惜这一异质相吸理论引导叔本华得出如此黯淡的结论，如果读者正准备结婚的话，最好不要读下面几段，以免翻悔；他的结论是：一个高度适合我们的孩子的人几乎从来不适合我们自己，不过我们当时由于被生命意志遮蔽视听，并不认识到这一点。

"互相投合与激情同时并存的爱情是极为罕见的幸运，"叔本华说。那个能使我们的孩子不至于生就硕大无比的下巴或特别阴柔的性格的人很少是能使我们终生幸福的人。追求个人幸福和追求健康的子女是两种截然相反的规划，而爱情却恶毒地使我们多年来相信二者是统一的。看到两个决不可能成为朋友的人结为夫妻，我们不必感到惊奇：

除了两性关系之外只会相互仇恨、蔑视甚至对对方厌恶之极的人竟为爱情所俘虏。物种的意志的力量远胜过个人的力量，因此情人对一切足以使他厌恶的特点视而不见，忽视一切，错判一切，把自己永远拴在情欲所钟的对象身上。他就是这样为幻觉所蒙蔽，一旦物种的意志得到了满足，这一幻觉就会消退，剩下的就是一个令人厌恶的终身伴侣。只有这样，我们才能解释为什么富有理性，甚至很出色的男人与泼妇，甚至妖婆结为连理，我们简直无法想象他们怎么会作出这样的选择……一个坠入情网的男人能够清楚地看到并且痛切地感觉到他的新娘身上难以容忍的缺点和性格，足以使他终身受难，却还不足以把他吓退……因为他追求的终极目标不是自身的利益，而是还没有出生的第三人的利益，尽管他在幻觉中以为是在追求自身的利益。

叔本华的理论意味着：生命意志如何强有力地推行自己的目标而不是我们的幸福，可以从一对情侣在做爱之后往往倍感无聊和惆怅中特别清楚地感受到。

　　　君不见，"*illico post coitum cachinnus auditur Diaboli?*"[①]

----

　　①　拉丁文，意为"交媾之后立即听到魔鬼的笑声？"——译者

所以,有一天,一个假小子般的女人和一个娘娘腔的男人走向婚礼的圣坛,除了出席婚礼的个别叔本华信徒外,连他们自己以及任何人都猜不到其真正动机。只有到日后,当生命意志的要求得到安抚,一个健壮的男孩在郊区的花园中踢球时,阴谋诡计才暴露。这对夫妇要么分手,要么在无言的敌视中共进晚餐。叔本华提出非此即彼的选择:

　　　　在缔结婚姻中似乎总有一方必须牺牲,不是个人利益就是物种利益。

　　不过他使我们毫不怀疑物种保证自己的利益的能力总是占上风:

　　　　下一代人的福祉是以这一代人为代价的。

　　男人付了账,然后故作漫不经心地问一句,是不是到他公寓中去喝一杯。她微笑低头望着地板,在桌子下面把餐巾纸越折越小。"那一定很愉快,真的,"她说,"但是我明天需要早起赶飞机到法兰克福去开会,5点半,可能更早。要不下回吧,一定会很愉快的,真的。"又一个微笑,餐巾纸在手中捏碎了。

　　她答应到了德国会打电话,说是不久会再见面,也许就在她回来的当天。他失望之情稍有安慰。但是直到约定的日子很晚的时候电话才响,她从法兰克福机场的电话亭中打来的。背后一片嘈杂，还夹杂着宣布飞往东方的航班起飞的刺耳声音。她告诉他从窗外能望见巨大的飞机，这个地方简直像地狱。

她说该死的汉莎航班误点了，她将设法在另外的航班上找一个座位，不过他不要等她。停顿一下之后，最坏的事得到了肯定。她接着说，她的生活目前有些复杂情况，真的，她不知道自己要什么，不过她知道自己需要空间和时间，如果他不介意的话，等她头脑清楚一点之后由她给他打电话。

1. 哲学家可能对我们为什么坠入情网提出了不太顺耳的解释，不过在令人反感中也有足以告慰之处——那就是知道我们的痛苦是正常的。我们不必为短短几天的希望所带来的巨大烦恼所困扰。一种足以推动我们去生儿育女的强大力量竟然会在目的达不到时悄然消退而不造成破坏，这本来就不合理。爱情如果不许诺给我们想象中最大的幸福，就不能引诱我们去承担生儿育女的重负。求爱遭拒后伤痛之深令我们吃惊，那是由于我们无知，不知道终成眷属意味着什么。我们决不应该认为自己如此痛苦是奇怪之事。如果不痛苦倒一定是缺了点什么。

2. 再者，我们不是天生不可爱，这本身并没有问题。我们并非性情乖张，面目可憎。好事不成，是因为我们不能同某一个特定的人生一个匀称的孩子。不必为此自怨自艾。总有一天我们会遇到一个特别欣赏我们并能对我们敞开胸怀的人（因为从生命意志的观点看，我们双方的下巴可形成理想的结合）。

3. 我们应该过一段时间就原谅对我们绝情的人，那不是他们的选择。每当某人以各种尴尬的方式表示自己需要空间和时间，不愿做出承诺，或害怕关系亲密时，这位绝情者只不过是努力把生命意志所下的本质上是潜意识的律令予以智能化而已。他们的理智可能欣赏我们的品质；而他们的生命意志却相反，并且以不容分说的方式告诉他们——那就是抽掉他们对我们的性欲。如果他们被智力比我们低下的人引诱过去，也不要责怪他们浅薄。据叔本华解释，我们应该记住：

在婚姻中追求的不是智力的享受，而是繁衍后代。

4. 每一次求爱遭拒都是造物反对生育的敕令，我们应该予以尊重，正如尊重闪电和火山爆发——确实可怕，但是我们无能为力。我们应该从以下的事实中得到慰藉：

男女之间缺乏爱欲等于宣告，他们可能生下的孩子将是一个结构不良的、缺乏内在和谐的、不幸的生物。

我们可能与爱人相得甚欢，但是造物却不高兴，那就更有理由服从造物而放弃爱情。

一时之间，男人倍感惆怅。周末他到巴特西公园散步，坐在泰晤士河边的一张长凳上。他身上带着一本歌德的《少

211

年维特之烦恼》的简装本,此书于1774年在莱比锡初版。成双成对的夫妇推着婴儿车或牵着孩子的手散步。一个穿蓝裙子,沾满巧克力的小女孩指着天空一架正向希思罗机场降落的飞机说:"爸爸,上帝是在那儿吗?"但是爸爸没工夫理会,情绪不佳,把她抱起来说他不知道,好像她是要他指路似的。一个4岁的小男孩骑着三轮脚踏车冲进了灌木丛,哭着喊妈妈,妈妈躺在铺在一块草地上的毯子上,刚刚闭上眼睛。她叫她丈夫去帮帮孩子。他气鼓鼓地说这回该轮到她了。她顶回去说该轮到他。他无言。她骂他废物,站了起来。一对老夫妇坐在旁边的长凳上默默地分食一块鸡蛋芥菜三明治。

1. 叔本华要我们不必为这种愁苦而惊讶。我们本不应该要求某种东西在一对夫妇或父母身上保持生命力。

2. 在叔本华的书斋里有许多自然科学的著作,其中有威廉·柯尔比和斯宾塞的《昆虫学导言》,佛朗索瓦·胡贝尔的《蜜蜂》以及卡代·德·沃的《鼹鼠的习性及捕杀法》。这位哲学家还读关于蚂蚁、甲壳虫、蜜蜂、苍蝇、蚂蚱、鼹鼠、候鸟的书,并且怀着悲天悯人和困惑不解的心情观察这些生物怎样地全都表现出热烈而无意义的对生命的依恋。他特别同情鼹鼠,一种发育不良的怪物,住在潮湿而狭隘的地道里,很少见天日,其初生儿长得像滑腻腻的软体虫,但还是尽一切力量求生存和传宗接代。

> 坚持不懈地用它巨大的铲状脚爪挖洞就是它们毕生的事业;周围是永远的长夜,它们的眼睛生来就是为了避光……它们受苦受难、毫无乐趣的一生到底获得了什么?生活的苦难和操心与得到的好处完全不相称。

在叔本华看来,世上所有的生命也都是同样地献身于同样无意义的生存。

> 看看那些可怜的蚂蚁忙个不停地辛勤劳动……多数昆虫的一生只不过是不停的劳动,为将来要破卵而出的幼虫准备粮食和住处。当幼虫吃完了粮食,到了化蝶的阶段,它们进入生命,只不过又周而复始地重复同样的劳动……我们不禁要问,这一切都有什么结果? ……除了饥饿和性欲得到满足之外,什么都没有,只是在无穷无尽的劳动的间歇中短暂的满足。

3. 哲学家无须再作类比了。我们追求爱情,同可能的对象在咖啡馆聊天,然后生儿育女,在这件事上不比鼹鼠的选择多,也不比它幸福。

4. 他不是想要使我们沮丧,而是要使我们摆脱期望,因

为期望引发怨恨。在失恋时听说幸福本来就不是题中之义,足以使人欣慰。奇怪的是,这位最阴暗的思想家却是最能鼓舞人的:

> 人惟一的先天的错误就是认为我们是生而为追求幸福的……只要我们坚持这一先天的错误……世界在我们看来就是充满了矛盾。因为每走一步,无论大小,我们必然会体验到这个世界和人生决不是为维持幸福生活而安排的……因是之故,几乎每一个年长的人脸上都挂着一种叫做失望的表情。

其实只要他们堕入情网时抱着正确的期待,就决不会那么失望了:

> 少年之所以烦恼和忧愁……皆因其坚信此生必定会得到幸福而孜孜以求。经常为希望所欺而生怨悔皆由此而来。我们梦中模糊的希望以变幻无常蛊惑人心的形象在我们眼前盘旋,撩拨我们去追寻其源头,最终归于虚妄……如

果年轻人能及时得到忠告和指导,从头脑中根除对这个世界抱很大期望的错误观念,他们将获益良多。

（三）

我们比鼹鼠总还有一项优势。我们同它们一样需要为生存而奋斗，为繁衍后代而求偶，但是除此之外我们还能去戏院、歌剧院和音乐厅，晚上睡在床上还能看小说、哲学书和史诗——叔本华正是从这些活动中找到至高无上的源泉，可以摆脱"生命意志"的需求。我们在艺术和哲学作品中找到的是我们自己的痛苦和奋斗的客观表述，通过声音、语言和形象予以诠释和再现。艺术家和哲学家不仅向我们展示我们的感受，而且以我们自己做不到的尖锐和智慧表达我们的体验；他们将我们生活的各个层面勾画出来，我们能认出是自己的，但是凭自己决不能理解得那么清楚。他们向我们解释我们的生存条件，助我们解惑，并减少孤立无援之感。我们也许不得不继续挖地洞，但是通过创造性的作品，至少能获得片刻的顿悟，洞察我们的苦难，从而可以免于苦难带来的震惊、孤立（甚至受迫害）之感。用叔本华的话来说，艺术与哲学以其不同的方式把痛苦转化为知识。

这位哲学家仰慕他母亲的朋友歌德，因为他把如许多的爱情的痛苦转化为知识，最著名的就是 25 岁时出版的使他享誉全欧洲的那部小说。《少年维特之烦恼》描述一名少年对一位女士的单相思——那迷人的夏绿蒂,她与维特对《威克菲尔子爵》一书有同好,身穿袖子上饰有粉红缎带的白裙;但此书同时也描述了成千上万读者的恋情(据说拿破仑就读过9遍)。最伟大的艺术作品是说给我们大家听的,尽管作者并不认识我们。叔本华如是说:

> ……诗人从生活中撷取特定的个体,准确地描述其个性,然而由此却启示了普遍的人性……他表面上只关注这一个,但事实上他所关注的是古往今来普天之下都存在的。因此,一些诗句,特别是诗剧中的句子,即使并非警句格言也经常适用于实际生活。

歌德的读者不但在《少年维特之烦恼》中认出了自己,而且也因而更加了解自己,因为歌德将一系列尴尬的、稍纵即逝的爱之瞬间明晰化了,读者以前可能经历过这种情愫,但自己当时并不知其深浅。他披露了爱情的某些规律,叔本华称之为浪漫心理的必要"思想"。例如,歌德把不爱者对待爱自己的人那种貌似慈爱实则极端残酷的态度描写得入木三分。在小说的后半,维特为自己的感情折磨得痛苦不堪,在夏绿蒂面前爆发出来:

> "夏绿蒂,"他哭道,"我再也不见你了!""为什么要这

样呢？"她回答说，"维特，你还是可以，而且一定要再见到我们的，不过别那么激动。噢！为什么你生来感情这样激烈，对一切身边的事物都那么激情冲动，不能自制！我求求你，"她拿起他的手接着说，"冷静点。想想你的精神、你的知识和你的天赋能给你带来那么多的快乐！"

我们不必生活在 18 世纪后半叶的德国就能充分体会其含义。世上故事比人少，同样的情节不断地重复，只是人名和背景有所变化。此即叔本华所谓："艺术的真谛就是以一概千千万。"反过来，意识到我们的境遇只不过是千千万之一，就足以感到慰藉。叔本华于 1818 和 1822 年两度访问过佛罗伦萨。他大概参观过圣马利亚·德尔·卡迈纳的布朗卡奇礼拜堂，里面有马萨乔①在 1425—1426 年间画的一系列壁画。

---

① Masaccio, Tommaso di Ser Giovanni（1401—1428），意大利文艺复兴时期著名画家，有"绘画开山祖"之誉，其画风影响到雕塑和建筑艺术。布朗卡奇礼拜堂的一组壁画是他与另外一位画家合作的主要代表作之一，其中"被逐出天堂的亚当和夏娃"是他的杰作。——译者

亚当和夏娃离开天堂时的痛苦并不单单属于他们自己。马萨乔通过这两个人物的面部表情和身体的姿态抓住了痛苦的本质，也就是痛苦这一概念本身。他的壁画是我们可能犯错误、我们的脆弱性的普遍象征。我们大家都是被驱逐出那天堂之园的。

读了一则爱情故事之后，失恋的求爱者就会超越自己；他不再是在迷茫中踽踽独行的受难者，而是庞大的人群中的一员。这些人自古以来就受繁衍后代的需要所驱使而爱上另外的人。这样，他的苦难给拔掉了芒刺，变得可以理解，而不是个人遭受的诅咒。对于能达到这种客观境界的人，叔本华作如下评论：

> 在他的生活和不幸的过程中，他着眼于人类整体的命运多于自己的命运，因而行为更像是个知者，而不是受难者。

我们在黑暗中掘地洞之余，一定要努力化眼泪为知识。

第六章

困难中的慰藉

（一）

很少有哲学家推崇悲苦。按照传统的看法，智慧的生活总是与努力减轻苦难、焦虑、绝望、愤怒、自轻和痛心相联系的。

（二）

弗里德里希·尼采指出，大多数哲学家从来都是"卷心菜头脑"①，而"命中注定，我是第一个像样的人"，他于1888年略带尴尬地承认这一点，"我非常害怕有一天我将被宣布为圣灵"；他把这一天定在第三个千禧年的黎明到来之时："让我们假设，到2000年左右，人们将获准读［我的著作］。"他认为只要他们读，就一定会喜欢：

> 我觉得手里拿一本我的书是任何人能赋予自己的最有

---

① 德文俗语"krautkops"，意谓头脑混乱而中空，犹如我国俗语"脑袋一团糨糊"。——译者

价值的显赫地位。我甚至猜想他拿书时会脱鞋,更不用说靴子了。

之所以为显赫,因为在众多"卷心菜头脑"中惟有尼采遗世独立,意识到凡是谋求自我完成的人都应该欢迎各式各样的困难。

> 如果可能的话——这"如果可能"实在是疯狂透顶的想法——你们不是想消灭困难吗? 而我们呢? 看来我们实在是更愿加剧困难,而且使它达到空前艰巨的程度!

尼采虽然按礼数给朋友寄去良好的祝愿,但是他心里明白他们更需要的是什么:

> 对于我所关心的人,我祝愿他们受苦受难、孤寂凄凉、疾病缠身、受尽虐待、备尝屈辱——我希望他们不得幸免于以下的体验:深刻的自轻自贱、缺乏自信的折磨、一败涂地的悲惨境地。

这足以说明为什么他的作品成为

> (人类)有史以来获得的最伟大的馈赠。

尽管这话是他自己说的。

（三）

不要被外表吓退。

通常第一次见面留下的……只是跃入眼帘的单一的特征，由此决定整个印象。于是，最和善、最讲理的人如果留着浓密的胡须，留下的印象只不过是大胡子的附属品——那就是军人型的，脾气暴躁，而且有时爱动武，结果人家就把他当做这样的人来对待。

（四）

　　他并不是从一开头就这样推崇困难的。对他最初的观点产生影响的是他21岁在莱比锡大学读书时发现的几位哲学家。1865年秋，他在莱比锡的布卢门街一家旧书店中顺手拿起一本《作为意志和表象的世界》，其作者已于5年前在300公里以西的法兰克福的寓所中去世：

> 　　我拿起一本完全陌生的（叔本华的）书，随便翻翻。不知道什么鬼精灵在耳边悄悄说："把这本书拿回去。"反正我就这么办了，这是违反惯例的，因为我通常从不轻率地买书。回家之后，我就抱着新获的宝贝倒在沙发一角，任凭这位活力充沛而忧郁阴沉的天才在我身上起作用。每一行都迸发出放弃、否定和听天由命。

　　这位老人改变了年轻人的一生。叔本华阐明：哲学智慧的精髓在于亚里士多德在《尼各马可伦理学》中所说：

> 　　审慎的人只争取摆脱痛苦而不争取欢乐。

　　对所有谋求心满意足的人来说，首先必须承认达到完

美是不可能的,这样就可以避免我们在追求完美的过程中最常遇到的麻烦和焦虑:

> (我们的)目标不应当指向生活中的欢乐和愉悦,而是指向尽可能避免那无数恶事……一个人最大的幸运就是没有经历巨大的身心痛苦而度过一生。

他下一次给住在瑙姆堡的寡母和 19 岁的妹妹写信时,不像平时那样汇报他的饮食和研究的进展,而代之以他的放弃和听天由命的新哲学:

> 我们知道生活是由苦难构成的;我们越是努力去享受它,就越受它的奴役,所以应当摈弃种种生活物品而实行禁欲。

这话使他母亲感到奇怪,她回信说她不喜欢“这种表现方式和这种见解,更喜欢一封满纸新近况的名副其实的信”。接着她劝她的儿子将心托付给上帝,并且好好吃饭。

但是叔本华的影响并不稍减。尼采开始小心翼翼地生活。在他开列的题为“个人的妄想”清单中,性占据突出的地位。他在瑙姆堡服兵役时把一张叔本华的照片放在书桌上,每当遇到困难时就叫道:“叔本华,救救我!”他 24 岁担任巴塞尔大学古典文献学的教授时进入了瓦格纳夫妇的小圈子,把他们联系在一起的是对这位法兰克福的悲观、审慎的智者的共同热爱。

（五）

这种迷恋延续了 10 年。尼采于 1876 年秋访问意大利，从此经历了思想的激变。他应一位艺术爱好者、富有的中年妇女玛尔维达·冯·迈森堡之邀与一群朋友在那不勒斯海湾边索伦托的一所别墅中住了几个月。"我从来没见过他那么欢快。他开心地放声大笑。"玛尔维达这样描述尼采对鲁宾纳奇别墅的第一反应。那别墅位于索伦托边缘的一条林阴道上，从起坐间眺望，海湾、伊斯基亚岛和维苏威山尽收眼底。屋前小花园内种着无花果、桔树和杉树，还有葡萄架通向海边。

别墅里的客人尽日游泳，游览庞贝、维苏威、卡普里，还有帕埃斯图姆的希腊神殿。吃的是清淡的橄榄油烹调的饭菜,晚间一起在起坐间读书:雅各布·布克哈特的希腊文明讲稿、蒙田、拉罗什富科、沃未纳格、拉布吕耶尔、司汤达、歌德的叙事诗《科林斯的新娘》和他的剧本《私生女》、希罗多德、修希底德、还有柏拉图的《法律篇》(不过也许是受蒙田坦承对柏拉图反感的影响,尼采对后者越来越厌烦:"柏拉图式的对话,那是一种自满而幼稚的辩证法,只有从来没有读过法国优秀作品的人才会感兴趣……柏拉图真是枯燥无味")。

尼采在地中海游泳,吃着不是牛油而是橄榄油烹调的菜肴,呼吸着温暖的空气,读着蒙田和司汤达的作品("这些小事——膳食、地点、天气、娱乐、关于自私的辩论——比任何迄今为止被认为重要的事都重要得多,超过人们的一切想象"),就在这期间他逐步改变了关于苦与乐的哲学,从而也改变了对困难的看法。1876年的10月底,他望着那不勒斯海湾日落,一种新的、非叔本华的对生存的信念在心中油然升起。他觉得他从一出生就已老去,如今在最后一刻得救,使他感动落泪。

(六)

1876年底他在致瓦格纳的信中宣布了他的转变:"如果我告诉你一件逐渐形成而突然进入我的意识的想法,你会不会感到惊讶？那就是不同意叔本华的教导——几乎在所有的总体性观念上我都不站在他一边。"

观念之一就是：既然如愿以偿是幻想，智者就应该致力于避免痛苦而不是追求快乐，如叔本华劝导的那样，"悄然退居一室，与灾祸隔绝"。现在尼采深感这一劝导怯懦而不真实，几年后他贬之为倒行逆施，企图"像胆小的麋鹿一样躲藏在森林里"。人的自我完成不是通过避免痛苦，而是通过承认痛苦是通向任何善的自然的、必经的步骤而达到的。

（七）

除了饮食和空气之外，促使尼采改变世界观的是他对历史上几位人物的反思，这几位人物的一生看来是真正地经历了自我完成，他们不愧为——用一个尼采词汇中最有争议的词来说——超人。

这个词名声不好，而且含义荒谬，主要不能怪尼采，而是由于他的妹妹伊丽莎白后来热衷于国家社会主义（尼采早在她与希特勒握手之前就称她为"那个心怀仇恨的反犹母鹅"），还由于尼采最早的盎格鲁-撒克逊诠释者的一项无意的决定，他们把一个卡通传奇中的英雄命名为超人。

但是尼采的超人与空中飞人和法西斯都没有关系。他

希特勒在魏玛接见伊丽莎白·尼采,1935年10月

给他母亲和妹妹的一封信中不经意的一句话更好地说明了
这个词的含义:

> 说实在的,在活着的人里没有一个是我在意的。我喜
> 欢的人都已在很久以前作古——比如加利亚尼①、亨利·
> 贝尔②以及蒙田。

他还可以加上另一位他崇拜的英雄:歌德。这四个人
是探索尼采成熟期心目中完美人生的最丰富的索引。

这几个人有许多共同点:富有好奇心、有艺术天才、对

---

① Abbé Ferdinando Galiani(1728—1787),18世纪著名意大利外交家、经济
学家和作家,是《货币》和《关于小麦贸易的对话》的作者。其思想在当
时属于前沿。——译者
② Henri Beyle,即《红与黑》的作者司汤达。——译者

蒙田(1533—1592)

加利亚尼(1728—1787)

歌德(1749—1832)

司汤达/亨利·贝尔(1783—1842)

性爱精力旺盛。尽管有阴暗面,他们都开怀大笑,不少人还常跳舞;他们热爱"温暖的阳光、鲜活的空气、南方的菜园、海风的气息,还有肉、蛋、水果快餐"。其中有些人具有与尼采十分相近的绞刑架式的幽默——从悲观的内心世界发出的欢快而恶毒的笑声。他们发掘了自己的才能,他们具有尼采称作"生命"的东西,那意味着勇气、野心、尊严、人格的力量、幽默感和独立性(与之相平行的就是没有故作正经、人云亦云、怨天尤人和谨小慎微)。

这几个人都是入世的。蒙田曾连任两届波尔多市市长,并曾骑马周游欧洲。出生于那不勒斯的加利亚尼曾任驻巴黎大使馆的秘书,并写过关于货币供应和粮食分配的著作(伏尔泰誉之为莫里哀的机智和柏拉图的智慧的结合)。歌德在魏玛宫廷中担任公职有 10 年之久;曾对改良农业、工业和济贫工作提出过建议;他还担负过外交使命,两次受到拿破仑接见。

他于 1787 年访问意大利时曾游览帕埃斯图姆的希腊神殿,爬过维苏威火山,逼近需要躲避碎石和泥浆的火山口。

尼采称他"了不起","是让我肃然起敬的最后一个德国人":"他对……现实活动加以利用。他没有遁世,而是溶入生活……他尽其所能担当大任……他要的是完整的总体;他为反对把理性、官感、感情和意志割裂开而奋斗。"

司汤达曾随拿破仑的军队转战欧洲,七访庞贝的废墟,在凌晨 5 时的满月下欣赏加德桥(罗马众多的竞技场都没有令我这样深深地陷入遐想……)。

尼采的英雄们也都多次堕入情网。"整个世界的运动都导向两性交欢,"这是蒙田的体验。歌德 74 岁时到马林巴德度假,迷上了一位 19 岁的漂亮女孩乌尔丽克·冯·莱未措,先请她出去喝茶,然后在散步时向她求婚(遭到拒绝)。司汤达熟悉并十分喜爱《维特》,也和它的作者一样多情,他的日记详细叙述几十年来的情场猎艳。他在 24 岁时随拿破仑的军队驻扎在德国,同旅店主人的女儿上了床,并在日记中得意地说她是"我所认识的第一个德国女人在一次高潮后筋疲力尽的。我用抚爱引发她的激情,她害怕极了"。

最后,这几个人都是艺术家("艺术是生命的伟大刺激,"尼采如是说),他们在完成《随笔集》、《想象自己是苏格拉底》①、《罗马挽歌》②和《论爱情》③时一定得到异乎寻常的满足。

(八)

尼采的意思是说,这些要素都是任何人要达到自我完成自然必需的。此外,他还添加了一个重要的细节:不经历十分愁苦,是达不到这些要素的:

---

① *Il Socrates immaginario*,18 世纪著名意大利作曲家帕伊西埃洛创作的讽刺歌剧,剧中人把自己想象成苏格拉底,笑料百出。这不是以上四个人之一的作品。——译者

② *Römische Elegien*,歌德的长诗。——译者

③ *De l' amour*,司汤达名著之一。——译者

苦与乐如此紧密相连,谁想得到多少这一面,就必须尝到多少另一面……你可以任择其一:是尽量少要快乐,简而言之就是无痛苦呢……还是尽量多要不快,以此为代价,得到迄今很少人享受到的丰富的内在的乐趣?如果你决定选择前者,宁愿减轻人类痛苦的程度,那么你也必须降低人类享乐的能力。

人的计划最圆满的完成看来是与某种程度的磨难分不开的,我们最大乐趣的源泉是与我们最大的痛苦别扭地联系在一起的:

试看那些最优秀、最完善的个人和民族的历史,请问有哪一棵大树长到这样骄人的高度没有经过风霜雨雪;请问,厄运和外界的阻力,某种仇恨、妒忌、怀疑、顽强抵制、强硬反对、吝啬、暴力,难道不都是有利的条件,无此则任何伟大,即使是美德,也难以成长起来?

(九)

何以故?因为没有人能够毫无经验而完成伟大的艺术作品,或是平步青云得到世俗的高位,或是初次尝试就成为情圣;在开始失败与后来的成功之间,在我们向往的功成名就之日和现在的间隔中必然充满痛苦、焦虑、妒忌和屈辱。我们受苦受难，因为我们不能自发地驾驭自我完成的要素。

尼采努力纠正这样一种观念：自我完成一定顺利到来，否则就根本实现不了。这种想法导致毁灭性的效果，因为它使我们过早地知难而退，而野蛮残暴本是几乎所有有价值的事物的合理需求，如果我们对这种残暴有所准备的话，那些困难本来是可以克服的。

我们可能想象蒙田的《随笔集》是完整地从他的头脑中跳出来的，于是把我们初次尝试写人生哲学时笔下艰涩看做自己天生无此才能。相反，我们应该好好看看这部杰作完成之前作者无比艰巨的推敲之功，看看那堆积如山的修改和补充稿。

《红与黑》、《昂利·勃吕拉传》和《论爱情》写来也不容易。司汤达的写作生涯是以一些拙劣的剧本大纲开始的。其中的一出故事围绕着一支流亡的军队在基伯龙登陆展开（人物包括威廉·皮特和查理·詹姆斯·福克斯），另一出是描写波拿巴掌权的过程，第三出——暂名《怕受管辖的人》——描写一个老人逐步滑向痴呆。司汤达在国家图书馆度过了许多周，从字典上抄录诸如"玩笑"、"可笑"和"滑稽"这类词的定义，但是还不足以改变他写剧本的笨拙手法。他的杰作是经过了几十年的艰苦劳动才问世的。

如果说多数文学作品都不如《红与黑》精美的话，尼采认为多半不是因为作者缺乏天赋，而是由于他们对需要经历多少痛苦有错误的看法。以下是写小说需要经历的艰辛：

> 一名小说家必备要素的配方是很容易提供的，但是要付诸实施，就需要某些品质，而这正是人们惯常说"我天赋不够"时所忽视的。只需写上百部小说的大纲，每部不超过两页，但是必须十分清晰，没有任何浮言虚字；每天都要写一段佚事，直到学会如何以内涵最丰富、最动人的形式来表达；必须不懈地收集、刻画各种人物典型；最重要的是要向别人讲述，并听别人讲述，注意观察和倾听对在场者产生的效果；应该像风景画家或服装设计师那样旅行……最后，应该思考人的行为的动机，不放过任何对此有所启发的标志，日夜不懈地收集这些材料。以上多方面的努力应该持续十多年；然后，书斋里创作出来的才有资格面世。

这一哲学思想是奇特的混合体，一方面是对人的潜力的极端信任（成功的机会是向我们每一个人敞开的，一如写小说);一方面是极端的残酷(写第一本小说之前须苦度十年愁惨的光阴)。

正是为了使我们习惯于痛苦的合理性,尼采花了许多时间谈山。

(十)

读尼采的著作每隔几页就会碰上关于爬山的叙述:

《瞧,这个人》:凡知道如何呼吸我的作品的气息的人就会知道那是山顶的空气,是健身的空气。必须生就适合这种空气的体质,否则就有感冒之虞。身临寒冰,孤寂难耐,但是万物在光明笼罩下多么宁静!呼吸多么自由!内心感受多么丰富!哲学,我迄今所理解和体验的哲学,就是自愿生活在高山的寒冰之中。

《论道德谱系》:(为理解我的哲学)需要不同于我们时代的另一种精神……需要适应高处稀薄的空气、适应一切意义上的严冬跋涉、天寒地冻和高山峻岭。

《人性,太人性的》:攀登真理的高山,你们决不会徒劳:或者今天更上一层楼,或者锻炼筋骨以便明天爬得更高。

《不合时宜的考察》:像哲学家一样尽量攀登纯净的冰

峰,登上高山之巅,扫尽一切云雾和混沌,只听到万物真元之声,粗犷而严峻,但字字清晰可懂!

　　无论从实际还是精神的意义上说,他就是属于高山的。尼采于1869年4月成为瑞士公民,可以说是瑞士最著名的哲学家。即便如此,他还是时常陷于一种大多数瑞士人都熟悉的情绪。他入瑞士籍一年之后向他母亲诉苦道:"我身为瑞士人深感痛苦!"

　　他35岁辞去巴塞尔大学的职位,开始在地中海沿岸过冬(多半在热那亚或尼斯),在阿尔卑斯山度夏——在瑞士东南部恩加丁地区海拔1800米的一个小村庄锡尔斯-玛丽亚,离莫里茨山只有几公里,来自意大利的风与寒冷的北方阵风在这里碰撞,把天空扫得如海一般湛蓝。

　　尼采于1879年6月首次访问恩加丁,立即爱上了这里的气候和地理环境。他告诉保罗·雷:"现在我可以呼吸到全欧洲最好的、最强壮的空气,它和我气质相同。"他给彼得·加斯特的信中说:"这不是瑞士……而是与之极不相同的地方,至少更像南方——要到墨西哥的高原俯瞰太平洋才能找到相似处(例如瓦哈卡),当然那里的蔬菜是热带的。总之,我要把这锡尔斯-玛丽亚据为己有。"在给他的同窗好友卡尔·冯·格斯多夫的信中,他写道:"我感到只有这里才是我真正的家,是我生于斯长于斯的地方。"

　　尼采在锡尔斯-玛丽亚租了一间可以眺望山景和松林

的农舍,在那里度过了7个夏天。他的大部分主要著作都是在那里完成的:《快乐的科学》、《查拉图斯特拉如是说》、《善恶的彼岸》、《论道德谱系》以及《偶像的黄昏》。他早晨5点起床,工作到中午,然后散步爬上环村的巍巍山峰:科尔瓦奇峰、拉格雷夫峰、马尼亚峰,这些奇峰峻岭野性未驯,像是最近才因地壳受到强大的地质压力而突起生成的。夜晚,他独自在室内吃一片火腿、鸡蛋和面包,早早就寝。("一个人如果不是每天至少三分之一的时间是怀着激情与人和书共度的,他怎么能成为思想家?")

今天,这村庄当然有一家博物馆。游人花几法郎就可以参观哲学家的卧室,据导游书介绍:"房间完全按照尼采当年朴实无华的面貌装修布置。"

但是,若要理解为什么尼采认为他的哲学和这里的山如此相近,最好绕过这居室,而去光顾锡尔斯-玛丽亚许多体育用品商店之一,购买登山靴、帆布背包、水瓶、手套、帐篷和一把尖镐。

爬上一次尼采故居几公里外的科尔瓦奇峰,比任何博物馆都能更好地解释尼采哲学的精神,解释他为何如此维护困难,为何背弃叔本华的麋鹿般的胆小。

山脚有一大片停车场、一排再生垃圾桶和一间垃圾车棚,还有一家餐馆,供应油腻腻的香肠和烧烤。

但是山顶却与此相反,美妙无比。可以望见整个恩加丁:塞格尔、席尔瓦普拉纳和圣莫里茨的碧绿的湖泊;向南望去,在与意大利交界处是巨大的塞拉和罗塞格冰川。空气中有一种非凡的静谧,似乎可以触摸世界的屋脊。高处使人喘不过气来,但又令人感到莫名的狂喜,不由人无端想笑,乃至大笑,是那种发自肺腑的纯真的笑,是因今生能见如此之美而迸发出的原始的欢快之情。

不过,回到尼采关于山的哲学教义,要爬上海拔3451米洵非易事。至少需要5个小时,必须紧随陡峭的山径,在岩石和茂密的松林中探寻路途,因空气稀薄而气短,层层加衣以对付山风,在终年积雪的山坡匍匐而行。

（十一）

尼采还提出过另一种登山的比喻。离他在锡尔斯－玛丽亚的小屋几步之遥有一条小道通向费克斯山谷，那是恩加丁最肥沃的地带。平缓的山坡得到充分的开垦。夏日里，成群的牛若有所思地啃着鲜亮碧绿的草，随着它们在一片片草场间移动，颈上的铃声叮当。

潺潺溪水流过田野，其声如泠泠清水注入玻璃杯中。除了一片片整修得完美无瑕的小型农场（每一片上都飘着国旗和乡旗）外，还有精心收拾的菜园，从那沃土里钻出来的花椰菜、甜菜、胡萝卜、莴苣如此苗壮，使人馋涎欲滴，恨不得像兔子那样趴下去咬它几口。

这地方能长出那样的莴苣是因为费克斯山谷是冰川形成的，这种冰层退去后的土壤的特点是含有丰富的矿物质。沿着河谷再往远处走，离开整齐的农场艰苦跋涉好几个小时，就来到了冰川本身，赫然大块，气势逼人，像是一张大桌布等着人去把它的皱褶拉平。然而这些褶子大如房屋,而且都是由刀刃般锋利的冰块形成,有时它们在夏日阳光下调整一下姿势,便发出痛苦的呻吟。

站在这冷酷的冰川边,很难想象这庞然大物怎么能和沿山谷几公里外的蔬菜和肥草联系起来,冰川显然是绿原的对立面,竟担负起肥沃土地的责任,简直不可思议。

尼采经常带着一支铅笔和一本皮面笔记本在费克斯山谷散步("只有散步时出现的思想才是有价值的"),以这种现象比喻人生的正负相倚,完美与困难相倚:

> 望着这些曾经是冰川覆盖的深沟空谷,我们很难设想有一天在同一地方可能出现草木葱茏、溪流灌溉的土地。人类历史也是一样:最野蛮的力量开辟了一条道路,主要是破坏性的;但是它的工作是必要的,为了以后更为优雅的文明能在此建造大厦。那些可怕的,被称作邪恶的能量却是人类的泥石建筑工和筑路工。

(十二)

不过,单有吓人的困难当然是远远不够的。一切人生都是艰难的;而其中有些得以实现完美,是对痛苦的态度使然。

每一次痛苦都是一个本能的信号,说明有些事不对头,而其孕育的结果是好是坏全赖承受者的智慧和力量。焦虑可能导致惊惶失措,也可能导致对缺失的准确分析。不公平感可能引出谋杀,也可能引出开创性的经济理论。妒忌可能引起怨恨,也可能激发起与对手竞争的决心,从而创作出杰作。

正如尼采最喜爱的蒙田在《随笔集》最后一章所述,生活的艺术在于善于利用逆境:

> 我们一定要学会忍受无法避免的苦难。一如世界的和声,我们的生活是由不和谐的和弦以及不同的音调组成的:柔和的、粗犷的、尖利的、平缓的、轻的和响的。如果一个音乐家只喜欢其中一部分,那他能唱什么呢? 他必须掌握所有这些,然后糅合在一起。同样的,我们也必须把善与恶糅合在一起,因为在我们的生活中二者本是同一物。

约三百年后,尼采重提同样的思想:

> 我们好比果实累累的田野,下面没有废弃不用的东西,君不见,任何情况下人和物都欢迎粪肥。

那么怎样才能果实累累呢?

（十三）

拉斐尔于 1483 年生于乌尔比诺,孩提时就显示出对绘画极大的兴趣,于是父亲带他到佩鲁贾去给著名的彼得罗·佩鲁吉诺当学徒。他不久就独立作画,到 20 岁之前已经画过乌尔比诺宫廷的几位人物的肖像以及卡斯特洛小城里的教堂的祭坛画,从乌尔比诺骑马向佩鲁贾的方向穿山路而行,大约一天可到卡斯特洛。

但是拉斐尔——这位尼采最喜爱的画家——自知还不是伟大的艺术家,因为他看到过两个人的作品:米开朗琪罗和达·芬奇。这些作品向他表明,他还没有能力画出人物的动态,而且尽管他很擅长几何画,还是没有掌握线条透视。这种妒忌有可能发展成变态心理,但是拉斐尔把它变做了肥料。

1504 年他 21 岁时离开乌尔比诺到佛罗伦萨去学习这两位大师的作品。他在市议会大厅中研究了他们的草图,在那里,达·芬奇和米开朗琪罗曾分别绘制关于安吉亚里战役和卡希纳战役的图。他吸取了他们两位的解剖图的手法,效法他们解剖和描画尸体的做法。他学习达·芬奇的《博士来拜》和《圣母子与圣安娜》的草图,并且仔细研究达·芬奇的一张不同寻常的画,这是他应一位贵族弗朗西斯科·德·焦孔多的要求为他的妻子画的肖像——一位带着神秘微笑的少妇。

拉斐尔努力的成绩是显而易见的。我们可以比较一下他在去佛罗伦萨之前画的"少妇像"和几年以后画的"少妇像"。

蒙娜(丽莎)启发拉斐尔画出半身坐姿,其中手臂起了金字塔底座的作用,还教给拉斐尔如何运用头、肩和手的坐标反差,使身体丰满起来。而他在乌尔比诺画的那位少妇则紧裹在衣服里,目光呆滞,双手被画面生硬地切掉了。佛罗伦萨的那位少妇则是动态的,舒坦自在。

拉斐尔的才华并非天成,他之伟大是由于对自卑感做出了明智的反应,而不如他的人就会因自卑而绝望。

这一成功之路提供了尼采式的教训,说明正确理解痛苦之益处。

不要讲什么天赋,生而知之! 可以列举出各式各样的伟人并没有多少天赋。他们的伟大是后天获得的,是通过一些人们不大愿意谈论的品质而成为我们所说的"天才"的:他们都是勤奋、认真的工匠,都是先把各部分做得合格了,才敢于从事整体的创作。他们不怕多花时间,因为他们从制作细小的次要部件中获得更多的乐趣,超过从辉煌的整体效果中得到的。

拉斐尔:尼科里尼-考波圣母像习作稿
尼科里尼-考波圣母像

用尼采的话来说,拉斐尔能够把自己道路上的困难"sublimieren"①、"vergeistigen"②、"aufheben"③,臻于成果斐然。

---

① 德文,意为"升华"。——译者
② 德文,意为"点化"。——译者
③ 德文,意为"扬弃"。——译者

（十四）

　　哲学家对园艺有很大的兴趣，既是实际的，又是形象的。他于1879年从巴塞尔大学去职后，就决心成为专业园艺家。"您知道，我性本爱朴素自然的生活，"他告诉他惊讶的母亲，"现在我更渴望过这样的生活。没有别的办法能改善我的健康。我需要真正的劳动，可以使我感到疲劳而没有精神压力。"他记得在瑙姆堡母亲的房子附近有一座古塔，他想租住，以便可以照料附近的园子。1879年9月他以极大的热情开始他的园艺生活——但是不久就遇到了问题。他的视力很弱，修枝时看不清楚，弯腰有困难，落叶又太多（那是秋天）。三星期后，他感到只好放弃了。

　　但是他对园艺的兴趣却在他的哲学中留下了踪影。在有些段落中，他建议我们像园丁一样对待困难。植物的根常常奇形怪状，面目可憎，但是对其潜力有信心的知者可以引导它们长出美丽的花朵和果实。人生亦然，在根部可能情感、处境都很艰难，但是经过精心培植，可以结出最伟大的成果和欢乐。

　　一个人可以像园丁一样处理自己的冲动，尽管极少人知道这一点，他可以把愤怒、怜悯、好奇、虚荣的幼苗培植得像棚架上美丽的果树一样果实累累，收益丰润。

但是我们大多数人都没认识到我们应该感激这些困难的幼苗。我们总是认为焦虑和妒忌不会给我们什么正当的教益，就把它们当做情感的杂草除掉了。如尼采所说：我们相信"高的东西是不允许从矮的长出来的，根本就不允许是成长起来的……一切一流的东西一定是 *causa sui*①"。

艺术、美、爱

愤怒、怜悯、好奇、虚荣

但是，尼采强调，"善与荣耀"是"与其对立面邪恶巧妙地相互关联，纠缠不清的"。"爱与恨，感激与复仇，温良与愤怒……是不可分的。"但这并不意味着它们必须同时表达出来，应该说，正面的事物可能是负面事物培植成功的结果。

　　仇恨、妒忌、贪婪、权欲等情感都是生命的必要条件……是贯穿于整个人生的经营中的基本要素。

———————

　　①　拉丁文，意为"天生的"。——译者

如果把所有的负面的根砍掉，也就等于扼杀了可能在枝头结出的正面的花果的元素。

使我们感到窘迫的不应是困难本身，而是我们无能让困难结出美丽的果实。

（十五）

尼采怀着无限景仰回顾古希腊人，正因为他们能赞赏这一观点。

尼采于1877年初与玛尔维达·冯·迈森堡同游距索伦托几公里的帕埃斯图姆，在黄昏中凝视那肃穆的神殿发思古之幽情，不由人不想象古希腊人是超常的巨人，这些神殿就是他们内心和他们社会内部存在的一种秩序的外在表现。

这是伟大的古典学家约翰·温克尔曼（1717—1768）的观点，并影响了几代德国大学教授。但是尼采提出的看

法是,古希腊文明决不来自肃穆宁静,而是来自最凶险的力量的升华:

> 一个时代,一个民族或个人能驾驭的情欲越强大,越凶险——因为他们有能力把它当做一种手段,那他们的文化达到的水平就越高。

那些神殿看起来很宁静,但它们是根部阴暗的幼苗经过精心培育长出的花朵。酒神狂欢节所表现的既是这阴暗面,又是驾驭它、培育它的努力。

> 最使希腊世界的观察家惊诧的,莫过于发现希腊人经常把发泄所有的情欲和本性中的邪恶倾向当作节日,甚至制定了一套正式的程序来庆祝再人性不过的内心世界……他们把这再人性不过的特点视为无法逃避的,决不加以贬斥,而宁愿通过社会和宗教的内部调节给予它二等的权利:凡是人性中有力量的,他们都称之为神,并刻在他们的天庭的墙壁上。他们并不排斥表现为邪恶品质的那些自然的冲动,而是设法加以调节,一旦发现足以为这些野性的洪水提供最无害的宣泄渠道的规范措施,就把它们限制在确定的仪式和固定的日子里。这就是古代一切道德的思想自由的根源。给邪恶和可疑的事物……以适当的发泄,而不是致力于彻底消灭之。

希腊人不是砍掉其敌人,而是施以教化。

一切情欲在某个时期都曾是纯粹的灾难,以它们的极端愚蠢扳倒其受害者。后来,在很久以后,情欲与精神相结合,实现了"精神化"。早先,由于情欲的愚蠢,人们向情欲本身开战:设法消灭它……消灭情欲和欲望只是为了避免受其愚蠢之害;而在今天看来,这种愚蠢造成的不愉快的后果只不过是愚蠢的一种急性发作。我们已经不再对牙医拔牙止痛感到惊奇。

只有对极度的艰难困苦作出明智的对应才能实现自我完成。性情浮躁的人很容易干脆拔掉一颗臼齿,或是刚到科尔瓦奇山峰的低坡处就弃之而去。尼采力主我们坚韧不拔。

(十六)

他还力主我们绝对不要酗酒,这并非巧合。

亲爱的妈妈:

今天写信是要禀告一桩我犯下的最令人不快、最痛苦之事。我实在行为不端,不知道您是否能原谅我。此刻我勉强提笔,心情极为沉重,特别是回想起复活节假期中我们在一起欢乐融洽的日子。上星期日,我喝醉了,没有任何借口,除了自己不知酒量多大,还有那天下午太兴奋了。

这是1863年春18岁的弗里德里希在学校附近阿腾堡厅堂中喝了4杯啤酒之后给他母亲弗兰齐斯卡写的信。几年之后,在波恩和莱比锡的大学中,他对他的同学们喜爱喝酒感到厌恶:"我常常对俱乐部中表达同学之谊的方式极为厌恶……有些人的啤酒拜物主义简直令我难以忍受。"

尼采在波恩大学的学生联谊会。二排向一边斜倾的是尼采。请注意底排联谊会的啤酒桶。

这一态度始终贯穿于哲学家的成年生活：

> 酒精饮料对我无益：每天一杯葡萄酒或啤酒已足以使
> 我的生活成为"泪泉"。慕尼黑是我的对立面居住之地。

他抱怨："德国的智慧中有多少啤酒！也许现代欧洲的
不满就是来源于我们的祖先整个中世纪都放纵于杯中
物……中世纪就意味着酒精毒害下的欧洲。"

1871年春，尼采同他的妹妹一起到卢加诺的花园饭店
度假。3月2—9日的账单显示他喝了19杯牛奶。

这不仅仅是个人的口味问题，他规劝每一个追求快乐
的人都绝对不要喝任何酒，绝对。

> 对于所有重精神的人，我无比认真地劝诫：绝对禁酒。
> 喝水足矣。

何以故？因为拉斐尔于1504年在乌尔比诺没有借酒来
逃避胸中的妒火，他跑到了佛罗伦萨学习如何成为伟大的
画家。因为司汤达在1805年没有借酒来逃避他因《怕受管
辖的人》失败而引起的绝望之情，他耕耘这一痛苦凡17年，
终于在1822年出版了《论爱情》：

> 如果你拒绝苦难在你身上逗留哪怕是1小时，如果你

总是早早地防范可能的痛苦于未然，如果你把苦难与不快当作应当消灭的邪恶与仇恨，当作生存的缺点，那么，很清楚，你心中怀有安逸的宗教。生活在安逸中的人啊，你们真不知人类幸福为何物，因为幸福与不幸是两姊妹，甚至是孪生姊妹，要么一起长大，要么一起永远保持矮小。

（十七）

尼采对酒精的敌视同时也说明他为什么敌视曾经流行一时的英国道德哲学：功利主义学派及其倡导者约翰·穆勒。功利主义者的论点是，在一个充满了道德模糊的世界上，衡量一种行为对或错的标准就是它带来多大的快乐或痛苦。穆勒认为：

> 行为之正确与其可能促进之幸福成正比，反之则为错误。幸福即快乐与无痛苦，不幸福即痛苦与丧失快乐。

功利主义思潮，甚至连同由此脱颖而出的那个国家，都令尼采愤怒不已：

> 欧洲的庸俗化，现代思想的平民主义皆源于英国。

253

人本来不是为追求幸福而奋斗的,只有英国人才是这样。

其实他自己当然也是为追求幸福而奋斗的,只不过他认为不能无痛苦地获得幸福,而功利主义者看来就是这样主张的:

所有这些以苦、乐——也就是从属的、次要的现象——来衡量事物的价值的思想模式是最为幼稚可笑的,任何具有创造意识和艺术家良知的人都嗤之以鼻。

提到艺术家的良知,因为艺术创作是最显著的例证,表明一种产生巨大成就感的活动总是需要经过巨大的苦难。假设司汤达以立竿见影的"苦"和"乐"来衡量他的艺术创作的价值,那么他决不会从《怕受管辖的人》进展到他的威力

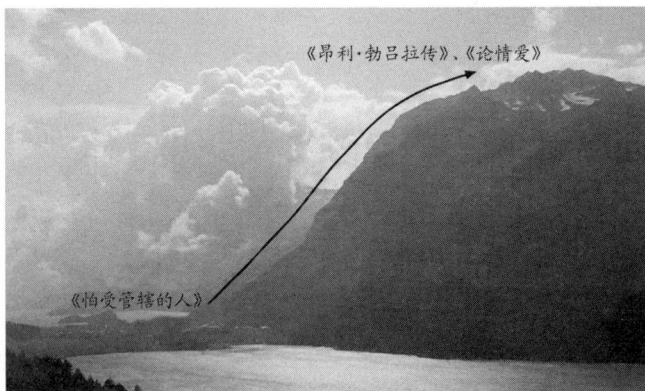

《昂利·勃吕拉传》、《论情爱》

《怕受管辖的人》

的高峰。

尼采要求我们不要停留在山下喝酒,而去接受攀登的痛苦。他还向市政规划者提出过建议:

> 从当前的存在中获得最大的收获和最大的享受的秘诀在于——危险地生活! 把你们的城市建立在维苏威火山坡上吧!

假如有人还是难耐酒瘾,而且此人对基督教评价不高,尼采提出另一个劝诫他的论点。他说任何喜欢喝酒的人从根本上持有基督教的世界观:

> 要我相信酒能使人高兴,我先得变成基督徒,也就是说,相信我认为特别荒唐之事。

(十八)

他对基督教的体验比对酒精多。他出生于莱比锡附近萨克森的一座名叫勒肯的小村庄。他的父亲卡尔·路德维希·尼采就是该村的教区牧师,他的虔诚母亲是牧师的女儿——戴维·厄恩斯特·奥勒在一小时路程外的波夫莱村布道。儿子(尼采)于 1844 年 10 月在勒肯教堂当地牧师会的主持下受洗。

弗里德里希 4 岁时父亲就去世了,他爱他的父亲并终生敬重他。1885 年,他打赢了一场与出版商的官司,得到一小笔钱,就为他父亲的墓定制了一大块墓碑,上面刻了一句《哥林多书》的语录:

"Die Liebe höret nimmer auf"①(《哥林多前书》第 3 章第 8 节)②

尼采回忆卡尔·路德维希说,"他是乡村牧师的完美体现。身材修长,五官端正,和蔼、慈祥。他因言语机智和富于同情心而到处受欢迎,农民都敬他爱他。他以精神导师的身份用言语和行动广施祝福。"

但是对父亲的爱并未阻止尼采对父亲以及一般基督教提供的对痛苦的慰藉抱有深刻的保留:

---

① 德语,意为"爱是永不止息的"。——译者
② "Corinthians"为《圣经·新约》中使徒圣保罗写给科林多教堂的使徒信件,共 2 封,称"前书","后书"。——译者

我向基督教会提出任何公诉人从未提出过的最严厉的控告。在我看来,基督教会是可以想见的最极端的腐蚀形式……一切事物都难逃它堕落之手……我称基督教为惟一的大诅咒,惟一的本质上的大堕落……

　　读《新约》时戴上手套是对的。接近这么多的不洁迫使人不得不如此……那里面一切都是怯懦,一切都是自欺,故意闭眼不看自己……难道还需要我说吗? 整个《新约》中只有一位孤独的人物是值得尊敬的,那就是罗马总督彼拉多①。

干脆说:

今天作为基督徒是不体面的。

（十九）

　　《新约》在我们遇到困难时如何安慰我们呢? 向我们暗示,许多困难实际不是困难而是美德:

---

① Ponce Pilate 或 Pontius Pilatus,古罗马犹地亚省总督(26—36),据称他有权决定耶稣的生死,他认为耶稣无罪,应予释放,但迫于犹太人的压力,还是把耶稣交出去钉十字架。后自杀。一说他已秘密皈依基督教,为罗马参议院判处死刑。——译者

若是有人为胆小所困扰,《新约》指出:

温柔的人有福了,因为他们必承受地土。(《马太福音》第5章第5节)

若是有人因为没有朋友而发愁,《新约》建议:

人为人子恨恶你们,拒绝你们,辱骂你们,弃掉你们的名,以为是恶,你们就有福了……因为你们在天上的赏赐是大的。(《路加福音》第6章第22—23节)

若是有人为在工作中受盘剥而发愁,《新约》劝告说:

你们作仆人的,要凡事听从你们肉身的主人……因你们知道从主那里必得着基业为赏赐。你们所侍奉的乃是主基督。(《歌罗西书》第3章第22—24节)

若是有人为没有钱而发愁,《新约》告诉我们:

骆驼穿过针的眼比财主进入神的国还容易呢。(《马可福音》第10章第25节)

此类话语与喝酒可能有所区别,不过尼采坚持认为本质上是相同的。基督教和酒精都有力量使我们相信,我们原来以为是自身的和这个世界的缺点都是不必介意的;二者都削弱我们培育我们的问题的决心;二者都剥夺我们自我完成的机会:

两种欧洲最大的毒品:酒精和基督教。

据尼采说,基督教是从罗马帝国的卑怯的奴隶的头脑中产生的;他们没有勇气去攀登山峰,所以创建出这样一种哲学,硬说他们所居的底层很让人喜欢。基督徒也希望享受自我完成的真正的内容(地位、性爱、智力超群、创造力),但是没有勇气忍受这些享受所必需经历的困难。所以他们就制造出一种伪善的信仰,谴责那些他们心里想要而又无力为之奋斗的东西,称赞那些他们本来不想要而正好拥有的东西。无力变成了"善",卑下变成了"谦恭",屈从自己所恨的人变成了"顺从",还有,用尼采的话来说,"无能复仇"变成了"宽恕"。每一种脆弱感都给封了一个神圣的名字,看起来像是"自愿获得的成就,是原来想要的,自己选择的,一项业绩,一项成就"。基督徒们迷恋于"安逸的宗教",于是在他们的价值体系中把容易得到的而不是应该向往的置于优先地位,这样就把生命的潜能抽干了。

(二十)

对困难持有"基督教"的态度的人并不限于基督徒;尼采认为这是一种永恒的可能性。当我们对于内心渴望而得不到的东西表示淡然时,我们就都变成了基督徒;当我们貌似轻松地说我们不需要爱,或是世俗的地位、金钱、成功、创造，乃至健康时，我们却恨得嘴角都歪了；我们默默地向我们公开放弃的东西开战，从墙垛后面打枪，躲在树上放冷枪。

尼采宁愿我们如何对待挫折呢？继续对我们所向往的东西保持信念，即便我们现在没有，也许永远得不到。换言之，抵制那种把难以得到的东西贬为邪恶的诱惑——也许尼采自己无比悲惨的人生给我们提供了这种行为方式最好的范例。

（二十一）

伊壁鸠鲁是他早期最喜爱的古代哲学家之一；他称之为"近古时期的灵魂抚慰者"，"最伟大的人物之一，以英雄-田园诗的方式讲哲学的发明家"。最令他神往的是伊壁鸠鲁关于与朋友共同生活乐在其中的思想。但是他极少体验与人同乐的满足。"我们生来就是心智的隐者，只有偶逢知音能谈一谈。"他30岁时创作一首关于孤独的赞美诗——《孤独颂》，终于不忍卒篇。

求偶的经历也不见得少一些愁苦，问题在于尼采的外表——海象式的特大胡须，还有他的腼腆使他的举止刻板僵硬，像一位退伍少校。1876年春，尼采旅游日内瓦时爱上了一名23岁的碧眼金发女郎，玛蒂尔德·特朗佩达。在一次交谈中谈到亨利·朗费罗的诗,尼采说他还没有见过朗费罗的"追求卓越"的德文版,玛蒂尔德说她家里有一本,愿意抄一份给他。尼采受到了鼓励,就请她出去散步。她把房东太太带来作陪。几天以后,尼采自告奋勇为她弹一曲钢琴。再下一次,她从这位巴塞尔大学31岁的古典哲学教授那里听到的是求婚。"难道你不认为我们两人在一起比各自单独生活会更好,更自由,因此更卓越吗?"顽皮的少校问道,"你敢不敢与我共同走完所有生活和思想的道路?"玛蒂尔德不敢。

一连串的类似的碰壁不断地伤害他。瓦格纳见他精神恒郁,健康不佳,认为只有两种解药:"要么结婚,要么写出一部歌剧。"但是尼采写不出歌剧,而且显然连像样的曲调也创作不出来。1872年7月,他寄给指挥家汉斯·冯·比洛①一首他创作的钢琴双重奏,请他给予坦诚的评论。比洛回答说,这是"我长期以来所见过写在乐谱纸上的最匪夷所思、最难听、最反音乐的一套音符",他怀疑尼采是否腿抽筋了。"你称你的乐曲为'骇人听闻',真是如此。"

瓦格纳却更加坚持己见,他一再劝他,"看在老天的分上,娶一个富婆吧!"他还同尼采的医生奥托·艾泽取得联系,并且告诉他自己猜想尼采的健康不佳是由于手淫过度。

---

① Hans von Bülow（1830—1894）,德国著名乐队指挥和钢琴家,为瓦格纳的学生。——译者

具有讽刺意义的是，瓦格纳不知道，尼采真正爱上的那一位富婆正是瓦格纳自己的妻子，科西玛。多年来，尼采一直用朋友式的关心的外衣掩盖他的感情。只有一次忍不住真情流露：1889 年 1 月，尼采寄给科西玛一张署名"酒神"的明信片，上面写道："阿里阿德涅，我爱你。"

不过，尼采间或也同意瓦格纳的关于婚姻的重要性的论点。他在给一位已婚友人弗朗兹·奥弗贝克的信中诉苦说："亏了你的妻子，你的境遇比我的好百倍。你们共同有一个巢，而我充其量有一个穴而已……偶与人接触就像是放假，是自我救赎。"

1882 年，他又升起希望，以为自己找到了一位合适的妻子，卢·安德烈斯-萨乐美，这是他最大的、最痛苦的恋爱。她 21 岁，美丽、聪慧、风骚，迷上了他的哲学。尼采一见倾心。他告诉她："我不想继续孤独下去，而要再学习做人。啊！实际上我什么都需要学！"他们在陶腾堡森林共度了两星期，在卢塞恩同他们共同的朋友保罗·雷照了一张不寻常的合影。

但是卢对尼采作为哲学家比作为丈夫更感兴趣。这次碰壁使尼采陷入长期的、强烈的悒郁之中。"现在我缺乏自信达到极点，"他向奥弗贝克诉说，"所有我听到的话都使我感到人们在蔑视我。"他特别怨恨他的母亲和妹妹，她们曾干预他与萨乐美的关系，现在同他断绝了来往，使他陷入更深的孤独。（"我不喜欢我的母亲，我妹妹的声音让我痛苦。

我跟她们在一起时总是要生病。")

　　事业上也不顺。尼采生前清醒时,他的著作销量从未超过2000册;多数都只售出几百册。这位作者只靠微薄的退休金和从一位姑母那里继承的一些股票维持生活,连新衣服都买不起,最后用他自己的话来说,"外表像一头剃了毛的山羊。"他只住最便宜的旅店,常常拖欠房租,连取暖费和他所喜爱的火腿香肠的费用都付不起。

　　他的健康很成问题。从学生时代起就病痛不断:头痛、消化不良、呕吐、晕眩、几乎失明,还有失眠。其中许多项都是梅毒的症状,几乎可以肯定他是在1865年2月间在科隆的一家妓院中染上的(尽管尼采自称他除了钢琴什么也没有碰过就出来了)。三年之后他在访问索伦托之后给玛尔维达·冯·迈森堡的一封信中称:"说到自苦和禁欲,我过去几年的生活堪与任何时代的苦行僧相比美……"他向医生的诉说是:"经常疼痛,有半身麻痹之感,与晕船的感觉非常相似,有时感到说话困难——这种感觉一天持续几小时。与此交替的是一种激烈的发作(最近一次发作迫使我吐了三天三夜,但求速死)。不能看书! 写也难得! 没法与人交往! 听不了音乐!"

最后,于1889年1月初,尼采在都灵的卡罗·阿尔贝托街头彻底崩溃了,他拥抱了一匹马,随即被送回他的住处,他在那里打算刺杀德国皇帝,策划一场反对反犹主义者的战争,越来越肯定自己是酒神、耶稣、天主、拿破仑、意大利国王、佛、亚历山大大帝、恺撒、伏尔泰、亚历山大·赫尔岑和理查德·瓦格纳——视几点钟而定;然后他就给塞进了一辆火车,运到德国的一家疯人院,以后由他的母亲和妹妹照看,直到11年后去世,享年55岁。

(二十二)

在难以忍受的孤独、微贱、贫困和疾病缠身之中,尼采没有表现出任何他所指责的基督徒的行径;他没有反对友谊,攻击名利、财富。加利亚尼和歌德仍然是他的英雄。尽管玛蒂尔德只不过想同他谈一次诗,他还是认为"对男人妄自菲薄的病来说,最好的治疗就是得到一位聪明的女士的爱"。尽管他病病歪歪,缺乏蒙田和司汤达的矫健骑术,他还是向往积极运动的生活:"一大清早,在精力最新鲜旺盛的时候埋头读书——我把这叫做罪恶!"

他为谋求幸福而艰苦奋斗,即使不成功,他也没有转而反对他曾经向往的东西。他始终坚信在他眼里一个高贵的人最重要的特点:做一个"不再弃绝"的人。

(二十三)

步行 7 小时之后,大部分是在雨中,我在筋疲力尽状态下到达了科尔瓦奇山峰,覆盖恩加丁山谷的云层就在脚下。我在背包里放了一瓶水、一块瑞士多孔干酪,还有从锡尔斯-玛丽亚村的艾德维斯旅馆带来的一个信封,我当天早晨在上面写了一段那位登山哲学家的语录,企图在海拔 3400 米的岩石上在山风中面对意大利读它。

尼采和他的牧师父亲一样,献身于抚慰人。和他父亲一样,他想向我们指出通向自我完成之路。但是他不同于牧师,也不同于把痛牙拔掉的牙医和毁掉不讨人喜欢的植物根的园丁,他认为困难是达到完成的关键性的必要前提,因此甜蜜的抚慰最终残酷多于助益。

人类最厉害的疾病在于他们与疾病斗争之道。表面上能治病的办法从长远来看比它要治的病还坏。临时有效的治疗、麻醉、镇静、所谓的安慰剂，被无知地当作治疗本身。人们忽视这样的事实……这些临时的缓解剂常常要病人付出更加全面深刻恶化的代价。

使我们感觉好些的不一定对我们好。使我们感到痛的不一定对我们不好。

把痛苦的状态笼统看作应该予以消灭的对立物，是极端愚蠢的，总的说来后果是灾难性的……几乎与想要消灭坏天气一样愚蠢。

The Consolations of Philosophy

Alain de Botton

Consolation for

I Consolation for Unpopularity

A few years ago, during a bitter New York winter, with an afternoon to spare before catching a flight to London, I found myself in a deserted gallery on the upper level of the Metropolitan Museum of Art. It was brightly lit, and aside from the soothing hum of an under-floor heating system, entirely silent. Having reached a surfeit of paintings in the Impressionist galleries, I was looking for a sign for the cafeteria – where I hoped to buy a glass of a certain variety of American chocolate milk of which I was at that time extremely fond – when my eye was caught by a canvas which a caption explained had been painted in Paris in the autumn of 1786 by the thirty-eight-year-old Jacques-Louis David.

Socrates, condemned to death by the people of Athens, prepares to drink a cup of hemlock, surrounded by woebegone friends. In the spring of 399 BC, three Athenian citizens had brought legal proceedings against the philosopher. They had accused him of failing to worship the city's gods, of introducing religious novelties and of corrupting the young men of Athens – and such was the severity of their charges, they had called for the death penalty.

Socrates had responded with legendary equanimity. Though afforded an opportunity to renounce his philosophy in court, he had sided with what he believed to be true rather than what he knew would be popular. In Plato's account he had defiantly told the jury:

> So long as I draw breath and have my faculties, I shall never stop practising philosophy and exhorting you and elucidating the truth for everyone that I meet ... And so gentlemen ... whether you acquit me or not, you know that I am not going to alter my conduct, not even if I have to die a hundred deaths.

And so he had been led to meet his end in an Athenian jail, his death marking a defining moment in the history of philosophy.

An indication of its significance may be the frequency with which it has been painted. In 1650 the French painter Charles-Alphonse Dufresnoy produced a *Death of Socrates*, now hanging in the Galleria Palatina in Florence (which has no cafeteria).

The eighteenth century witnessed the zenith of interest in Socrates' death, particularly after Diderot drew attention to its painterly potential in a passage in his *Treatise on Dramatic Poetry*.

Jacques-Louis David received his commission in the spring of 1786 from Charles-Michel Trudaine de la Sablière, a wealthy member of the Parlement and a gifted Greek scholar. The terms were generous, 6,000 livres upfront, with a further 3,000 on delivery (Louis XVI had paid only 6,000 livres for the larger *Oath of the Horatii*). When the picture was exhibited at the Salon of 1787, it was at once judged the finest of the Socratic ends. Sir Joshua Reynolds thought it 'the most exquisite and admirable effort of art which has appeared since the *Cappella Sistina*, and the *Stanze* of Raphael. The picture would have done honour to Athens in the age of Pericles.'

I bought five postcard Davids in the museum gift-shop and later, flying over the ice fields of Newfoundland (turned a luminous green by a full moon and a cloudless sky), examined one while picking at a pale evening meal left on the table in front of me by a stewardess during a misjudged snooze.

Plato sits at the foot of the bed, a pen and a scroll beside him, silent witness to the injustice of the state. He had been twenty-nine at the time of Socrates' death, but David turned him into an old man, grey-haired and grave. Through the passageway, Socrates' wife, Xanthippe, is escorted from the prison cell by warders. Seven friends are in various stages of lamentation. Socrates' closest companion Crito, seated beside him, gazes at the master with devotion and concern. But the philosopher, bolt upright, with an athlete's torso and biceps, shows neither apprehension nor regret. That a large number of Athenians have denounced him as foolish has not shaken him in his convictions. David had planned to paint Socrates in the act of swallowing poison, but the poet André Chenier suggested that there would be greater dramatic tension if he was shown finishing a philosophical point while at the same time reaching serenely for the hemlock that would end his life, symbolizing both obedience to the laws of Athens and allegiance to his calling. We are witnessing the last edifying moments of a transcendent being.

If the postcard struck me so forcefully, it was perhaps because the behaviour it depicted contrasted so sharply with my own. In conversations, my priority was to be liked, rather than to speak the truth. A desire to please led me to laugh at modest jokes like a parent on the opening night of a school play. With strangers, I adopted the servile manner of a concierge greeting wealthy clients in a hotel − salival enthusiasm born of a morbid, indiscriminate desire for affection. I did not publicly doubt ideas to which the majority was committed. I sought the approval of figures of authority and after encounters with them, worried at length whether they had thought me acceptable. When passing through customs or driving alongside police cars, I harboured a confused wish for the uniformed officials to think well of me.

But the philosopher had not buckled before unpopularity and the condemnation of the state. He had not retracted his thoughts because others had complained. Moreover, his confidence had sprung from a more profound source than hot-headedness or bull-like courage. It had been grounded in philosophy. Philosophy had supplied Socrates with convictions in which he had been able to have rational, as opposed to hysterical, confidence when faced with disapproval.

That night, above the ice lands, such independence of mind was a revelation and an incitement. It promised a counterweight to a supine tendency to follow socially sanctioned practices and ideas.

In Socrates' life and death lay an invitation to intelligent scepticism.

And more generally, the subject of which the Greek philosopher was the supreme symbol seemed to offer an invitation to take on a task at once profound and laughable: to become wise through philosophy. In spite of the vast differences between the many thinkers described as philosophers across time (people in actuality so diverse that had they been gathered together at a giant cocktail party, they would not only have had nothing to say to one another, but would most probably have come to blows after a few drinks), it seemed possible to discern a small group of men, separated by centuries, sharing a loose allegiance to a vision of philosophy suggested by the Greek etymology of the word – *philo*, love; *sophia*, wisdom – a group bound by a common interest in saying a few consoling and practical things about the causes of our greatest griefs. It was to these men I would turn.

2

Every society has notions of what one should believe and how one should behave in order to avoid suspicion and unpopularity. Some of these societal conventions are given explicit formulation in a legal code, others are more intuitively held in a vast body of ethical and practical judgements described as 'common sense', which dictates what we should wear, which financial values we should adopt, whom we should esteem, which etiquette we should follow and what domestic life we should lead. To start questioning these conventions would seem bizarre, even aggressive. If common sense is cordoned off from questions, it is because its judgements are deemed plainly too sensible to be the targets of scrutiny.

It would scarcely be acceptable, for example, to ask in the course of an ordinary conversation what our society holds to be the purpose of work.

Or to ask a recently married couple to explain in full the reasons behind their decision.

Or to question holiday-makers in detail about the assumptions behind their trip.

Ancient Greeks had as many common-sense conventions and would have held on to them as tenaciously. One weekend, while browsing in a second-hand bookshop in Bloomsbury, I came upon a series of history books originally intended for children, containing a host of photographs and handsome illustrations. The series included *See Inside an Egyptian Town*, *See Inside a Castle* and a volume I acquired along with an encyclopedia of poisonous plants, *See Inside an Ancient Greek Town*.

There was information on how it had been considered normal to dress in the city states of Greece in the fifth century BC.

The book explained that the Greeks had believed in many gods, gods of love, hunting and war, gods with power over the harvest, fire and sea. Before embarking on any venture they had prayed to them either in a temple or in a small shrine at home, and sacrificed animals in their honour. It had been expensive: Athena cost a cow; Artemis and Aphrodite a goat; Asclepius a hen or cock.

The Greeks had felt sanguine about owning slaves. In the fifth century BC, in Athens alone, there were, at any one time, 80—100,000 slaves, one slave to every three of the free population.

The Greeks had been highly militaristic, too, worshipping courage on the battlefield. To be considered an adequate male, one had to know how to scythe the heads off adversaries. The Athenian soldier ending the career of a Persian (painted on a plate at the time of the Second Persian War) indicated the appropriate behaviour.

Women had been entirely under the thumb of their husbands and fathers. They had taken no part in politics or public life, and had been unable either to inherit property or to own money. They had normally married at thirteen, their husbands chosen for them by their fathers irrespective of emotional compatibility.

None of which would have seemed remarkable to the contemporaries of Socrates. They would have been confounded and angered to be asked exactly why they sacrificed cocks to Asclepius or why men needed to kill to be virtuous. It would have appeared as obtuse as wondering why spring followed winter or why ice was cold.

But it is not only the hostility of others that may prevent us from questioning the status quo. Our will to doubt can be just as powerfully sapped by an internal sense that societal conventions must have a sound basis, even if we are not sure exactly what this may be, because they have been adhered to by a great many people for a long time. It seems implausible that our society could be gravely mistaken in its beliefs and at the same time that we would be alone in noticing the fact. We stifle our doubts and follow the flock because we cannot conceive of ourselves as pioneers of hitherto unknown, difficult truths.

It is for help in overcoming our meekness that we may turn to the philosopher.

3

1. *The life*

He was born in Athens in 469 BC, his father Sophroniscus was believed to have been a sculptor, his mother Phaenarete a midwife. In his youth, Socrates was a pupil of the philosopher Archelaus, and thereafter practised philosophy without ever writing any of it down. He did not charge for his lessons and so slid into poverty; though he had little concern for material

275

possessions. He wore the same cloak throughout the year and almost always walked barefoot (it was said he had been born to spite shoemakers). By the time of his death he was married and the father of three sons. His wife, Xanthippe, was of notoriously foul temper (when asked why he had married her, he replied that horse-trainers needed to practise on the most spirited animals). He spent much time out of the house, conversing with friends in the public places of Athens. They appreciated his wisdom and sense of humour. Few can have appreciated his looks. He was short, bearded and bald, with a curious rolling gait, and a face variously likened by acquaintances to the head of a crab, a satyr or a grotesque. His nose was flat, his lips large, and his prominent swollen eyes sat beneath a pair of unruly brows.

But his most curious feature was a habit of approaching Athenians of every class, age and occupation and bluntly asking them, without worrying whether they would think him eccentric or infuriating, to explain with precision why they held certain commonsense beliefs and what they took to be the meaning of life – as one surprised general reported:

> Whenever anyone comes face to face with Socrates and has a conversation with him, what invariably happens is that, although he may have started on a completely different subject first, Socrates will keep heading him off as they're talking until he has him trapped into giving an account of his present life-style and the way he has spent his life in the past. And once he has him trapped, Socrates won't let him go before he has well and truly cross-examined him from every angle.

He was helped in his habit by climate and urban planning. Athens was warm for half the year, which increased opportunities for conversing without formal introduction with people outdoors. Activities which in northern lands unfolded behind the mud walls of sombre, smoke-filled huts needed no shelter from the benevolent Attic skies. It was common to linger in the agora, under the colonnades of the Painted Stoa or the Stoa of Zeus Eleutherios, and talk to strangers in the late afternoon, the privileged hours between the practicalities of high noon and the anxieties of night.

The size of the city ensured conviviality. Around 240, 000 people lived within Athens and its port. No more than an hour was needed to walk from one end of the city to the other, from Piraeus to Aigeus gate. Inhabitants could feel connected like pupils at a school or guests at a wedding. It wasn't only fanatics and drunkards who began conversations with strangers in public.

If we refrain from questioning the status quo, it is − aside from the weather and the size of our cities − primarily because we associate what is popular with what is right. The sandalless philosopher raised a plethora of questions to determine whether what was popular happened to make any sense.

2. *The rule of common sense*

Many found the questions maddening. Some teased him. A few would kill him. In *The Clouds*, performed for the first time at the theatre of Dionysus in the spring of 423 BC, Aristophanes offered Athenians a caricature of the philosopher in their midst who refused to accept common sense without investigating its logic at impudent length. The actor playing Socrates appeared on stage in a basket suspended from a crane, for he claimed his mind worked better at high altitude. He was immersed in such important thoughts that he had no time to wash or to perform household tasks, his cloak was therefore malodorous and his home infested with vermin, but at least he could consider life's most vital questions. These included: how many of its own lengths can a flea jump? And do gnats hum through their mouths or their anuses? Though Aristophanes omitted to elaborate on the results of

277

Socrates' questions, the audience must have been left with an adequate sense of their relevance.

Aristophanes was articulating a familiar criticism of intellectuals: that through their questions they drift further from sensible views than those who have never ventured to analyse matters in a systematic way. Dividing the playwright and the philosopher was a contrasting assessment of the adequacy of ordinary explanations. Whereas sane people could in Aristophanes' eyes rest in the knowledge that fleas jumped far given their size and that gnats made a noise from somewhere, Socrates stood accused of a manic suspicion of common sense and of harbouring a perverse hunger for complicated, inane alternatives.

To which Socrates would have replied that in certain cases, though perhaps not those involving fleas, common sense might warrant more profound inquiry. After brief conversations with many Athenians, popular views on how to lead a good life, views described as normal and so beyond question by the majority, revealed surprising inadequacies of which the confident manner of their proponents had given no indication. Contrary to what Aristophanes hoped, it seemed that those Socrates spoke to barely knew what they were talking about.

3. *Two conversations*

One afternoon in Athens, to follow Plato's *Laches*, the philosopher came upon two esteemed generals, Nicias and Laches. The generals had fought the Spartan armies in the battles of the Peloponnesian War, and had earned the respect of the city's elders and the admiration of the young. Both were to die as soldiers: Laches in the battle of Mantinea in 418 BC, Nicias in the ill-fated expedition to Sicily in 413 BC. No portrait of them survives, though one imagines that in battle they might have resembled two horsemen on a section of the Parthenon frieze.

The generals were attached to one common-sense idea. They believed that in order to be courageous, a person had to belong to an army, advance in battle and kill adversaries. But on encountering them under open skies, Socrates felt inclined to ask a few more questions:

SOCRATES: Let's try to say what courage is, Laches.

LACHES: My word, Socrates, that's not difficult! If a man is
    prepared to stand in the ranks, face up to the enemy and not
    run away, you can be sure that he's courageous.

But Socrates remembered that at the battle of Plataea in 479 BC, a Greek force under the Spartan regent Pausanias had initially retreated, then courageously defeated the Persian army under Mardonius:

SOCRATES: At the battle of Plataea, so the story goes, the
    Spartans came up against [the Persians], but weren't
    willing to stand and fight, and fell back. The Persians broke
    ranks in pursuit; but then the Spartans wheeled round
    fighting like cavalry and hence won that part of the battle.

Forced to think again, Laches came forward with a second common-sense idea: that courage was a kind of endurance. But endurance could, Socrates pointed out, be directed towards rash ends. To distinguish true courage from delirium, another element would be required. Laches' companion Nicias, guided by Socrates, proposed that courage would have to involve knowledge, an awareness of good and evil, and could not always be limited to warfare.

In only a brief outdoor conversation, great inadequacies had been discovered in the standard definition of a much-admired Athenian virtue. It had been shown not to take into account the possibility of courage off the battlefield or the importance of knowledge being combined with endurance. The issue might have seemed trifling but its implications were immense. If a general had previously been taught that ordering his army to retreat was cowardly, even when it seemed the only sensible manoeuvre, then the redefinition broadened his options and emboldened him against criticism.

In Plato's *Meno*, Socrates was again in conversation with someone supremely confident of the truth of a common-sense idea. Meno was an imperious aristocrat who was visiting Attica from his native Thessaly and had an idea about the relation of money to virtue. In order to be virtuous, he explained to Socrates, one had to be very rich, and poverty was invariably a personal failing rather than an accident.

We lack a portrait of Meno, too, though on looking through a Greek men's magazine in the lobby of an Athenian hotel, I imagined that he might have borne a resemblance to a man drinking champagne in an illuminated swimming pool.

The virtuous man, Meno confidently informed Socrates, was someone of great wealth who could afford good things. Socrates asked a few more questions:

SOCRATES: By good do you mean such things as health and wealth?

MENO: I include the acquisition of both gold and silver, and of high and honourable office in the state.

SOCRATES: Are these the only kind of good things you recognize?

MENO: Yes, I mean everything of that sort.

SOCRATES: ... DO you add 'just and righteous' to the word 'acquisition', or doesn't it make any difference to you? Do you call it virtue all the same even if they are unjustly acquired?

MENO: Certainly not.

SOCRATES: SO it seems that justice or temperance or piety, or some other part of virtue must attach to the acquisition [of gold and silver] ... In fact, lack of gold and silver, if it results from a failure to acquire them ... in circumstances which would have made their acquisition unjust, is itself virtue.

MENO: It looks like it.

SOCRATES: Then to have such goods is no more virtue than
to lack them ...

MENO: Your conclusion seems inescapable.

In a few moments, Meno had been shown that money and
influence were not in themselves necessary and sufficient features
of virtue. Rich people could be admirable, but this depended on
how their wealth had been acquired, just as poverty could not by
itself reveal anything of the moral worth of an individual. There
was no binding reason for a wealthy man to assume that his assets
guaranteed his virtue; and no binding reason for a poor one to
imagine that his indigence was a sign of depravity.

4. *Why others may not know*

The topics may have dated, but the underlying moral has not:
other people may be wrong, even when they are in important
positions, even when they are espousing beliefs held for centuries
by vast majorities. And the reason is simple: they have not
examined their beliefs logically.

Meno and the generals held unsound ideas because they had
absorbed the prevailing norms without testing their logic. To point
out the peculiarity of their passivity, Socrates compared living
without thinking systematically to practising an activity like
pottery or shoemaking without following or even knowing of
technical procedures. One would never imagine that a good pot or
shoe could result from intuition alone; why then assume that the
more complex task of directing one's life could be undertaken
without any sustained reflection on premises or goals?

Perhaps because we don't believe that directing our lives is in fact
complicated. Certain difficult activities look very difficult from
the outside, while other, equally difficult activities look very
easy. Arriving at sound views on how to live falls into the second

category, making a pot or a shoe into the first.

Making it was clearly a formidable task. Clay first had to be brought to Athens, usually from a large pit at Cape Kolias 7 miles south of the city, and placed on a wheel, spun at between 50 and 150 rotations per minute, the speed inversely proportional to the diameter of the part being moulded (the narrower the pot, the faster the wheel). Then came sponging, scraping, brushing and handlemaking.

Next, the vase had to be coated with a black glaze made from fine compact clay mixed with potash. Once the glaze was dry, the vase was placed in a kiln, heated to 800℃ with the air vent open. It turned a deep red, the result of clay hardening into ferric oxide (Fe_2O_3). Thereafter, it was fired to 950℃ with the air vent closed and wet leaves added to the kiln for moisture, which turned the body of the vase a greyish black and the glaze a sintered black (magnetite, Fe_3O_4). After a few hours, the air vent was reopened, the leaves raked out and the temperature allowed to drop to 900℃. While the glaze retained the black of the second firing, the body of the vase returned to the deep red of the first.

It isn't surprising that few Athenians were drawn to spin their own vases without thinking. Pottery looks as difficult as it is. Unfortunately, arriving at good ethical ideas doesn't, belonging instead to a troublesome class of superficially simple but inherently complex activities.

Socrates encourages us not to be unnerved by the confidence of people who fail to respect this complexity and formulate their views without at least as much rigour as a potter. What is declared obvious and 'natural' rarely is so. Recognition of this should teach us to think that the world is more flexible than it seems, for the established views have frequently emerged not through a process of faultless reasoning, but through centuries of intellectual muddle.

There may be no good reason for things to be the way they are.

5. *How to think for oneself*

The philosopher does not only help us to conceive that others may be wrong, he offers us a simple method by which we can ourselves determine what is right. Few philosophers have had a more minimal sense of what is needed to begin a thinking life. We do not need years of formal education and a leisured existence. Anyone with a curious and well-ordered mind who seeks to evaluate a common-sense belief can start a conversation with a friend in a city street and, by following a Socratic method, may arrive at one or two ground-breaking ideas in under half an hour.

Socrates' method of examining common sense is observable in all Plato's early and middle dialogues and, because it follows consistent steps, may without injustice be presented in the language of a recipe book or manual, and applied to any belief one is asked to accept or feels inclined to rebel against. The correctness of a statement cannot, the method suggests, be determined by whether it is held by a majority or has been believed for a long time by important people. A correct statement is one incapable of being rationally contradicted. A statement is true if it cannot be disproved. If it can, however many believe it, however grand they may be, it must be false and we are right to doubt it.

The Socratic method for thinking

1. Locate a statement confidently described as common sense.

   Acting courageously involves not retreating in battle.

   Being virtuous requires money.

2. Imagine for a moment that, despite the confidence of the person proposing it, the statement is false. Search for situations or contexts where the statement would not be true.

   Could one ever be courageous and yet retreat in battle?

Could one ever stay firm in battle and yet not be courageous?

Could one ever have money and not be virtuous?
Could one ever have no money and be virtuous?

3. If an exception is found, the definition must be false or at least imprecise.

It is possible to be courageous and retreat.
It is possible to stay firm in battle yet not be courageous.

It is possible to have money and be a crook.
It is possible to be poor and virtuous.

4. The initial statement must be nuanced to take the exception into account.

Acting courageously can involve both retreat and advance in battle.

People who have money can be described as virtuous only if they have acquired it in a virtuous way, and some people with no money can be virtuous when they have lived through situations where it was impossible to be virtuous and make money.

5. If one subsequently finds exceptions to the improved statements, the process should be repeated. The truth, in so far as a human being is able to attain such a thing, lies in a statement which it seems impossible to disprove. It is by finding out what something is not that one comes closest to understanding what it is.

6. The product of thought is, whatever Aristophanes insinuated, superior to the product of intuition.

It may of course be possible to arrive at truths without philosophizing. Without following a Socratic method, we may realize that people with no money may be called virtuous if they have lived through situations in which it was impossible to be virtuous and make money, or that acting courageously can involve retreat in battle. But we risk not knowing how to respond to people who don't agree with us, unless we have first thought through the objections to our position logically. We may be silenced by impressive figures who tell us forcefully that money is essential to virtue and that only effeminates retreat in battle. Lacking counterarguments to lend us strength (the battle of Plataea and enrichment in a corrupt society), we will have to propose limply or petulantly that we feel we are right, without being able to explain why.

Socrates described a correct belief held without an awareness of how to respond rationally to objections as *true opinion*, and contrasted it unfavourably with *knowledge*, which involved understanding not only why something was true, but also why its alternatives were false. He likened the two versions of the truth to beautiful works by the great sculptor Daedalus. A truth produced by intuition was like a statue set down without support on an outdoor plinth.

A strong wind could at any time knock it over. But a truth supported by reasons and an awareness of counterarguments was like a statue anchored to the ground by tethering cables.

Socrates' method of thinking promised us a way to develop opinions in which we could, even if confronted with a storm, feel veritable confidence.

4

In his seventieth year, Socrates ran into a hurricane. Three Athenians − the poet Meletus, the politician Anytus and the orator Lycon − decided that he was a strange and evil man. They claimed that he had failed to worship the city's gods, had corrupted the social fabric of Athens and had turned young men against their fathers. They believed it was right that he should be silenced, and perhaps even killed.

The city of Athens had established procedures for distinguishing right from wrong. On the south side of the agora stood the Court of the Heliasts, a large building with wooden benches for a jury at one end, and a prosecution and defendant's platform at the other. Trials began with a speech from the prosecution, followed by a speech from the defence. Then a jury numbering between 200 and 2,500 people would indicate where the truth lay by a ballot or a show of hands. This method of deciding right from wrong by counting the number of people in favour of a proposition was used throughout Athenian political and legal life. Two or three times a month, all male citizens, some 30,000, were invited to gather on Pnyx hill south-west of the agora to decide on important questions of state by a show of hands. For the city, the opinion of the majority had been equated with the truth.

There were 500 citizens in the jury on the day of Socrates' trial. The prosecution began by asking them to consider that the philosopher standing before them was a dishonest man. He had inquired into things below the earth and in the sky, he was a heretic, he had resorted to shifty rhetorical devices to make weaker arguments defeat stronger ones, and he had been a vicious influence on the young, intentionally corrupting them through his conversations.

Socrates tried to answer the charges. He explained that he had never held theories about the heavens nor investigated things below the earth, he was not a heretic and very much believed in divine activity; he had never corrupted the youth of Athens – it was just that some young men with wealthy fathers and plenty of free time had imitated his questioning method, and annoyed important people by showing them up as know-nothings. If he had corrupted anyone, it could only have been unintentionally, for there was no point in wilfully exerting a bad influence on companions, because one risked being harmed by them in turn. And if he had corrupted people only unintentionally, then the correct procedure was a quiet word to set him straight, not a court case.

He admitted that he had led what might seem a peculiar life:

> I have neglected the things that concern most people – making money, managing an estate, gaining military or civic honours, or other positions of power, or joining political clubs and parties which have formed in our cities.

However, his pursuit of philosophy had been motivated by a simple desire to improve the lives of Athenians:

> I tried to persuade each of you not to think more of practical advantages than of his mental and moral well-being.

Such was his commitment to philosophy, he explained, that he was unable to give up the activity even if the jury made it the condition for his acquittal:

> I shall go on saying in my usual way, 'My very good friend, you are an Athenian and belong to a city which is the greatest and most famous in the world for its wisdom and strength. Are you not ashamed that you give your attention to acquiring as much money as possible, and similarly with reputation and honour, and give no attention or thought to truth and understanding and the perfection of your soul?' And should any of you dispute that, and profess that he does care about such things, I won't let him go straight away nor leave him, but will question and examine and put him to the test ... I shall do this to everyone I meet, young or old, foreigner or fellow-citizen.

It was the turn of the jury of 500 to make up their minds. After brief deliberation 220 decided Socrates wasn't guilty; 280 that he was. The philosopher responded wryly: 'I didn't think the margin would be so narrow.' But he did not lose confidence; there was no hesitation or alarm; he maintained faith in a philosophical project that had been declared conclusively misconceived by a majority 56 per cent of his audience.

If we cannot match such composure, if we are prone to burst into tears after only a few harsh words about our character or achievements, it may be because the approval of others forms an essential part of our capacity to believe that we are right. We feel justified in taking unpopularity seriously not only for pragmatic reasons, for reasons of promotion or survival, but more importantly because being jeered at can seem an unequivocal sign that we have gone astray.

Socrates would naturally have conceded that there are times when we are in the wrong and should be made to doubt our views, but he would have added a vital detail to alter our sense of truth's relation to unpopularity: errors in our thought and way of life can at no point and in no way ever be proven simply by the fact that we have run into opposition.

What should worry us is not the number of people who oppose us, but how good their reasons are for doing so. We should therefore divert our attention away from the presence of unpopularity to the explanations for it. It may be frightening to hear that a high proportion of a community holds us to be wrong, but before abandoning our position, we should consider the method by which their conclusions have been reached. It is the soundness of their method of thinking that should determine the weight we give to their disapproval.

We seem afflicted by the opposite tendency: to listen to everyone, to be upset by every unkind word and sarcastic observation. We fail to ask ourselves the cardinal and most consoling question: on what basis has this dark censure been made? We treat with equal seriousness the objections of the critic who has thought rigorously and honestly and those of the critic who has acted out of misanthropy and envy.

We should take time to look behind the criticism. As Socrates had learned, the thinking at its basis, though carefully disguised, may be badly awry. Under the influence of passing moods, our critics may have fumbled towards conclusions. They may have acted from impulse and prejudice, and used their status to ennoble their hunches. They may have built up their thoughts like inebriated amateur potters.

Unfortunately, unlike in pottery, it is initially extremely hard to tell a good product of thought from a poor one. It isn't difficult to identify the pot made by the inebriated craftsman and the one by the sober colleague.

It is harder immediately to identify the superior definition.

ἡ φρόνιμος καρτερία ἔστιν ἀνδρεία.	ἀνδρεῖός ἐστι ὃς ἂν ἐν τῇ τάξει μένων μάχηται τοῖς πολεμίοις.
Courage is intelligent endurance.	The man who stands in the ranks and fights the enemy is courageous.

A bad thought delivered authoritatively, though without evidence of how it was put together, can for a time carry all the weight of a sound one. But we acquire a misplaced respect for others when we concentrate solely on their conclusions − which is why Socrates urged us to dwell on the logic they used to reach them. Even if we cannot escape the consequences of opposition, we will at least be spared the debilitating sense of standing in error.

The idea had first emerged some time before the trial, during a conversation between Socrates and Polus, a well-known teacher of rhetoric visiting Athens from Sicily. Polus had some chilling political views, of whose truth he wished ardently to convince Socrates. The teacher argued that there was at heart no happier life for a human being than to be a dictator, for dictatorship enabled one to act as one pleased, to throw enemies in prison, confiscate their property and execute them.

Socrates listened politely, then answered with a series of logical arguments attempting to show that happiness lay in doing good. But Polus dug in his heels and affirmed his position by pointing out that dictators were often revered by huge numbers of people. He mentioned Archelaus, the king of Macedon, who had murdered his uncle, his cousin and a seven-year-old legitimate heir and yet continued to enjoy great public support in Athens. The number of people who liked Archelaus was a sign, concluded Polus, that his theory on dictatorship was correct.

Socrates courteously admitted that it might be very easy to find people who liked Archelaus, and harder to find anyone to support the view that doing good brought one happiness: 'If you feel like calling witnesses to claim that what I'm saying is wrong, you can count on your position being supported by almost everyone in Athens,' explained Socrates, 'whether they were born and bred here or elsewhere.'

You'd have the support of Nicias the son of Niceratus, if you wanted, along with his brothers, who between them have a whole row of tripods standing in the precinct of Dionysus. You'd have the support of Aristocrates the son of Scellius as well ... You could call on the whole of Pericles' household, if you felt like it, or any other Athenian family you care to choose.

But what Socrates zealously denied was that this widespread support for Polus's argument could on its own in any way prove it correct:

The trouble is, Polus, you're trying to use on me the kind of rhetorical refutation which people in lawcourts think is successful. There too people think they're proving the other side wrong if they produce a large number of eminent witnesses in support of the points they're making, when their opponent can only come up with a single witness or none at all. But this kind of reputation is completely worthless in the context of the truth, since it's perfectly possible for someone to be defeated in court by a horde of witnesses who have no more than apparent respectability and who all happen to testify against him.

True respectability stems not from the will of the majority but from proper reasoning. When we are making vases, we should listen to the advice of those who know about turning glaze into Fe_3O_4 at 800 ℃; when we are making a ship, it is the verdict of those who construct triremes that should worry us; and when we are considering ethical matters – how to be happy and courageous and just and good – we should not be intimidated by bad thinking, even if it issues from the lips of teachers of rhetoric, mighty generals and well-dressed aristocrats from Thessaly.

It sounded élitist, and it was. Not everyone is worth listening to. Yet Socrates' élitism had no trace of snobbery or prejudice. He might have discriminated in the views he attended to, but the discrimination operated not on the basis of class or money, nor on the basis of military record or nationality, but on the basis of reason, which was – as he stressed – a faculty accessible to all.

To follow the Socratic example we should, when faced with criticism, behave like athletes training for the Olympic games. Information on sport was further supplied by *See Inside an Ancient Greek Town*.

Imagine we're athletes. Our trainer has suggested an exercise to strengthen our calves for the javelin. It requires us to stand on one leg and lift weights. It looks peculiar to outsiders, who mock and complain that we are throwing away our chances of success. In the baths, we overhear a man explain to another that we are ἡμῖν μέλει μᾶλλον τὸ τά σκέλη καλὰ ἐπιδεικνύναι ἢ τὸ βοηθεῖν τῇ πόλει πρὸς τὴν ὀλυμπιονίκην. (More interested in showing off a set of calf muscles than helping the city win the games.) Cruel, but no grounds for alarm if we listen to Socrates in conversation with his friend Crito:

SOCRATES: When a man is ... taking [his training] seriously, does he pay attention to all praise and criticism and opinion indiscriminately, or only when it comes from the one qualified person, the actual doctor or trainer ?

CRITO: Only when it comes from the one qualified person.

SOCRATES: Then he should be afraid of the criticism and welcome the praise of the one qualified person, but not those of the general public.

CRITO: Obviously.

SOCRATES: He ought to regulate his actions and exercises and eating and drinking by the judgement of his instructor, who has expert knowledge, not by the opinions of the rest of the public.

The value of criticism will depend on the thought processes of critics, not on their number or rank:

Don't you think it a good principle that one shouldn't respect all human opinions, but only some and not others ... that one should respect the good ones, but not the bad ones? ... And good ones are those of people with understanding, whereas bad ones are those of people without it ...

So my good friend, we shouldn't care all that much about what the populace will say of us, but about what the expert on matters of justice and injustice will say.

The jurors on the benches of the Court of the Heliasts were no experts. They included an unusual number of the old and the warwounded, who looked to jury work as an easy source of additional income. The salary was three obols a day, less than a manual labourer's, but helpful if one was sixty-three and bored at home. The only qualifications were citizenship, a sound mind and an absence of debts – though soundness of mind was not judged by Socratic criteria, more the ability to walk in a straight line and produce one's name when asked. Members of the jury fell asleep during trials, rarely had experience of similar cases or relevant laws, and were given no guidance on how to reach verdicts.

Socrates' own jury had arrived with violent prejudices. They had been influenced by Aristophanes' caricature of Socrates, and felt that the philosopher had played a role in the disasters that had befallen the once-mighty city at the end of the century. The Peloponnesian War had finished in catastrophe, a Spartan – Persian alliance had brought Athens to her knees, the city had been blockaded, her fleet destroyed and her empire dismembered. Plagues had broken out in poorer districts, and democracy had been suppressed by a dictatorship guilty of executing a thousand citizens. For Socrates' enemies, it was more than coincidence that many of the dictators had once spent time with the philosopher. Critias and Charmides had discussed ethical matters with Socrates, and it seemed all they had acquired as a result was a lust for murder.

What could have accounted for Athens's spectacular fall from grace? Why had the greatest city in Hellas, which seventy-five years before had defeated the Persians on land at Plataea and at sea at Mycale, been forced to endure a succession of humiliations? The man in the dirty cloak who wandered the streets asking the obvious seemed one ready, entirely flawed explanation.

Socrates understood that he had no chance. He lacked even the time to make a case. Defendants had only minutes to address a jury, until the water had run from one jar to another in the court clock:

> I am convinced that I never wronged anyone intentionally, but
> I cannot convince you of this, because we have so little time
> for discussion. If it was your practice, as it is with other
> nations, to give not one day but several to the hearing of
> capital trials, I believe that you might have been convinced;
> but under present conditions it is not so easy to dispose of grave
> allegations in a short space of time.

An Athenian courtroom was no forum for the discovery of the truth. It was a rapid encounter with a collection of the aged and one-legged who had not submitted their beliefs to rational examination and were waiting for the water to run from one jar to the other.

It must have been difficult to hold this in mind, it must have required the kind of strength accrued during years in conversation with ordinary Athenians: *the strength, under certain circumstances, not to take the views of others seriously.* Socrates was not wilful, he did not dismiss these views out of misanthropy, which would have contravened his faith in the potential for rationality in every human being. But he had been up at dawn for most of his life talking to Athenians; he knew how their minds worked and had seen that unfortunately they frequently didn't, even if he hoped they would some day. He had observed their tendency to take positions on a whim and to follow accepted opinions without questioning them. It wasn't arrogance to keep this before him at a moment of supreme opposition.

He possessed the self-belief of a rational man who understands that his enemies are liable not to be thinking properly, even if he is far from claiming that his own thoughts are invariably sound. Their disapproval could kill him; it did not have to make him wrong.

Of course, he might have renounced his philosophy and saved his life. Even after he had been found guilty, he could have escaped the death penalty, but wasted the opportunity through intransigence. We should not look to Socrates for advice on escaping a death sentence; we should look to him as an extreme example of how to maintain confidence in an intelligent position which has met with illogical opposition.

The philosopher's speech rose to an emotional finale:

> If you put me to death, you will not easily find anyone to take my place. The fact is, if I may put the point in a somewhat comical way, that I have been literally attached by God to our city, as though it were a large thoroughbred horse which because of its great size is inclined to be lazy and needs the stimulation of a gadfly ... If you take my advice you will spare my life. I suspect, however, that before long you will awake from your drowsing, and in your annoyance you will take

Anytus's advice and finish me off with a single slap; and then
you will go on sleeping.

He was not mistaken. When the magistrate called for a second,
final verdict, 360 members of the jury voted for the philosopher to
be put to death. The jurors went home; the condemned man was
escorted to prison.

5

It must have been dark and close, and the sounds coming up from
the street would have included jeers from Athenians anticipating
the end of the satyr-faced thinker. He would have been killed at
once had the sentence not coincided with the annual Athenian
mission to Delos, during which, tradition decreed, the city could
not put anyone to death. Socrates' good nature attracted the
sympathy of the prison warder, who alleviated his last days by
allowing him to receive visitors. A stream of them came: Phaedo,
Crito, Crito's son Critobulus, Apollodorus, Hermogenes, Epigenes,
Aeschines, Antisthenes, Ctesippus, Menexenus, Simmias,
Cebes, Phaedondas, Euclides and Terpsion. They could not
disguise their distress at seeing a man who had only ever displayed
great kindness and curiosity towards others waiting to meet his end
like a criminal.

Though David's canvas presented Socrates surrounded by
devastated friends, we should remember that their devotion stood
out in a sea of misunderstanding and hatred.

To counterpoint the mood in the prison cell and introduce
variety, Diderot might have urged a few of the many prospective
hemlock painters to capture the mood of other Athenians at the
idea of Socrates' death – which might have resulted in paintings
with titles like *Five Jurors Playing Cards after a Day in Court* or
The Accusers Finishing Dinner and Looking Forward to Bed. A
painter with a taste for pathos could more plainly have chosen to

title these scenes *The Death of Socrates*.

When the appointed day came, Socrates was alone in remaining calm. His wife and three children were brought to see him, but Xanthippe's cries were so hysterical, Socrates asked that she be ushered away. His friends were quieter though no less tearful. Even the prison warder, who had seen many go to their deaths, was moved to address an awkward farewell:

> 'In your time here, I've known you to be the most generous and gentlest and best of men who have ever come to this place ... You know the message I've come to bring: goodbye, then, and try to bear the inevitable as easily as you can. ' And with this he turned away in tears and went off.

Then came the executioner, bearing a cup of crushed hemlock:
> When he saw the man Socrates said: 'Well, my friend, you're an expert in these things: what must one do?' 'Simply drink it,' he said, 'and walk about till a heaviness comes over your legs; then lie down, and it will act by itself. ' And with this he held out the cup to Socrates. He took it perfectly calmly ... without a tremor or any change of colour or countenance ... He pressed the cup to his lips, and drank it off with good humour and without the least distaste. Till then most of us had been able to restrain our tears fairly well [narrated by Phaedo] ; but when we saw he was drinking, that he'd actually drunk it, we could do so no longer. In my own case, the tears came pouring out in spite of myself ... Even before me, Crito had moved away when he was unable to restrain his tears. And Apollodorus, who even earlier had been continuously in tears, now burst forth into such a storm of weeping and grieving, that he made everyone present break down except Socrates himself.

The philosopher implored his companions to calm themselves – 'What a way to behave, my strange friends!' he mocked – then stood up and walked around the prison cell so the poison could take effect. When his legs began to feel heavy, he lay down on his back and the sensation left his feet and legs; as the poison moved upwards and reached his chest, he gradually lost consciousness. His breathing became slow. Once he saw that his best friend's eyes had grown fixed, Crito reached over and closed them:

And that [said Phaedo] ... was the end of our companion, who was, we can fairly say, of all those of his time whom we knew, the bravest and also the wisest and most upright man.

It is hard not to start crying oneself. Perhaps because Socrates is said to have had a bulbous head and peculiar widely-spaced eyes, the scene of his death made me think of an afternoon on which I had wept while watching a tape of *The Elephant Man*.

It seemed that both men had suffered one of the saddest of fates – to be good and yet judged evil.

We might never have been jeered at for a physical deformity, nor condemned to death for our life's work, but there is something universal in the scenario of being misunderstood of which these stories are tragic, consummate examples. Social life is beset with disparities between others' perceptions of us and our reality. We are accused of stupidity when we are being cautious. Our shyness is taken for arrogance and our desire to please for sycophancy. We struggle to clear up a misunderstanding, but our throat goes dry and the words found are not the ones meant. Bitter enemies are appointed to positions of power over us, and denounce us to others. In the hatred unfairly directed towards an innocent philosopher we recognize an echo of the hurt we ourselves encounter at the hands of those who are either unable or unwilling to do us justice.

But there is redemption in the story, too. Soon after the philosopher's death the mood began to change. Isocrates reported that the audience watching Euripides' *Palamedes* burst into tears when Socrates' name was mentioned; Diodorus said that his accusers were eventually lynched by the people of Athens.

Plutarch tells us that the Athenians developed such hatred for the accusers that they refused to bathe with them and ostracized them socially until, in despair, they hanged themselves. Diogenes Laertius recounts that only a short while after Socrates' death the city condemned Meletus to death, banished Anytus and Lycon and erected a costly bronze statue of Socrates crafted by the great Lysippus.

The philosopher had predicted that Athens would eventually see things his way, and it did. Such redemption can be hard to believe in. We forget that time may be needed for prejudices to fall away and envy to recede. The story encourages us to interpret our own unpopularity other than through the mocking eyes of local juries. Socrates was judged by 500 men of limited intelligence who harboured irrational suspicions because Athens had lost the Peloponnesian War and the defendant looked strange. And yet he maintained faith in the judgement of wider courts. Though we inhabit one place at one time, through this example, we may imaginatively project ourselves into other lands and eras which promise to judge us with greater objectivity. We may not convince local juries in time to help ourselves, but we can be consoled by the prospect of posterity's verdict.

Yet there is a danger that Socrates' death will seduce us for the wrong reasons. It may foster a sentimental belief in a secure connection between being hated by the majority and being right. It can seem the destiny of geniuses and saints to suffer early misunderstanding, then to be accorded bronze statues by Lysippus. We may be neither geniuses nor saints. We may simply be privileging the stance of defiance over good reasons for it, childishly trusting that we are never so right as when others tell us we are wrong.

This was not Socrates' intention. It would be as naïve to hold that unpopularity is synonymous with truth as to believe that it is synonymous with error. The validity of an idea or action is determined not by whether it is widely believed or widely reviled but by whether it obeys the rules of logic. It is not because an argument is denounced by a majority that it is wrong nor, for those drawn to heroic defiance, that it is right.

The philosopher offered us a way out of two powerful delusions: that we should always or never listen to the dictates of public opinion.

To follow his example, we will best be rewarded if we strive instead to listen always to the dictates of reason.

II Consolation for Not Having Enough Money

1

Happiness, an acquisition list

1. A neoclassical Georgian house in the centre of London. Chelsea (Paradise Walk, Markham Square), Kensington (the southern part of Campden Hill Road, Hornton Street), Holland Park (Aubrey Road). In appearance, similar to the front elevation of the Royal Society of Arts designed by the Adam brothers (1772—4). To catch the pale light of late London afternoons, large Venetian windows offset by Ionic columns (and an arched tympanum with anthemions).
   In the first-floor drawing room, a ceiling and a chimney-piece like Robert Adam's design for the library at Kenwood House.

2. A jet stationed at Farnborough or Biggin Hill (a Dassault Falcon 900C or Gulfstream IV) with avionics for the nervous flyer, ground-proximity warning system, turbulence-detecting radar and CAT II autopilot. On the tail-fin, to replace the standard stripes, a detail from a still life, a fish by Velázquez or three lemons by Sánchez Cotán from the *Fruit and Vegetables* in the Prado.

3. The Villa Orsetti in Marlia near Lucca. From the bedroom, views over water, and the sound of fountains. At the back of the house, a magnolia Delavayi growing along the wall, a terrace for winter, a great tree for summer and a lawn for games. Sheltered gardens indulgent to fig and nectarine. Squares of cypresses, rows of lavender, orange trees and an olive orchard.

4. A library with a large desk, a fireplace and a view on to a garden. Early editions with the comforting smell of old books, pages yellowed and rough to the touch. On top of shelves, busts of great thinkers and astrological globes. Like the design of the library for a house for William III of Holland.

5. A dining room like that at Belton House in Lincolnshire. A long oak table seating twelve. Frequent dinners with the same friends. The conversation intelligent but playful. Always affectionate. A thoughtful chef and considerate staff to remove any administrative difficulties (the chef adept at zucchini pancakes, tagliatelle with white truffles, fish soup, risotto, quail, John Dory and roast chicken). A small drawing room to retire to for tea and chocolates.

6. A bed built into a niche in the wall (like one by Jean-François Blondel in Paris). Starched linen changed every day, cold to the cheek. The bed huge; toes do not touch the end of the bed; one *wallows*. Recessed cabinets for water and biscuits, and another for a television.

7. An immense bathroom with a tub in the middle on a raised platform, made of marble with cobalt-blue seashell designs. Taps that can be operated with the sole of the foot and release water in a broad, gentle stream. A skylight visible from the bath. Heated limestone floors. On the walls, reproductions of the frescos on the precinct of the Temple of Isis in Pompeii.

8. Money sufficient to allow one to live on the interest of the interest.

9. For weekends, a penthouse apartment at the tip of the Ile de la Cité decorated with pieces from the noblest period of French furniture (and the weakest of government), the reign of Louis XVI. A half-moon commode by Grevenich, a console by Saunier, a bonheur-du-jour by Vandercruse-La Croix. Lazy mornings reading *Pariscope* in bed, eating *pain au chocolat* on Sèvres china and chatting about existence with, and occasionally teasing, a reincarnation of Giovanni Bellini's *Madonna* (from the Galleria dell'Accademia in Venice), whose melancholy expression would belie a dry sense of

humour and spontaneity – and who would dress in Agnès B and Max Mara for walks around the Marais.

2

An anomaly among an often pleasure-hating and austere fraternity, there was one philosopher who seemed to understand and want to help. 'I don't know how I shall conceive of the good,' he wrote, 'if I take away the pleasures of taste, if I take away sexual pleasure, if I take away the pleasure of hearing, and if I take away the sweet emotions that are caused by the sight of beautiful forms.'

Epicurus was born in 341 BC on the verdant island of Samos, a few miles off the coast of Western Asia Minor. He took early to philosophy, travelling from the age of fourteen to hear lessons from the Platonist Pamphilus and the atomic philosopher Nausiphanes. But he found he could not agree with much of what they taught and by his late twenties had decided to arrange his thoughts into his own philosophy of life. He was said to have written 300 books on almost everything, including *On Love*, *On Music*, *On Just Dealing*, *On Human Life* (in four books) and *On Nature* (in thirty-seven books), though by a catastrophic series of mishaps, almost all were lost over the centuries, leaving his philosophy to be reconstructed from a few surviving fragments and the testimony of later Epicureans.

What immediately distinguished his philosophy was an emphasis on the importance of sensual pleasure: 'Pleasure is the beginning and the goal of a happy life,' asserted Epicurus, confirming what many had long thought but philosophy had rarely accepted. The philosopher confessed his love of excellent food: 'The beginning and root of every good is the pleasure of the stomach. Even wisdom and culture must be referred to this.' Philosophy properly performed was to be nothing less than a guide to pleasure:

The man who alleges that he is not yet ready for philosophy or

that the time for it has passed him by, is like the man who says
that he is either too young or too old for happiness.

Few philosophers had ever made such frank admissions of their
interest in a pleasurable lifestyle. It shocked many, especially
when they heard that Epicurus had attracted the support of some
wealthy people, first in Lampsacus in the Dardanelles, and then in
Athens, and had used their money to set up a philosophical
establishment to promote happiness. The school admitted both
men and women, and encouraged them to live and study pleasure
together. The idea of what was going on inside the school
appeared at once titillating and morally reprehensible.

There were frequent leaks from disgruntled Epicureans detailing
activities between lectures. Timocrates, the brother of Epicurus's
associate Metrodorus, spread a rumour that Epicurus had to vomit
twice a day because he ate so much. And Diotimus the Stoic took the
unkind step of publishing fifty lewd letters which he said had been
written by Epicurus when he'd been drunk and sexually frenzied.

Despite these criticisms, Epicurus's teachings continued to attract
support. They spread across the Mediterranean world; schools for
pleasure were founded in Syria, Judaea, Egypt, Italy and Gaul;
and the philosophy remained influential for the next 500 years,
only gradually to be extinguished by the hostility of forbidding
barbarians and Christians during the decline of the Roman Empire
in the West. Even then, Epicurus's name entered many languages
in adjectival form as a tribute to his interests (*Oxford English
Dictionary*: ' Epicurean: devoted to the pursuit of pleasure;
hence, luxurious, sensual, gluttonous').

Browsing in a newsagent in London 2,340 years after the
philosopher's birth, I came upon copies of *Epicurean Life*, a
quarterly magazine with articles on hotels, yachts and restaurants,
printed on paper with the sheen of a well-polished apple.

The tenor of Epicurus's interests was further suggested by The Epicurean, a restaurant in a small Worcestershire town, which offered its clientele, seated on high-backed chairs in a hushed dining room, dinners of seared sea scallops and cep risotto with truffles.

3

The consistency of the associations provoked by Epicurus's philosophy throughout the ages, from Diotimus the Stoic to the editors of *Epicurean Life*, testifies to the way in which, once the word 'pleasure' has been mentioned, it seems obvious what is entailed. 'What do I need for a happy life?' is far from a challenging question when money is no object.

Yet 'What do I need for a *healthy life*?' can be more difficult to answer when, for example, we are afflicted by bizarre recurring headaches or an acute throb in the stomach area after evening meals. We know there is a problem; it can be hard to know the solution.

In pain, the mind is prone to consider some strange cures: leeches, bleeding, nettle stews, trepanning. An atrocious pain pulses in the temples and at the base of the head, as though the whole cranium had been placed in a clamp and tightened. The head feels as if it may soon explode. What seems intuitively most necessary is to let some air into the skull. The sufferer requests that a friend place his head on a table and drill a small hole in the side. He dies hours later of a brain haemorrhage.

If consulting a good doctor is generally thought advisable despite the sombre atmosphere of many surgery waiting rooms, it is because someone who has thought rationally and deeply about how the body works is likely to arrive at better ideas about how to be healthy than someone who has followed a hunch. Medicine presupposes a hierarchy between the confusion the lay person will be in about what is wrong with them, and the more accurate knowledge available to doctors reasoning logically. Doctors are required to compensate for their patients' lack, at times fatal, of bodily self-knowledge.

At the heart of Epicureanism is the thought that we are as bad at intuitively answering 'What will make me happy?' as 'What will make me healthy?' The answer which most rapidly comes to mind is liable to be as faulty. Our souls do not spell out their troubles more clearly than our bodies, and our intuitive diagnoses are rarely any more accurate. Trepanning might serve as a symbol of the difficulties of understanding our psychological as much as our physiological selves.

A man feels dissatisfied. He has trouble rising in the morning and is surly and distracted with his family. Intuitively, he places the blame on his choice of occupation and begins searching for an alternative, despite the high costs of doing so. It was the last time I would turn to *See Inside an Ancient Greek Town*.

Deciding rapidly that he would be happy in the fish business, the man acquires a net and an expensive stall in the market-place. And yet his melancholy does not abate.

We are often, in the words of the Epicurean poet Lucretius, like ' a sick man ignorant of the cause of his malady'.

It is because they understand bodily maladies better than we can that we seek doctors. We should turn to philosophers for the same reason when our soul is unwell – and judge them according to a similar criterion:

> Just as medicine confers no benefit if it does not drive away
> physical illness, so philosophy is useless if it does not drive
> away the suffering of the mind.

The task of philosophy was, for Epicurus, to help us interpret our indistinct pulses of distress and desire and thereby save us from mistaken schemes for happiness. We were to cease acting on first impulses, and instead investigate the rationality of our desires according to a method of questioning close to that used by Socrates in evaluating ethical definitions over a hundred years earlier. And by providing what might at times feel like counter-intuitive diagnoses of our ailments, philosophy would – Epicurus promised – guide us to superior cures and true happiness.

4

Those who had heard the rumours must have been surprised to discover the real tastes of the philosopher of pleasure. There was no grand house. The food was simple, Epicurus drank water rather than wine, and was happy with a dinner of bread, vegetables and a palmful of olives. ' Send me a pot of cheese, so that I may have a feast whenever I like,' he asked a friend. Such were the tastes of a man who had described pleasure as the purpose of life.

He had not meant to deceive. His devotion to pleasure was far greater than even the orgy accusers could have imagined. It was just that after rational analysis, he had come to some striking conclusions about what actually made life pleasurable – and fortunately for those lacking a large income, it seemed that the essential ingredients of pleasure, however elusive, were not very expensive.

Happiness, an Epicurean acquisition list

1. Friendship

On returning to Athens in 306 BC at the age of thirty-five, Epicurus settled on an unusual domestic arrangement. He located a large house a few miles from the centre of Athens, in the Melite district between the market-place and the harbour at Piraeus, and moved in with a group of friends. He was joined by Metrodorus and his sister, the mathematician Polyaenus, Hermarchus, Leonteus and his wife Themista, and a merchant called Idomeneus (who soon married Metrodorus's sister). There was enough space in the house for the friends to have their own quarters, and there were common rooms for meals and conversations.

Epicurus observed that:

Of all the things that wisdom provides to help one live one's entire life in happiness, the greatest by far is the possession of friendship.

Such was his attachment to congenial company, Epicurus recommended that one try never to eat alone:

Before you eat or drink anything, consider carefully who you eat or drink with rather than what you eat or drink: for feeding without a friend is the life of a lion or a wolf.

The household of Epicurus resembled a large family, but there was seemingly no sullenness nor sense of confinement, only sympathy and gentleness.

We don't exist unless there is someone who can see us existing, what we say has no meaning until someone can understand, while to be surrounded by friends is constantly to have our identity confirmed; their knowledge and care for us have the power to pull us from our numbness. In small comments, many of them teasing, they reveal they know our foibles and accept them and so, in turn, accept that we have a place in the world. We can ask them 'Isn't he frightening?' or 'Do you ever feel that...?' and be understood, rather than encounter the puzzled ' No, not particularly' – which can make us feel, even when in company, as lonely as polar explorers.

True friends do not evaluate us according to worldly criteria, it is the core self they are interested in; like ideal parents, their love for us remains unaffected by our appearance or position in the social hierarchy, and so we have no qualms in dressing in old clothes and revealing that we have made little money this year. The desire for riches should perhaps not always be understood as a simple hunger for a luxurious life, a more important motive might

309

be the wish to be appreciated and treated nicely. We may seek a fortune for no greater reason than to secure the respect and attention of people who would otherwise look straight through us. Epicurus, discerning our underlying need, recognized that a handful of true friends could deliver the love and respect that even a fortune may not.

2. Freedom

Epicurus and his friends made a second radical innovation. In order not to have to work for people they didn't like and answer to potentially humiliating whims, they removed themselves from employment in the commercial world of Athens ('We must free ourselves from the prison of everyday affairs and politics'), and began what could best have been described as a commune, accepting a simpler way of life in exchange for independence. They would have less money but would never again have to follow the commands of odious superiors.

So they bought a garden near their house, a little outside the old Dipylon gate, and grew a range of vegetables for the kitchen, probably *bliton* (cabbage), *krommyon* (onion) and *kinara* (ancestor of the modern artichoke, of which the bottom was edible but not the scales). Their diet was neither luxurious nor abundant, but it was flavoursome and nutritious. As Epicurus explained to his friend Menoeceus, '[The wise man] chooses not the greatest quantity of food but the most pleasant. '

Simplicity did not affect the friends' sense of status because, by distancing themselves from the values of Athens, they had ceased to judge themselves on a material basis. There was no need to be embarrassed by bare walls, and no benefit in showing off gold. Among a group of friends living outside the political and economic centre of the city, there was – in the financial sense – nothing to prove.

3. Thought

There are few better remedies for anxiety than thought. In writing a problem down or airing it in conversation we let its essential aspects emerge. And by knowing its character, we remove, if not the problem itself, then its secondary, aggravating characteristics: confusion, displacement, surprise.

There was much encouragement to think in the Garden, as Epicurus's community became known. Many of the friends were writers. According to Diogenes Laertius, Metrodorus, for one, wrote twelve works, among them the lost *Way of Wisdom* and *Of Epicurus's Weak Health*. In the common rooms of the house in Melite and in the vegetable garden, there must have been unbroken opportunities to examine problems with people as intelligent as they were sympathetic.

Epicurus was especially concerned that he and his friends learn to analyse their anxieties about money, illness, death and the supernatural. If one thought rationally about mortality, one would, Epicurus argued, realize that there was nothing but oblivion after death, and that ' what is no trouble when it arrives is an idle worry in anticipation. ' It was senseless to alarm oneself in advance about a state which one would never experience:

> There is nothing dreadful in life for the man who has truly
> comprehended that there is nothing terrible in not living.

Sober analysis calmed the mind; it spared Epicurus's friends the furtive glimpses of difficulties that would have haunted them in the unreflective environment beyond the Garden.

∞

Wealth is of course unlikely ever to make anyone miserable. But the crux of Epicurus's argument is that if we have money without friends, freedom and an analysed life, *we will never be truly* happy. And if we have them, but are missing the fortune, *we will never be unhappy.*

To highlight what is essential for happiness and what may, if one is denied prosperity through social injustice or economic turmoil, be forgone without great regrets, Epicurus divided our needs into three categories:

> Of the desires, some are natural and necessary. Others are natural but unnecessary. And there are desires that are neither natural nor necessary.

WHAT IS AND IS NOT ESSENTIAL FOR HAPPINESS

Natural and necessary	Natural but unnecessary	Neither natural nor necessary
Friends	Grand house	Fame
Freedom	Private baths	Power
Thought (about main sources of anxiety: death, illness, poverty, superstition)	Banquets Servants Fish, meat	
Food, shelter, clothes		

Crucially for those unable to make or afraid of losing money, Epicurus's tripartite division suggested that happiness was dependent on some complex psychological goods but relatively independent of material ones, beyond the means required to purchase some warm clothes, somewhere to live and something to eat – a set of priorities designed to provoke thought in those who had equated happiness with the fruition of grand financial schemes, and misery with a modest income.

To plot the Epicurean relation between money and happiness on a graph, money's capacity to deliver happiness is already present in small salaries and will not rise with the largest. We will not cease being happy with greater outlay, but we will not, Epicurus insisted, *surpass* levels of happiness already available to those on a limited income.

RELATION OF HAPPINESS TO MONEY FOR SOMEONE WITH FRIENDS, FREEDOM, ETC.

Amount of money spent

The analysis depended on a particular understanding of happiness. For Epicurus, we are happy if we are not in *active* pain. Because we suffer active pain if we lack nutrients and clothes, we must have enough money to buy them. But suffering is too strong a word to describe what will occur if we are obliged to wear an ordinary cardigan rather than a cashmere one or to eat a sandwich rather than sea scallops. Hence the argument that:

Plain dishes offer the same pleasure as a luxurious table, when the pain that comes from want is taken away.

Whether we regularly eat meals like the one on the right or like the one on the left cannot be the decisive factor in our state of mind.

As for eating meat, it relieves neither any of our nature's stress nor a desire whose non-satisfaction would give rise to pain... What it contributes to is not life's maintenance but variation of pleasures ... like drinking of exotic wines, all of which our

313

nature is quite capable of doing without.

It may be tempting to attribute this disparagement of luxury to the primitive range of products available to the rich in the undeveloped economy of Hellenistic Greece. Yet the argument may still be defended by pointing to an imbalance in the ratio of price to happiness in products of later ages.

We would not be happy with the vehicle on the left but no friends; with a villa but no freedom; with linen sheets but too much anxiety to sleep. So long as essential non-material needs are unattended, the line on the graph of happiness will remain stubbornly low.

RELATION OF HAPPINESS TO MONEY FOR SOMEONE WITHOUT FRIENDS, FREEDOM, ETC.

Nothing satisfies the man who is not satisfied with a little.

To avoid acquiring what we do not need or regretting what we cannot afford, we should ask rigorously the moment we desire an expensive object whether we are right to do so. We should undertake a series of thought experiments in which we imagine ourselves projected in time to the moment when our desires have been realized, in order to gauge our likely degree of happiness:

> The following method of inquiry must be applied to every desire: What will happen to me if what I long for is accomplished? What will happen if it is not accomplished?

A method which, though no examples of it survive, must have followed at least five steps – which may without injustice be sketched in the language of an instruction manual or recipe book.

1. Identify a project for happiness.

   In order to be happy on holiday, I must live in a villa.

2. Imagine that the project may be false. Look for exceptions to the supposed link between the desired object and happiness. Could one possess the desired object but not be happy? Could one be happy but not have the desired object?

   Could I spend money on a villa and still not be happy?

   Could I be happy on holiday and not spend as much money as on a villa?

3. If an exception is found, the desired object cannot be a necessary and sufficient cause of happiness.

   It is possible to have a miserable time in a villa if, for example, I feel friendless and isolated.

   It is possible for me to be happy in a tent if, for example, I am with someone I love and feel appreciated by.

4. In order to be accurate about producing happiness, the initial project must be nuanced to take the exception into account.

   In so far as I can be happy in an expensive villa, this depends on being with someone I love and feel appreciated by.

   I can be happy without spending money on a villa, as long as I am with someone I love and feel appreciated by.

315

5. True needs may now seem very different from the confused initial desire.

Happiness depends more on the possession of a congenial companion than a well-decorated villa.

5

Why, then, if expensive things cannot bring us remarkable joy, are we so powerfully drawn to them? Because of an error similar to that of the migraine sufferer who drills a hole in the side of his skull: because expensive objects can feel like plausible solutions to needs we don't understand. Objects mimic in a material dimension what we require in a psychological one. We need to rearrange our minds but are lured towards new shelves. We buy a cashmere cardigan as a substitute for the counsel of friends.

We are not solely to blame for our confusions. Our weak understanding of our needs is aggravated by what Epicurus termed the 'idle opinions' of those around us, which do not reflect the natural hierarchy of our needs, emphasizing luxury and riches, seldom friendship, freedom and thought. The prevalence of idle opinion is no coincidence. It is in the interests of commercial enterprises to skew the hierarchy of our needs, to promote a material vision of the good and downplay an unsaleable one.

And the way we are enticed is through the sly association of superfluous objects with our other, forgotten needs.

It may be a jeep we end up buying, but it was – for Epicurus – freedom we were looking for.

It may be the aperitif we purchase, but it was – for Epicurus – friendship we were after.

It may be fine bathing accoutrements we acquire, but it was – for Epicurus – thought that would have brought us calm.

To counteract the power of luxurious images Epicureans appreciated the importance of advertising.

In the AD 120s, in the central market-place of Oinoanda, a town of 10,000 inhabitants in the south-western corner of Asia Minor, an enormous stone colonnade 80 metres long and nearly 4 metres high was erected and inscribed with Epicurean slogans for the attention of shoppers:

> Luxurious foods and drinks... in no way produce freedom from harm and a healthy condition in the flesh.
> One must regard wealth beyond what is natural as of no more use than water to a container that is full to overflowing.
> Real value is generated not by theatres and baths and perfumes and ointments ... but by natural science.

The wall had been paid for by Diogenes, one of Oinoanda's wealthiest citizens, who had sought, 400 years after Epicurus and his friends had opened the Garden in Athens, to share with his fellow inhabitants the secrets of happiness he had discovered in Epicurus's philosophy. As he explained on one corner of the wall:

> Having already reached the sunset of my life (being almost on the verge of departure from the world on account of old age), I wanted, before being overtaken by death, to compose a fine anthem to celebrate the fullness of pleasure and so to help now those who are well-constituted. Now, if only one person, or two or three or four or five or six... were in a bad predicament, I should address them individually... but as the majority of people suffer from a common disease, as in a plague, with their false notions about things, and as their number is increasing (for in mutual emulation they catch the disease from each other, like sheep)... I wished to use this stoa to advertise publicly medicines that bring salvation.

The massive limestone wall contained some 25,000 words advertising all aspects of Epicurus's thought, mentioning the importance of friendship and of the analysis of anxieties. Inhabitants shopping in the boutiques of Oinoanda had been warned in detail that they could expect little happiness from the activity.

Advertising would not be so prevalent if we were not such suggestible creatures. We want things when they are beautifully presented on walls, and lose interest when they are ignored or not well spoken of. Lucretius lamented the way in which what we want is 'chosen by hearsay rather than by the evidence of [our] own senses'.

Unfortunately, there is no shortage of desirable images of luxurious products and costly surroundings, fewer of ordinary settings and individuals. We receive little encouragement to attend to modest gratifications – playing with a child, conversations with a friend, an afternoon in the sun, a clean house, cheese spread across fresh bread ('Send me a pot of cheese, so that I may have a feast whenever I like'). It is not these elements which are celebrated in the pages of *Epicurean Life*.

Art may help to correct the bias. Lucretius lent force to Epicurus's intellectual defence of simplicity by helping us, in superlative Latin verse, to feel the pleasures of inexpensive things:

We find that the requirements of our bodily nature are few indeed, no more than is necessary to banish pain, and also to spread out many pleasures for ourselves. Nature does not periodically seek anything more gratifying than this, not complaining if there are no golden images of youths about the house who are holding flaming torches in their right hands to illuminate banquets that go on long into the night. What does it matter if the hall doesn't

Ergo corpoream ad naturam
pauca videmus
esse opus omnino, quae demant
cumque dolorem.
delicias quoque uti multas
substernere possint
gratius interdum, neque natura
ipsa requirit,
si non aurea sunt iuvenum
simulacra per aedes
lampadas igniferas manibus
retinentia dextris,
lumina nocturnis epulis ut
suppeditentur,

sparkle with silver and gleam with gold, and no carved and gilded rafters ring to the music of the lute? Nature doesn't miss these luxuries when people can recline in company on the soft grass by a running stream under the branches of a tall tree and refresh their bodies pleasurably at small expense. Better still if the weather smiles on them, and the season of the year stipples the green grass with flowers.	*nec domus argento fulget auroque renidet* *nec citharae reboant laqueata aurataque templa,* *cum tamen inter se prostrati in gramine molli* *propter aquae rivum sub ramis arboris altae* *non magnis opibus iucunde corpora curant,* *praesertim cum tempestas adridet et anni* *tempora conspergunt viridantis floribus herbas.*

It is hard to measure the effect on commercial activity in the Greco-Roman world of Lucretius's poem. It is hard to know whether shoppers in Oinoanda discovered what they needed and ceased buying what they didn't because of the giant advertisement in their midst. But it is possible that a well-mounted Epicurean advertising campaign would have the power to precipitate global economic collapse. Because, for Epicurus, most businesses stimulate unnecessary desires in people who fail to understand their true needs, levels of consumption would be destroyed by greater selfawareness and appreciation of simplicity. Epicurus would not have been perturbed:

> When measured by the natural purpose of life, poverty is great wealth; limitless wealth, great poverty.

It points us to a choice: on the one hand, societies which stimulate unnecessary desires but achieve enormous economic strengths as a result; and on the other, Epicurean societies which would provide for essential material needs but could never raise living standards beyond subsistence level. There would be no mighty monuments in an Epicurean world, no technological advances and little incentive to trade with distant continents. A society in which people were more limited in their needs would also be one of few resources. And yet – if we are to believe the philosopher – such a society would not be unhappy. Lucretius articulated the choice. In a world without Epicurean values:

> Mankind is perpetually the victim of a pointless and futile martyrdom, fretting life away in fruitless worries through failure to realise what limit is set to acquisition and to the growth of genuine pleasure.

But at the same time:

> It is this discontent that has driven life steadily onward, out to the high seas...

We can imagine Epicurus's response. However impressive our ventures on to the high seas, the only way to evaluate their merits is according to the pleasure they inspire:

> It is to pleasure that we have recourse, using the feeling as our standard for judging every good.

And because an increase in the wealth of societies seems not to guarantee an increase in happiness, Epicurus would have suggested that the needs which expensive goods cater to cannot be those on which our happiness depends.

6

Happiness, an acquisition list

1. A hut.
2.

3. To avoid superiors, patronization, infighting and competition.
4. Thought.
5. A reincarnation of Giovanni Bellini's *Madonna* (from the Galleria dell'Accademia in Venice), whose melancholy expression would belie a dry sense of humour and spontaneity — and who would dress in manmade fibres from the sales racks of modest department stores.

Happiness may be difficult to attain. The obstacles are not primarily financial.

Ⅲ Consolation for Frustration

1

Thirteen years before painting the *Death of Socrates*, Jacques-Louis David attended to another ancient philosopher who met his end with extraordinary calm, amidst the hysterical tears of friends and family.

The *Death of Seneca*, painted in 1773 by the twenty-five-year-old David, depicted the Stoic philosopher's last moments in a villa outside Rome in April AD 65. A centurion had arrived at the house a few hours before with instructions from the emperor that Seneca should take his own life forthwith. A conspiracy had been discovered to remove the twenty-eight-year-old Nero from the throne, and the emperor, maniacal and unbridled, was seeking indiscriminate revenge. Though there was no evidence to link Seneca to the conspiracy, though he had worked as the imperial tutor for five years and as a loyal aide for a decade, Nero ordered the death for good measure. He had by this point already murdered his halfbrother Britannicus, his mother Agrippina and his wife Octavia; he had disposed of a large number of senators and equestrians by feeding them to crocodiles and lions; and he had sung while Rome burned to the ground in the great fire of 64.

When they learned of Nero's command, Seneca's companions blanched and began to weep, but the philosopher, in the account provided by Tacitus and read by David, remained unperturbed, and strived to check their tears and revive their courage:

> Where had their philosophy gone, he asked, and that resolution against impending misfortunes which they had encouraged in each other over so many years? 'Surely nobody was unaware that Nero was cruel!' he added. 'After murdering his mother and brother, it only remained for him to kill his teacher and tutor.'

He turned to his wife Paulina, embraced her tenderly ('very different from his philosophical imperturbability' – Tacitus) and

asked her to take consolation in his well-spent life. But she could
not countenance an existence without him, and asked to be
allowed to cut her veins in turn. Seneca did not deny her wish:

> I will not grudge your setting so fine an example. We can die
> with equal fortitude, though yours will be the nobler end.

But because the emperor had no desire to increase his reputation
for cruelty, when his guards noticed that Paulina had taken a knife
to her veins, they seized it against her will and bandaged up her
wrists.

Her husband's suicide began to falter. Blood did not flow fast
enough from his aged body, even after he had cut the veins in his
ankles and behind his knees. So in a self-conscious echo of the
death in Athens 464 years previously, Seneca asked his doctor to
prepare a cup of hemlock. He had long considered Socrates the
exemplar of how one might, through philosophy, rise above
external circumstance (and in a letter written a few years before
Nero's command, had explained his admiration):

> He was much tried at home, whether we think of his wife, a
> woman of rough manners and shrewish tongue, or of the
> children ... He lived either in time of war or under tyrants ...
> but all these measures changed the soul of Socrates so little that
> they did not even change his features. What wonderful and rare
> distinction! He maintained this attitude up to the very end ...
> amid all the disturbances of Fortune, he was undisturbed.

But Seneca's desire to follow the Athenian was in vain. He drank
the hemlock and it had no effect. After two fruitless attempts, he
finally asked to be placed in a vapour-bath, where he suffocated
to death slowly, in torment but with equanimity, undisturbed by
the disturbances of Fortune.

David's rococo version of the scene was not the first, nor the
finest. Seneca appeared more like a reclining pasha than a dying
philosopher. Paulina, thrusting her bared right breast forward,

was dressed for grand opera rather than Imperial Rome. Yet David's rendering of the moment fitted, however clumsily, into a lengthy history of admiration for the manner in which the Roman endured his appalling fate.

Though his wishes had come into sudden, extreme conflict with reality, Seneca had not succumbed to ordinary frailties; reality's shocking demands had been met with dignity. Through his death, Seneca had helped to create an enduring association, together with other Stoic thinkers, between the very word 'philosophical' and a temperate, self-possessed approach to disaster. He had from the first conceived of philosophy as a discipline to assist human beings in overcoming conflicts between their wishes and reality. As Tacitus had reported, Seneca's response to his weeping companions had been to ask, as though the two were essentially one, where their *philosophy* had gone, and where their resolution against impending misfortunes.

Throughout his life, Seneca had faced and witnessed around him exceptional disasters. Earthquakes had shattered Pompeii; Rome and Lugdunum had burnt to the ground; the people of Rome and her empire had been subjected to Nero, and before him Caligula, or as Suetonius more accurately termed him, 'the Monster', who had 'on one occasion ... cried angrily, "I wish all you Romans had only one neck!"'

Seneca had suffered personal losses, too. He had trained for a career in politics, but in his early twenties had succumbed to suspected tuberculosis, which had lasted six years and led to suicidal depression. His late entry into politics had coincided with Caligula's rise to power. Even after the Monster's murder in 41, his position had been precarious. A plot by the Empress Messalina had, through no fault of Seneca's, resulted in his disgrace and eight years of exile on the island of Corsica. When he had finally been recalled to Rome, it had been to take on against his will the most fateful job in the imperial administration – tutor to Agrippina's twelve-year-old son, Lucius Domitius Ahenobarbus, who would fifteen years later order him to kill himself in front of his wife and family.

Seneca knew why he had been able to withstand the anxieties:
> I owe my life to [philosophy], and that is the least of my obligations to it.

His experiences had taught him a comprehensive dictionary of frustration, his intellect a series of responses to them. Years of philosophy had prepared him for the catastrophic day Nero's centurion had struck at the villa door.

2

A Senecan dictionary of frustration

Introduction

Though the terrain of frustration may be vast – from a stubbed toe to an untimely death – at the heart of every frustration lies a basic structure: the collision of a wish with an unyielding reality.

The collisions begin in earliest infancy, with the discovery that the sources of our satisfaction lie beyond our control and that the world does not reliably conform to our desires.

And yet, for Seneca, in so far as we can ever attain wisdom, it is by learning not to aggravate the world's obstinacy through our own responses, through spasms of rage, self-pity, anxiety, bitterness, self-righteousness and paranoia.

A single idea recurs throughout his work: that we best endure those frustrations which we have prepared ourselves for and understand and are hurt most by those we least expected and cannot fathom. Philosophy must reconcile us to the true dimensions of reality, and so spare us, if not frustration itself, then at least its panoply of pernicious accompanying emotions.

Her task is to prepare for our wishes the softest landing possible on the adamantine wall of reality.

Anger

The ultimate infantile collision. We cannot find the remote control or the keys, the road is blocked, the restaurant full – and so we slam doors, deracinate plants and howl.

1. The philosopher held it to be a kind of madness:

    There is no swifter way to insanity. Many [angry people]... call down death on their children, poverty on themselves, ruin on their home, denying that they are angry, just as the mad deny their insanity. Enemies to their closest friends ... heedless of the law ... they do everything by force ... The greatest of ills has seized them, one that surpasses all other vices.

2. In calmer moments, the angry may apologize and explain that they were overwhelmed by a power stronger than themselves, that is, stronger than their reason. ' They ' , their rational selves, did not mean the insults and regret the shouting; ' they ' lost control to darker forces within. The angry hereby appeal to a predominant view of the mind in which the reasoning faculty, the seat of the true self, is depicted as occasionally assaulted by passionate feelings which reason neither identifies with nor can be held responsible for.

    This account runs directly counter to Seneca's view of the mind, according to which anger results not from an uncontrollable eruption of the passions, but from a basic (and correctable) error of reasoning. Reason does not always govern our actions, he conceded: if we are sprinkled with cold water, our body gives us no choice but to shiver; if fingers are flicked over our eyes, we have to blink. But anger does not belong in the category of involuntary physical movement, it can only break out on the back of certain rationally held *ideas*; if we can only change the ideas, we will change our propensity to anger.

3. And in the Senecan view what makes us angry are dangerously optimistic notions about what the world and other people are like.

4. How badly we react to frustration is critically determined by what we think of as normal. We may be frustrated that it is raining, but our familiarity with showers means we are unlikely ever to respond to one with anger. Our frustrations are tempered by what we understand we can expect from the world, by our experience of what it is normal to hope for. We aren't overwhelmed by anger whenever we are denied an object we desire, only when we believe ourselves entitled to obtain it. Our greatest furies spring from events which violate our sense of the ground rules of existence.

5. With money, one could have expected to lead a very comfortable life in Ancient Rome. Many of Seneca's friends had large houses in the capital and villas in the countryside. There were baths, colonnaded gardens, fountains, mosaics, frescos and gilded couches. There were retinues of slaves to prepare the food, look after the children and tend the garden.

6. Nevertheless, there seemed an unusual level of rage among the privileged. ' Prosperity fosters bad tempers, ' wrote Seneca, after observing his wealthy friends ranting around him because life had not turned out as they had hoped.

Seneca knew of a wealthy man, Vedius Pollio, a friend of the Emperor Augustus, whose slave once dropped a tray of crystal glasses during a party. Vedius hated the sound of breaking glass and grew so furious that he ordered the slave to be thrown into a pool of lampreys.

7. Such rages are never beyond explanation. Vedius Pollio was angry for an identifiable reason: because he believed in a world in which glasses do not get broken at parties. We shout when we can't find the remote control because of an implicit belief in a world in which remote controls do not get mislaid. Rage is caused by a conviction, almost comic in its optimistic origins (however tragic in its effects), that a given frustration has not been written into the contract of life.

8. We should be more careful. Seneca tried to adjust the scale of our expectations so that we would not bellow so loudly when these were dashed:

> *When dinner comes a few minutes late:*
> What need is there to kick the table over? To smash the goblets?
> To bang yourself against columns?
> *When there's a buzzing sound:*
> Why should a fly infuriate you which no one has taken enough trouble to drive off, or a dog which gets in your way, or a key dropped by a careless servant?
> *When something disturbs the calm of the dining room:*
> Why go and fetch the whip in the middle of dinner, just because the slaves are talking?

We must reconcile ourselves to the necessary imperfectibility of existence:

> Is it surprising that the wicked should do wicked deeds, or unprecedented that your enemy should harm or your friend annoy you, that your son should fall into error or your servant misbehave?

We will cease to be so angry once we cease to be so hopeful.

Shock

An aeroplane belonging to the Swiss national airline, carrying 229 people, takes off on a scheduled flight from New York to

Geneva. Fifty minutes out of Kennedy Airport, as the stewardesses roll their trolleys down the aisles of the McDonald Douglas MD −11, the captain reports smoke in the cockpit. Ten minutes later, the plane disappears off the radar. The gigantic machine, each of its wings 52 metres long, crashes into the placid seas off Halifax, Nova Scotia, killing all on board. Rescue workers speak of the difficulty of identifying what were, only hours before, humans with lives and plans. Briefcases are found floating in the sea.

1. If we do not dwell on the risk of sudden disaster and pay a price for our innocence, it is because reality comprises two cruelly confusing characteristics: on the one hand, continuity and reliability lasting across generations; on the other, unheralded cataclysms. We find ourselves divided between a plausible invitation to assume that tomorrow will be much like today and the possibility that we will meet with an appalling event after which nothing will ever be the same again. It is because we have such powerful incentives to neglect the latter that Seneca invoked a goddess.

2. She was to be found on the back of many Roman coins, holding a cornucopia in one hand and a rudder in the other. She was beautiful and usually wore a light tunic and a coy smile. Her name was Fortune. She had originated as a fertility goddess, the firstborn of Jupiter, and was honoured with a festival on the 25th of May and with temples throughout Italy, visited by the barren and farmers in search of rain. But gradually her remit had widened, she had become associated with money, advancement, love and health. The cornucopia was a symbol of her power to bestow favours, the rudder a symbol of her more sinister power to change destinies. She could scatter gifts, then with terrifying speed shift the rudder's course, maintaining an imperturbable smile as she watched us

choke to death on a fishbone or disappear in a landslide.

3. Because we are injured most by what we do not expect, and because we must expect everything ('There is nothing which Fortune does not dare'), we must, proposed Seneca, hold the possibility of disaster in mind at all times. No one should undertake a journey by car, or walk down the stairs, or say goodbye to a friend, without an awareness, which Seneca would have wished to be neither gruesome nor unnecessarily dramatic, of fatal possibilities.

4. For evidence of how little is needed for all to come to nought, we have only to hold up our wrists and study for a moment the pulses of blood through our fragile, greenish veins:

> What is man? A vessel that the slightest shaking, the slightest toss will break ... A body weak and fragile, naked, in its natural state defenceless, dependent upon another's help and exposed to all the affronts of Fortune.

5. Lugdunum had been one of the most prosperous Roman settlements in Gaul. At the junction of the Arar and Rhone rivers, it enjoyed a privileged position as a crossroads of trade and military routes. The city contained elegant baths and theatres and a government mint. Then in August 64 a spark slipped out of hand and grew into a fire that spread through the narrow streets, terrified inhabitants levering themselves from windows at its approach. Flames licked from house to house and by the time the sun had risen the whole of Lugdunum, from suburb to market, from temple to baths, had burnt to cinders. The survivors were left destitute in only the soot-covered clothes they stood in, their noble buildings roasted beyond recognition. The blaze was so rapid, it took longer for news of the disaster to reach Rome than for the city to burn:

> You say: 'I did not think it would happen.' Do you think there is anything that will not happen, when you know that it

is possible to happen, when you see that it has already happened ... ?

6. On the fifth of February 62, similar disaster struck the province of Campania. The earth trembled, and large sections of Pompeii collapsed. In the months that followed, many inhabitants decided to leave Campania for other parts of the peninsula. Their move suggested to Seneca that they believed there was somewhere on earth, in Liguria or Calabria, where they might be wholly safe, out of reach of Fortune's will. To which he replied with an argument, persuasive in spite of its geological dubiousness:

> Who promises them better foundations for this or that soil to stand on? All places have the same conditions and if they have not yet had an earthquake, they can none the less have quakes. Perhaps tonight or before tonight, today will split open the spot where you stand securely. How do you know whether conditions will henceforth be better in those places against which Fortune has already exhausted her strength or in those places which are supported on their own ruins? We are mistaken if we believe any part of the world is exempt and safe ... Nature has not created anything in such a way that it is immobile.

7. At the time of Caligula's accession to the throne, away from high politics in a household in Rome, a mother lost her son. Metilius had been short of his twenty-fifth birthday and a young man of exceptional promise. He had been close to his mother Marcia, and his death devastated her. She withdrew from social life and sank into mourning. Her friends watched with compassion and hoped for a day when she would regain a measure of composure. She didn't. A year passed, then another and a third, and still Marcia came no closer to overcoming her grief. After three years she was as tearful as she had been on the very day of his funeral. Seneca sent her a

letter. He expressed enormous sympathies, but gently continued, ' the question at issue between us [is] whether grief ought to be *deep* or *neverending*. '

Marcia was rebelling against what seemed like an occurrence at once dreadful and rare − and all the more dreadful because it was rare. Around her were mothers who still had their sons, young men beginning their careers, serving in the army or entering politics. Why had hers been taken from her?

8. The death was unusual and terrible, but it was not − Seneca ventured − abnormal. If Marcia looked beyond a restricted circle, she would come upon a woefully long list of sons whom Fortune had killed. Octavia had lost her son, Livia her son, Cornelia hers; so had Xenophon, Paulus, Lucius Bibulus, Lucius Sulla, Augustus and Scipio. By averting her gaze from early deaths, Marcia had, understandably but perilously, denied them a place in her conception of the normal:

   We never anticipate evils before they actually arrive ... So many funerals pass our doors, yet we never dwell on death. So many deaths are untimely, yet we make plans for our own infants: how they will don the toga, serve in the army, and succeed to their father's property.

   The children might live, but how ingenuous to believe that they were guaranteed to survive to maturity − even to dinner-time:

   No promise has been given you for this night − no, I have suggested too long a respite − no promise has been given even for this *hour*.

   There is dangerous innocence in the expectation of a future formed on the basis of probability. Any accident to which a human has been subject, however rare, however distant in time, is a possibility we must ready ourselves for.

9. Because Fortune's long benevolent periods risk seducing us into somnolence, Seneca entreated us to spare a little time each day

to think of her. We do not know what will happen next; we must expect something. In the early morning, we should undertake what Seneca termed a *praemeditatio*, a meditation in advance, on all the sorrows of mind and body to which the goddess may subsequently subject us.

A SENECAN PRAEMEDITATIO

[The wise] will start each day with the thought...
Fortune gives us nothing which we can really own.
Nothing, whether public or private, is stable; the destinies of men, no less than those of cities, are in a whirl.
Whatever structure has been reared by a long sequence of years, at the cost of great toil and through the great kindness of the gods, is scattered and dispersed in a single day. No, he who has said 'a day' has granted too long a postponement to swift misfortune; an hour, an instant of time, suffices for the overthrow of empires.
How often have cities in Asia, how often in Achaia, been laid low by a single shock of earthquake? How many towns in Syria, how many in Macedonia, have been swallowed up? How often has this kind of devastation laid Cyprus in ruins?
We live in the middle of things which have all been destined to die. Mortal have you been born, to mortals have you given birth.
Reckon on everything, expect everything.

10. The same could naturally have been conveyed in other ways. In more sober philosophical language, one could say that a subject's agency is only one of the causal factors determining events in the course of his or her life. Seneca resorted instead to continual hyperbole:

Whenever anyone falls at your side or behind you, cry out:
'Fortune, you will not deceive me, you will not fall upon me confident and heedless. I know what you are planning.

It is true that you struck someone else, but you aimed at me. '

(The original ends with a final, more rousing alliteration:
Quotiens aliquis ad latus aut pone tergum ceciderit,
exclama: ' Non decipies me, fortuna, nec securum aut
neglegentem opprimes. Scio quid pares; alium quidem
percussisti, sed me petisti. ')

11. If most philosophers feel no need to write like this, it is
because they trust that, so long as an argument is logical, the
style in which it is presented to the reader will not determine
its effectiveness. Seneca believed in a different picture of the
mind. Arguments are like eels: however logical, they may
slip from the mind's weak grasp unless fixed there by imagery
and style. We need metaphors to derive a sense of what
cannot be seen or touched, or else we will forget.

The goddess of Fortune, in spite of her unphilosophical,
religious roots, was the perfect image to keep our exposure to
accident continually within our minds, conflating a range of
threats to our security into one ghastly anthropomorphic
enemy.

Sense of injustice

*A feeling that the rules of justice have been violated, rules which
dictate that if we are honourable, we will be rewarded, and that
if we are bad, we will be punished – a sense of justice inculcated
in the earliest education of children, and found in most religious
texts, for example, in the book of Deuteronomy, which explains
that the godly person ' shall be like a tree planted by the rivers of
water ... and whatsoever he doeth shall prosper. The ungodly are
not so: but are like chaff which the wind driveth away. '*

Goodness $\longrightarrow$ Reward
Evil $\longrightarrow$ Punishment

In cases where one acts correctly but still suffers disaster, one is left bewildered and unable to fit the event into a scheme of justice. The world seems absurd. One alternates between a feeling that one may after all have been bad and this is why one was punished, and the feeling that one truly was not bad and therefore must have fallen victim to a catastrophic failure in the administration of justice. The continuing belief that the world is fundamentally just is implied in the very complaint that there has been an injustice.

1. Justice was not an ideology that had helped Marcia.

2. It had forced her to oscillate between a debilitating feeling that her son Metilius had been taken away from her because she was bad, and at other moments, a feeling of outrage with the world that Metilius had died given that she had always been essentially good.

3. But we cannot always explain our destiny by referring to our moral worth; we may be cursed and blessed without justice behind either. Not everything which happens *to* us occurs with reference to something *about* us.

   Metilius hadn't died because his mother was bad, nor was the world unfair because his mother was good and yet he had died. His death was, in Seneca's image, the work of Fortune, and the goddess was no moral judge. She did not evaluate her victims like the god of Deuteronomy and reward them according to merit. She inflicted harm with the moral blindness of a hurricane.

4. Seneca knew in himself the sapping impulse to interpret failures according to a misguided model of justice. Upon the accession of Claudius in early 41, he became a pawn in a plan by the Empress Messalina to rid herself of Caligula's sister, Julia Livilla. The empress accused Julia of having an adulterous

affair and falsely named Seneca as her lover. He was in an instant stripped of family, money, friends, reputation and his political career, and sent into exile on the island of Corsica, one of the most desolate parts of Rome's vast empire.

He would have endured periods of self-blame alternating with feelings of bitterness. He would have reproached himself for misreading the political situation with regard to Messalina, and resented the way his loyalty and talents had been rewarded by Claudius.

Both moods were based on a picture of a moral universe where external circumstances reflected internal qualities. It was a relief from this punitive schema to remember Fortune:

I do not allow [Fortune] to pass sentence upon myself.

Seneca's political failure did not have to be read as retribution for sins, it was no rational punishment meted out after examination of the evidence by an all-seeing Providence in a divine courtroom; it was a cruel but morally meaningless by-product of the machinations of a rancorous Empress. Seneca was not only distancing himself from disgrace. The imperial official he had been had not deserved all the credit for his status either.

The interventions of Fortune, whether kindly or diabolical, introduced a random element into human destinies.

Anxiety

A condition of agitation about an uncertain situation which one both wishes will turn out for the best and fears may turn out for the worst. Typically leaves sufferers unable to derive enjoyment from supposedly pleasurable activities, cultural, sexual or social.

Even in sublime settings the anxious will remain preoccupied by private anticipations of ruin and may prefer to be left alone in a room.

1. The traditional form of comfort is reassurance. One explains to the anxious that their fears are exaggerated and that events are sure to unfold in a desired direction.

2. But reassurance can be the cruellest antidote to anxiety. Our rosy predictions both leave the anxious unprepared for the worst, and unwittingly imply that it would be disastrous if the worst came to pass. Seneca more wisely asks us to consider that bad things probably will occur, but adds that they are unlikely ever to be as bad as we fear.

3. In February 63, Seneca's friend Lucilius, a civil servant working in Sicily, learned of a lawsuit against him which threatened to end his career and disgrace his name for ever. He wrote to Seneca.

   'You may expect that I will advise you to picture a happy outcome, and to rest in the allurements of hope,' replied the philosopher, but 'I am going to conduct you to peace of mind through another route' – which culminated in the advice:

   > If you wish to put off all worry, assume that what you fear *may* happen is certainly *going* to happen.

   Seneca wagered that once we look rationally at what will occur if our desires are not fulfilled, we will almost certainly find that the underlying problems are more modest than the anxieties they have bred. Lucilius had grounds for sadness but not hysteria:

   > If you lose this case, can anything more severe happen to you than being sent into exile or led to prison? ... 'I may become a poor man'; I shall then be one among many. 'I may be exiled'; I shall then regard myself as though I had been born in the place to which I'll be sent. 'They may put me in chains.' What then? Am I free from bonds now?

   Prison and exile were bad, but – the linchpin of the argument – not as bad as the desperate Lucilius might have feared before scrutinizing the anxiety.

4. It follows that wealthy individuals fearing the loss of their fortune should never be reassured with remarks about the improbability of their ruin. They should spend a few days in a draughty room on a diet of thin soup and stale bread. Seneca had taken the counsel from one of his favourite philosophers:

> The great hedonist teacher Epicurus used to observe certain periods during which he would be niggardly in satisfying hunger, with the object of seeing ... whether it was worth going to much trouble to make the deficit good.

The wealthy would, Seneca promised, soon come to an important realization:

> 'Is this really the condition that I feared?' ... Endure [this poverty] for three or four days at a time, sometimes for more ... and I assure you ... you will understand that a man's peace of mind does not depend upon Fortune.

5. Many Romans found it surprising, even ridiculous, to discover that the philosopher proffering such advice lived in considerable luxury himself. By his early forties, Seneca had accumulated enough money through his political career to acquire villas and farms. He ate well, and developed a love of expensive furniture, in particular, citrus-wood tables with ivory legs.

He resented suggestions that there was something unphilosophical in his behaviour:

> Stop preventing philosophers from possessing money; no one has condemned wisdom to poverty.

And with touching pragmatism:

> I will despise whatever lies in the domain of Fortune, but if a choice is offered, I will choose the better half.

6. It wasn't hypocrisy. Stoicism does not recommend poverty; it recommends that we neither fear nor despise it. It considers wealth to be, in the technical formulation, a *productum*, a

preferred thing – neither an essential one nor a crime. Stoics may live with as many gifts of Fortune as the foolish. Their houses can be as grand, their furniture as beautiful. They are identified as wise by only one detail: how they would respond to sudden poverty. They would walk away from the house and the servants without rage or despair.

7. The idea that a wise person should be able to walk away from *all* Fortune's gifts calmly was Stoicism's most extreme, peculiar claim, given that Fortune grants us not only houses and money but also our friends, our family, even our bodies:

> The wise man can lose nothing. He has everything invested in himself.

> The wise man is self-sufficient ... if he loses a hand through disease or war, or if some accident puts out one or both of his eyes, he will be satisfied with what is left.

Which sounds absurd, unless we refine our notion of what Seneca meant by 'satisfied'. We should not be happy to lose an eye, but life would be possible even if we did so. The right number of eyes and hands is a *productum*. Two examples of the position:

> The wise man will not despise himself even if he has the stature of a dwarf, but he nevertheless wishes to be tall.

> The wise man is self-sufficient in that he *can* do without friends, not that he *desires* to do without them.

8. Seneca's wisdom was more than theoretical. Exiled to Corsica, he found himself abruptly stripped of all luxuries. The island had been a Roman possession since 238 BC, but it had not enjoyed the benefits of civilization. The few Romans on the island rarely settled outside two colonies on the east coast, Aleria and Mariana, and it was unlikely that Seneca was allowed to inhabit them, for he complained of hearing only 'barbaric speech' around him, and was associated with a

forbidding building near Luri at the northern tip of the island known since ancient times as 'Seneca's Tower'.

Conditions must have contrasted painfully with life in Rome. But in a letter to his mother, the former wealthy statesman explained that he had managed to accommodate himself to his circumstances, thanks to years of morning premeditations and periods of thin soup:

> Never did I trust Fortune, even when she seemed to be offering peace. All those blessings which she kindly bestowed on me – money, public office, influence – I relegated to a place from which she could take them back without disturbing me. Between them and me, I have kept a wide gap, and so she has merely *taken* them, not *torn* them from me.

Feelings of being mocked by

(i) inanimate objects

A sense that one's wishes are being purposefully frustrated by a pencil which drops off a table or a drawer that refuses to open. The frustration caused by the inanimate object is compounded by a sense that it holds one in contempt. It is acting in a frustrating way in order to signal that it does not share the view of one's intelligence or status to which one is attached and to which others subscribe.

(ii) animate objects

A similarly acute pain arising from the impression that other people are silently ridiculing one's character.

On arrival at a hotel in Sweden I am accompanied to my room by an employee who offers to carry my luggage. 'It will be far too heavy for a man like you,' he smiles, emphasizing 'man' to imply its opposite. He has Nordic blond hair (perhaps a skier, a hunter of elk; in past centuries, a warrior) and a determined expression. 'Monsieur will enjoy the room,' he says. It is unclear why he has called me 'Monsieur', knowing that I have come from London, and the use of 'will' smacks of an order. The suggestion becomes plainly incongruous, and evidence of conspiracy, when the room turns out to suffer from traffic noise, a faulty shower and a broken television.

In otherwise shy, quiet people, feelings of being slyly mocked may boil over into sudden shouting and acts of cruelty – even murder.

1. It is tempting, when we are hurt, to believe that the thing which hurt us *intended* to do so. It is tempting to move from a sentence with clauses connected by 'and' to one with clauses connected by 'in order to'; to move from thinking that 'The pencil fell off the table *and* now I am annoyed' to the view that 'The pencil fell off the table *in order to* annoy me.'

2. Seneca collected examples of such feelings of persecution by inanimate objects. Herodotus's *Histories* provided one. Cyrus, the king of Persia and the founder of its great empire, owned a beautiful white horse which he always rode into battle. In the spring of 539 BC King Cyrus declared war on the Assyrians in hope of expanding his territory, and set off with a large army for their capital, Babylon, on the banks of the Euphrates river. The march went well, until the army reached the river Gyndes, which flowed down from the Matienian mountains into the Tigris. The Gyndes was known to be perilous even in the summer, and at this time of year was brown and foaming, swollen with the winter rains. The king's generals counselled delay, but Cyrus was not daunted and gave orders for an immediate crossing. Yet as the boats were being readied, Cyrus's horse slipped away unnoticed and attempted to swim across the river. The current seized the beast, toppled it and swept it downstream to its death.

   Cyrus was livid. The river had dared to make away with his sacred white horse, the horse of the warrior who had ground

Croesus into the dust and terrified the Greeks. He screamed and cursed, and at the height of his fury decided to pay back the Gyndes for its insolence. He vowed to punish the river by making it so weak that a woman would in future be able to cross it without so much as wetting her knees.

Setting aside plans for the expansion of his empire, Cyrus divided his army into two parts, marked out 180 small canals running off from each bank of the river in various directions and ordered his men to start digging, which they did for an entire summer, their morale broken, all hope of a quick defeat of the Assyrians gone. And when they were finished, the once-rapid Gyndes was split into 360 separate channels through which water flowed so languidly that astonished local women could indeed wander across the trickling stream without hoisting their skirts. His anger assuaged, the King of Persia instructed his exhausted army to resume the march to Babylon.

3. Seneca collected similar examples of feelings of persecution at the hands of animate objects. One concerned the Roman governor of Syria, Gnaeus Piso, a brave general but a troubled soul. When a soldier returned from a period of leave without the friend he had set out with and claimed to have no idea where he had gone, Piso judged that the soldier was lying; he had killed his friend, and would have to pay with his life.

The condemned man swore he hadn't murdered anyone and begged for time for an inquiry to be made, but Piso knew better and had the soldier escorted to his death without delay.

However, as the centurion in charge was preparing to cut off the soldier's head, the missing companion arrived at the gates of the camp. The army broke into spontaneous applause and the relieved centurion called off the execution.

Piso took the news less well. Hearing the cheers, he felt them to be mocking his judgement. He grew red and angry, so angry that he summoned his guards and ordered both men to be executed, the soldier who hadn't committed murder and the one who hadn't been murdered. And because he was by this point feeling very persecuted, Piso also sent the centurion off to his death for good measure.

4. The governor of Syria had at once interpreted the applause of his soldiers as a wish to undermine his authority and to question his judgement. Cyrus had at once interpreted the river's manslaughter of his horse as murder.

   Seneca had an explanation for such errors of judgement; it lay with 'a certain abjectness of spirit' in men like Cyrus and Piso. Behind their readiness to anticipate insult lay a fear of deserving ridicule. When we suspect that we are appropriate targets for hurt, it does not take much for us to believe that someone or something is out to hurt us:

   > 'So and so did not give me an audience today, though he gave it to others'; 'he haughtily repulsed or openly laughed at my conversation'; 'he did not give me the seat of honour, but placed me at the foot of the table. '

   There may be innocent grounds. He didn't give me an audience today, because he would prefer to see me next week. It seemed like he was laughing at me, but it was a facial tic. These are not the first explanations to come into our minds when we are abject of spirit.

5. So we must endeavour to surround our initial impressions with a fireguard and refuse to act at once on their precepts. We must ask ourselves if someone who has not answered a letter is *necessarily* being tardy to annoy us, and if the missing keys have *necessarily* been stolen:

   > [The wise do] not put a wrong construction upon everything.

6. And the reason why they are able not to was indirectly explained by Seneca in a letter to Lucilius, the day he came

upon a sentence in one of the works of the philosopher Hecato:
I shall tell you what I liked today in [his writings]; it is
these words: 'What progress, you ask, have I made? *I
have begun to be a friend to myself.*' That was indeed a
great benefit; ... you may be sure that such a man is a
friend to all mankind.

7. There is an easy way to measure our inner levels of abjectness
and friendliness to ourselves: we should examine how well we
respond to noise. Seneca lived near a gymnasium. The walls
were thin and the racket was continuous. He described the
problem to Lucilius:

Imagine what a variety of noises reverberates around my
ears! ... For example, when a strenuous gentleman is
exercising himself by swinging lead weights, when he is
working hard, or else pretends to be working hard, I can
hear him grunting; and whenever he releases his pent-up
breath, I can hear him panting in wheezy, high-pitched
tones. When my attention turns to a less active type who is
happy with an ordinary, inexpensive massage, I can hear the
smack of a hand pummelling his shoulders ... One should
add to this the arresting of an occasional reveller or
pickpocket, the racket of the man who always likes to hear
his own voice in the bathroom ... the hair-plucker with his
shrill, penetrating cry ... then the cake seller with his varied
cries, the sausage man, the confectioner and everyone
hawking for the catering shops.

8. Those who are unfriendly with themselves find it hard to
imagine that the cake seller is shouting *in order to sell cakes.*
The builder on the ground floor of a hotel in Rome (1) may be
pretending to repair a wall, but his real intention is to tease the
man trying to read a book in a room on the upper level (2).

Abject interpretation: The builder is hammering *in order to*
annoy me.

Friendly interpretation: The builder is hammering *and* I am annoyed.

9. To calm us down in noisy streets, we should trust that those making a noise know nothing of us. We should place a fireguard between the noise outside and an internal sense of deserving punishment. We should not import into scenarios where they don't belong pessimistic interpretations of others' motives. Thereafter, noise will never be pleasant, but it will not have to make us furious:

All outdoors may be bedlam, provided that there is no disturbance within.

3

Of course, there would be few great human achievements if we accepted all frustrations. The motor of our ingenuity is the question ' Does it have to be like this?', from which arise political reforms, scientific developments, improved relationships, better books. The Romans were consummate at refusing frustration. They hated winter cold and developed under-floor heating. They didn't wish to walk on muddy roads and so paved them. In the middle of the first century AD the Roman inhabitants of Nîmes in Provence decided they wanted more water for their city than nature had granted them, and so spent a hundred million sesterces building an extraordinary symbol of human resistance to the status quo. To the north of Nîmes, near Uzès, Roman engineers found a water source strong enough to irrigate the baths and fountains of their city, and drew up plans to divert the water 50 miles through mountains and across valleys in a system of aqueducts and under-ground pipes. When the engineers confronted the cavernous gorge of the river Gard, they did not despair at nature's obstacle but erected a massive three-tiered aqueduct, 360 metres long and 48 metres high, capable of carrying 35,000 cubic metres of water a day – so that the inhabitants of Nîmes would never be forced to suffer the frustration of a shallow bath.

Unfortunately, the mental faculties which search so assiduously for alternatives are hard to arrest. They continue to play out scenarios of change and progress even when there is no hope of altering reality. To generate the energy required to spur us to action, we are reminded by jolts of discomfort – anxiety, pain, outrage, offence – that reality is not as we would wish it. Yet these jolts have served no purpose if we cannot subsequently effect improvement, if we lose our peace of mind but are unable to divert rivers; which is why, for Seneca, wisdom lies in correctly discerning where we are free to mould reality according to our wishes and where we must accept the unalterable with tranquillity.

The Stoics had another image with which to evoke our condition as creatures at times able to effect change yet always subject to external necessities. We are like dogs who have been tied to an unpredictable cart. Our leash is long enough to give us a degree of leeway, but not long enough to allow us to wander wherever we please.

The metaphor had been formulated by the Stoic philosophers Zeno and Chrysippus and reported by the Roman Bishop Hippolytus:

> When a dog is tied to a cart, if it wants to follow, it is pulled *and* follows, making its spontaneous act *coincide with* necessity. But if the dog does not follow, it will be compelled in any case. So it is with men too: even if they don't want to, they will be compelled to follow what is destined.

A dog will naturally hope to go wherever it pleases. But as Zeno and Chrysippus's metaphor implies, if it cannot, then it is better for the animal to be *trotting* behind the cart rather than *dragged and strangled* by it. Though the dog's first impulse may be to fight against the sudden swerve of the cart in an awful direction, his sorrows will only be compounded by his resistance.

As Seneca put it:

> An animal, struggling against the noose, tightens it ... there is no yoke so tight that it will not hurt the animal less if it pulls *with* it than if it fights *against* it. The one alleviation for overwhelming evils is to endure and bow to necessity.

To reduce the violence of our mutiny against events which veer away from our intentions, we should reflect that we, too, are never without a leash around our neck. The wise will learn to identify what is necessary and follow it at once, rather than exhaust themselves in protest. When a wise man is told that his suitcase has been lost in transit, he will resign himself in seconds to the fact. Seneca reported how the founder of Stoicism had behaved upon the loss of his possessions:

> When Zeno received news of a shipwreck and heard that all his luggage had been sunk, he said, 'Fortune bids me to be a less encumbered philosopher.'

It may sound like a recipe for passivity and quietude, encouragement to resign ourselves to frustrations that might have been overcome. It could leave us without heart to build even a diminutive aqueduct like that in Bornègre, in a valley a few kilometres north of the Pont du Gard, a modest 17 metres long and 4 metres high.

But Seneca's point is more subtle. It is no less unreasonable to accept something as necessary when it *isn't* as to rebel against something when it *is*. We can as easily go astray by accepting the unnecessary and denying the possible, as by denying the necessary and wishing for the impossible. It is for reason to make the distinction.

Whatever the similarities between ourselves and a dog on a leash, we have a critical advantage: we have reason and the dog doesn't. So the animal does not at first grasp that he is even tied to a leash, nor understand the connection between the swerves of the cart and the pain in his neck. He will be confused by the changes in direction, it will be hard for him to calculate the cart's trajectory, and so he will suffer constant painful jolts. But reason enables us to theorize with accuracy about the path of our cart, which offers us a chance, unique among living beings, to increase our sense of freedom by ensuring a good slack between ourselves and necessity. Reason allows us to determine when our wishes are in irrevocable conflict with reality, and then bids us to submit ourselves willingly, rather than angrily or bitterly, to necessities. We may be powerless to alter certain events, but we remain free to choose our attitude towards them, and it is in our spontaneous acceptance of necessity that we find our distinctive freedom.

In February 62, Seneca came up against an unalterable reality. Nero ceased to listen to his old tutor, he shunned his company, encouraged slander of him at court and appointed a bloodthirsty praetorian prefect, Ofonius Tigellinus, to assist him in indulging his taste for random murder and sexual cruelty. Virgins were taken off the streets of Rome and brought to the emperor's chambers. Senators' wives were forced to participate in orgies, and saw their husbands killed in front of them. Nero roamed the city at night disguised as an ordinary citizen and slashed the throats of passers-by in back alleys. He fell in love with a young boy who he wished could have been a girl, and so he castrated him and went through a mock wedding ceremony. Romans wryly joked that their lives would have been more tolerable if Nero's father Domitius had married that sort of a woman. Knowing he was in extreme danger, Seneca attempted to withdraw from court and remain quietly in his villa outside Rome. Twice he offered his resignation; twice Nero refused, embracing him tightly and swearing that he would rather die than harm his beloved tutor. Nothing in Seneca's experience could allow him to believe such promises.

He turned to philosophy. He could not escape Nero, and what he could not change, reason asked him to accept. During what might have been intolerably anxious years, Seneca devoted himself to the study of nature. He began writing a book about the earth and the planets. He looked at the vast sky and the constellation of the heavens, he studied the unbounded sea and the high mountains. He observed flashes of lightning and speculated on their origins:

> A lightning bolt is fire that has been compressed and hurled violently. Sometimes we take up water in our two clasped hands and pressing our palms together squirt out water the way a pump does. Suppose something like this occurs in the clouds. The constricted space of the compressed clouds forces out the air that is between them and by means of this pressure sets the air afire and hurls it the way a catapult does.

He considered earthquakes and decided they were the result of air trapped inside the earth that had sought a way out, a form of geological flatulence:

> Among the arguments that prove earthquakes occur because of moving air, this is one you shouldn't hesitate to put forward: when a great tremor has exhausted its rage against cities and countries, another equal to it cannot follow. After the largest shock, there are only gentle quakes because the first tremor, acting with greater vehemence, has created an exit for the struggling air.

It hardly mattered that Seneca's science was faulty; it was more significant that a man whose life could at any time have been cut short by the caprice of a murderous emperor appeared to gain immense relief from the spectacle of nature – perhaps because in mighty natural phenomena lie reminders of all that we are powerless to change, of all that we must accept. Glaciers, volcanoes, earthquakes and hurricanes stand as impressive symbols of what exceeds us. In the human world, we grow to believe that we may always alter our destinies, and hope and worry accordingly. It is apparent from the heedless pounding of the oceans or the flight of comets across the night sky that there are forces entirely indifferent to our desires. The indifference is not nature's alone; humans can wield equally blind powers over their fellows, but it is nature which gives us a most elegant lesson in the necessities to which we are subject:

> Winter brings on cold weather; and we must shiver. Summer returns, with its heat; and we must sweat. Unseasonable weather upsets the health; and we must fall ill. In certain places we may meet with wild beasts, or with men who are more destructive than any beasts ... And we cannot change this order of things ... it is to this law [of Nature] that our souls must adjust themselves, this they should follow, this they should obey ... That which you cannot reform, it is best to endure.

Seneca began his book on nature as soon as he had first offered Nero his resignation. He was granted three years. Then in April 65, Piso's plot against the emperor was uncovered, and a centurion dispatched to the philosopher's villa. He was ready. Topless Paulina and her maids might have collapsed into tears –

– but Seneca had learned to follow the cart obediently, and slit his veins without protest. As he had reminded Marcia on the loss of her son Metilius:

> What need is there to weep over parts of life?
> The whole of it calls for tears.

IV Consolation for Inadequacy

After centuries of neglect, at times hostility, after being scattered and burnt and surviving only in partial forms in the vaults and libraries of monasteries, the wisdom of ancient Greece and Rome returned triumphantly to favour in the sixteenth century. Among the intellectual élites of Europe, a consensus emerged that the finest thinking the world had yet known had occurred in the minds of a handful of geniuses in the city states of Greece and the Italian peninsula between the construction of the Parthenon and the sack of Rome − and that there was no greater imperative for the educated than to familiarize themselves with the richness of these works. Major new editions were prepared of, among others, Plato, Lucretius, Seneca, Aristotle, Catullus, Longinus and Cicero, and selections from the classics − Erasmus's *Apophthegmata* and *Adages*, Stobeus's *Sententiae*, Antonio de Guevara's *Golden Epistles* and Petrus Crinitus's *Honorable Learning* − spread into libraries across Europe.

In south-western France, on the summit of a wooded hill 30 miles east of Bordeaux, sat a handsome castle made of yellow stone with dark-red roofs.

It was home to a middle-aged nobleman, his wife Françoise, his daughter Léonor, their staff and their animals (chickens, goats, dogs and horses). Michel de Montaigne's grandfather had bought the property in 1477 from the proceeds of the famliy salt-fish business, his father had added some wings and extended the land under cultivation, and the son had been looking after it since the age of thirty-five, though he had little interest in household management and knew almost nothing about farming ('I can scarcely tell my cabbages from my lettuces').

He preferred to pass his time in a circular library on the third floor of a tower at one corner of the castle: 'I spend most days of my life there, and most hours of each day. '

The library had three windows (with what Montaigne described as ' splendid and unhampered views '), a desk, a chair and, arranged on five tiers of shelves in a semicircle, about a thousand volumes of philosophy, history, poetry and religion. It was here that Montaigne read Socrates' (' the wisest man that ever was ') steadfast address to the impatient jurors of Athens in a Latin edition of Plato translated by Marsilio Ficino; here that he read Epicurus's vision of happiness in Diogenes Laertius's *Lives* and Lucretius's *De Rerum Natura*, edited by Denys Lambin in 1563; and here that he read and re-read Seneca (an author ' strikingly suited to my humour') in a new set of his works printed in Basle in 1557.

He had been initiated in the classics at an early age. He had been taught Latin as a first language. By seven or eight, he had read Ovid's *Metamorphoses*. Before he was sixteen, he had bought a set of Virgil and knew intimately the *Aeneid*, as well as Terence, Plautus and the *Commentaries* of Caesar. And such was his devotion to books that, after working as a counsellor in the Parlement of Bordeaux for thirteen years, he retired with the idea of devoting himself entirely to them. Reading was the solace of his life:

> It consoles me in my retreat; it relieves me of the weight of distressing idleness and, at any time, can rid me of boring company. It blunts the stabs of pain whenever pain is not too overpowering and extreme. To distract me from morose thoughts, I simply need to have recourse to books.

But the library shelves, with their implication of an unbounded admiration for the life of the mind, did not tell the full story. One had to look more closely around the library, stand in the middle of the room and tilt one's head to the ceiling: in the mid-1570s Montaigne had a set of fifty-seven short inscriptions culled from the Bible and the classics painted across the wooden beams, and these suggested some profound reservations about the benefits of having a mind:

The happiest life is to be without thought. – Sophocles

Have you seen a man who thinks he is wise? You have more to hope for from a madman than from him. – Proverbs

There is nothing certain but uncertainty, nothing more miserable and more proud than man. – pliny

Everything is too complicated for men to be able to understand. – Ecclesiastes

Ancient philosophers had believed that our powers of reason could afford us a happiness and greatness denied to other creatures. Reason allowed us to control our passions and to correct the false notions prompted by our instincts. Reason tempered the wild demands of our bodies and led us to a balanced relationship with our appetites for food and sex. Reason was a sophisticated, almost divine, tool offering us mastery over the world and ourselves.

In the *Tusculan Disputations*, of which there was a copy in the round library, Cicero had heaped praise upon the benefits of intellectual work:

There is no occupation so sweet as scholarship; scholarship is the means of making known to us, while still in this world, the infinity of matter, the immense grandeur of Nature, the heavens, the lands and the seas. Scholarship has taught us piety, moderation, greatness of heart; it snatches our souls from darkness and shows them all things, the high and the low, the first, the last and everything in between; scholarship furnishes us with the means of living well and happily; it teaches us how to spend our lives without discontent and without vexation.

Though he owned a thousand books and had benefited from a fine classical education, this laudation so infuriated Montaigne, it ran so contrary to the spirit of the library beams, that he expressed his indignation with uncharacteristic ferocity:

> Man is a wretched creature ... just listen to him bragging ... Is this fellow describing the properties of almighty and everlasting God! In practice, thousands of little women in their villages have lived more gentle, more equable and more constant lives than [Cicero].

The Roman philosopher had overlooked how violently unhappy most scholars were; he had arrogantly disregarded the appalling troubles for which human beings, alone among all other creatures, had been singled out − troubles which might in dark moments leave us regretting that we had not been born ants or tortoises.

Or goats. I found her in the yard of a farm a few kilometres from Montaigne's château, in the hamlet of Les Gauchers.

She had never read the *Tusculan Disputations* nor Cicero's *On the Laws*. And yet she seemed content, nibbling at stray pieces of lettuce, occasionally shaking her head like an elderly woman expressing quiet disagreement. It was not an unenviable existence.

Montaigne was himself struck by, and elaborated upon the advantages of living as an animal rather than as a reasoning human with a large library. Animals knew instinctively how to help themselves when they were sick: goats could pick out dittany from a thousand other plants if they were wounded, tortoises automatically looked for origanum when they were bitten by vipers, and storks could give themselves salt-water enemas. By contrast, humans were forced to rely on expensive, misguided doctors (medicine chests were filled with absurd prescriptions: 'the urine of a lizard, the droppings of an elephant, the liver of a mole, blood drawn from under the right wing of a white pigeon, and for those of us with colic paroxysms, triturated rat shit').

Animals also instinctively understood complex ideas without suffering long periods of study. Tunny-fish were spontaneous experts in astrology. 'Wherever they may be when they are surprised by the winter solstice, there they remain until the following equinox,' reported Montaigne. They understood geometry and arithmetic, too, for they swam together in groups in the shape of a perfect cube: 'If you count one line of them you have the count of the whole school, since the same figure applies to their depth, breadth and length.' Dogs had an innate grasp of dialectical logic. Montaigne mentioned one who, looking for his master, came upon a three-pronged fork in the road. He first looked down one road, then another, and then ran down the third after concluding that his master must have chosen it:

> Here was pure dialectic: the dog made use of disjunctive and
> copulative propositions and adequately enumerated the parts.
> Does it matter whether he learned all this from himself or from
> the *Dialectica* of George of Trebizond?

Animals frequently had the upper hand in love as well. Montaigne read enviously of an elephant who had fallen in love with a flowerseller in Alexandria. When being led through the market, he knew how to slip his wrinkled trunk through her neckband and would massage her breasts with a dexterity no human could match.

And without trying, the humblest farm animal could exceed the philosophical detachment of the wisest sages of antiquity. The Greek philosopher Pyrrho once travelled on a ship which ran into a fierce storm. All around him passengers began to panic, afraid that the mutinous waves would shatter their fragile craft. But one passenger did not lose his composure and sat quietly in a corner, wearing a tranquil expression. He was a pig:

> Dare we conclude that the benefit of reason (which we praise
> so highly and on account of which we esteem ourselves to be
> lords and masters of all creation) was placed in us for our
> torment? What use is knowledge if, for its sake, we lose the

calm and repose which we should enjoy without it and if it makes our condition worse than that of Pyrrho's pig?

It was questionable whether the mind gave us anything to be grateful for:

> We have been allotted inconstancy, hesitation, doubt, pain, superstition, worries about what will happen (even after we are dead), ambition, greed, jealousy, envy, unruly, insane and untameable appetites, war, lies, disloyalty, backbiting and curiosity. We take pride in our fair, discursive reason and our capacity to judge and to know, but we have bought them at a price which is strangely excessive.

If offered a choice, Montaigne would in the end perhaps not have opted to live as a goat − but only just. Cicero had presented the benevolent picture of reason. Sixteen centuries later, it was for Montaigne to introduce the adverse:

> To learn that we have said or done a stupid thing is nothing, we must learn a more ample and important lesson: *that we are but blockheads.*

− the biggest blockheads of all being philosophers like Cicero who had never suspected they might even be such things. Misplaced confidence in reason was the well-spring of idiocy − and, indirectly, also of inadequacy.

Beneath his painted beams, Montaigne had outlined a new kind of philosophy, one which acknowledged how far we were from the rational, serene creatures whom most of the ancient thinkers had taken us to be. We were for the most part hysterical and demented, gross and agitated souls beside whom animals were in many respects paragons of health and virtue − an unfortunate reality which philosophy was obliged to reflect, but rarely did:

> Our life consists partly in madness, partly in wisdom: whoever writes about it merely respectfully and by rule leaves more than half of it behind.

And yet if we accepted our frailties, and ceased claiming a

mastery we did not have, we stood to find – in Montaigne's generous, redemptive philosophy – that we were ultimately still adequate in our own distinctive half-wise, half-blockheadish way.

2

On Sexual Inadequacy

How problematic to have both a body and a mind, for the former stands in almost monstrous contrast to the latter's dignity and intelligence. Our bodies smell, ache, sag, pulse, throb and age. They force us to fart and burp, and to abandon sensible plans in order to lie in bed with people, sweating and letting out intense sounds reminiscent of coyotes calling out to one another across the barren wastes of the American deserts. Our bodies hold our minds hostage to their whims and rhythms. Our whole perspective on life can be altered by the digestion of a heavy lunch. 'I feel quite a different person before and after a meal,' concurred Montaigne:

> When good health and a fine sunny day smile at me, I am quite
> debonair; give me an ingrowing toe-nail, and I am touchy,
> badtempered and unapproachable.

Even the greatest philosophers have not been spared bodily humiliation. 'Imagine Plato struck down by epilepsy or apoplexy,' proposed Montaigne, 'then challenge him to get any help from all those noble and splendid faculties of his soul.' Or imagine that in the middle of a symposium, Plato had been struck by a need to fart:

> That sphincter which serves to discharge our stomachs has
> dilations and contractions proper to itself, independent of our
> wishes or even opposed to them.

Montaigne heard of a man who knew how to fart at will, and on occasion arranged a sequence of farts in a metrical accompaniment to poetry, but such mastery did not contravene his general observation that our bodies have the upper hand over our minds,

and that the sphincter is ' most indiscreet and disorderly '.
Montaigne even heard a tragic case of one behind ' so stormy and
churlish that it has obliged its master to fart forth wind constantly
and unremittingly for forty years and is thus bringing him to his
death. '

No wonder we may be tempted to deny our uncomfortable,
insulting coexistence with these vessels. Montaigne met a woman
who, acutely aware of how repulsive her digestive organs were,
tried to live as though she didn't have any:

[This] lady (amongst the greatest) ... shares the opinion that
chewing distorts the face, derogating greatly from women's
grace and beauty; so when hungry, she avoids appearing in
public. And I know a man who cannot tolerate watching people
eat nor others watching him do so: he shuns all company even
more when he fills his belly than when he empties it.

Montaigne knew men so overwhelmed by their sexual longings
that they ended their torment through castration. Others tried to
suppress their lust by applying snow-and-vinegar compresses to
their overactive testicles. The Emperor Maximilian, conscious of
a conflict between being regal and having a body, ordered that no
one should see him naked, particularly below the waist. He
expressly requested in his will that he be buried in a set of linen
underpants. ' He should have added a codicil, ' noted Montaigne,
' saying that the man who pulled them on ought to be blindfolded. '

However drawn we may be towards such radical measures,
Montaigne's philosophy is one of reconciliation: ' The most
uncouth of our afflictions is to despise our being. ' Rather than
trying to cut ourselves in two, we should cease waging civil war
on our perplexing physical envelopes and learn to accept them as
unalterable facts of our condition, neither so terrible nor so
humiliating.

In the summer of 1993, L. and I travelled to northern Portugal for a holiday. We drove along the villages of the Minho, then spent a few days south of Viana do Castelo. It was here, on the last night of our holiday, in a small hotel overlooking the sea, that I realized − quite without warning − that I could no longer make love. It would hardly have been possible to surmount, let alone mention the experience, if I had not, a few months before going to Portugal, come across the twenty-first chapter of the first volume of Montaigne's *Essays*.

The author recounted therein that a friend of his had heard a man explain how he had lost his erection just as he prepared to enter a woman. The embarrassment of the detumescence struck Montaigne's friend with such force, that the next time he was in bed with a woman, he could not banish it from his mind, and the fear of the same catastrophe befalling him grew so overwhelming that it prevented his own penis from stiffening. From then on, however much he desired a woman, he could not attain an erection, and the ignoble memory of every misadventure taunted and tyrannized him with increasing force.

Montaigne's friend had grown impotent after failing to achieve the unwavering rational command over his penis that he assumed to be an indispensable feature of normal manhood. Montaigne did not blame the penis: ' Except for genuine impotence, never again are you incapable if you are capable of doing it once. ' It was the oppressive notion that we had complete mental control over our bodies, and the horror of departing from this portrait of normality, that had left the man unable to perform. The solution was to redraw the portrait; it was by accepting a loss of command over the penis as a harmless possibility in love-making that one could preempt its occurrence − as the stricken man eventually discovered. In bed with a woman, he learnt to:

> admit beforehand that he was subject to this infirmity and spoke
> openly about it, so relieving the tensions within his soul. By

bearing the malady as something to be expected, his sense of
constriction grew less and weighed less heavily on him.

Montaigne's frankness allowed the tensions in the reader's own
soul to be relieved. The penis's abrupt moods were removed from
the Cimmerian recesses of wordless shame and reconsidered with
the unshockable, worldly eye of a philosopher whom nothing
bodily could repulse. A sense of personal culpability was lessened
by what Montaigne described as:

> [The universal] disobedience of this member which thrusts
> itself forward so inopportunely when we do not want it to, and
> which so inopportunely lets us down when we most need it.

A man who failed with his mistress and was unable to do any
more than mumble an apology could regain his forces and soothe
the anxieties of his beloved by accepting that his impotence
belonged to a broad realm of sexual mishaps, neither very rare nor
very peculiar. Montaigne knew a Gascon nobleman who, after
failing to maintain an erection with a woman, fled home, cut off
his penis and sent it to the lady ' to atone for his offence '.
Montaigne proposed instead that:

> If [couples] are not ready, they should not try to rush things.
> Rather than fall into perpetual wretchedness by being struck
> with despair at a first rejection, it is better ... to wait for an
> opportune moment ... a man who suffers a rejection should
> make gentle assays and overtures with various little sallies; he
> should not stubbornly persist in proving himself inadequate once
> and for all.

It was a new language, unsensational and intimate, with which to
articulate the loneliest moments of our sexuality. Cutting a path
into the private sorrows of the bedchamber, Montaigne drained
them of their ignominy, attempting all the while to reconcile us to
our bodily selves. His courage in mentioning what is secretly lived
but rarely heard expands the range of what we can dare to express
to our lovers and to ourselves − a courage founded on Montaigne's

conviction that nothing that can happen to man is inhuman, that 'every man bears the whole Form of the human condition,' a condition which includes — we do not need to blush nor hate ourselves for it — the risk of an occasional rebellious flaccidity in the penis.

Montaigne attributed our problems with our bodies in part to an absence of honest discussion about them in polite circles. Representative stories and images do not tend to identify feminine grace with a strong interest in love-making, nor authority with the possession of a sphincter or penis. Pictures of kings and ladies do not encourage us to think of these eminent souls breaking wind or making love. Montaigne filled out the picture in blunt, beautiful French:

> *Au plus eslevé throne du monde si ne sommes assis que sus nostre cul.*
> Upon the highest throne in the world, we are seated, still, upon our arses.
> *Les Roys et les philosophes fientent, et les dames aussi.*
> Kings and philosophers shit: and so do ladies.

He could have put it otherwise. Instead of '*cul*', '*derrière*' or '*fesses*'. Instead of '*fienter*', '*aller au cabinet*'. Randle Cotgrave's *Dictionarie of the French and English Tongues (for the furtherance of young Learners, and the advantage of all others that endeavour to arrive at the most exactly knowledge of the French language)*, printed in London in 1611, explained that '*fienter*' referred particularly to the excretions of vermin and badgers. If Montaigne felt the need for such strong language, it was to correct an equally strong denial of the body in works of philosophy and in drawing rooms. The view that ladies never had to wash their hands and kings had no behinds had made it timely to remind the world that they shat and had arses:

The genital activities of mankind are so natural, so necessary and so right: what have they done to make us never dare to mention them without embarrassment and to exclude them from serious orderly conversation? We are not afraid to utter the words *kill*, *thieve*, or *betray*; but those others we only dare to mutter through our teeth.

In the vicinity of Montaigne's château were several beech-tree forests, one to the north near the village of Castillon-la-Bataille, another to the east near St Vivien. Montaigne's daughter Léonor must have known their silences and their grandeur. She was not encouraged to know their name: the French for ' beech tree ' is '*fouteau*'. The French for ' fuck' *is* '*foutre*'.

' My daughter − I have no other children − is of an age when the more passionate girls are legally allowed to marry,' Montaigne explained of Léonor, then about fourteen:

> She is slender and gentle; by complexion she is young for her age, having been quietly brought up on her own by her mother; she is only just learning to throw off her childish innocence. She was reading from a French book in my presence when she came across the name of that well-known tree *fouteau*. The woman she has for governess pulled her up short rather rudely and made her jump over that awkward ditch.

Twenty coarse lackeys could not, Montaigne wryly remarked, have taught Léonor more about what lurked beneath '*fouteau*' than a stern injunction to longjump over the word. But for the governess, or the ' old crone ' as her employer more bluntly termed her, the leap was essential because a young woman could not easily combine dignity with a knowledge of what might occur if in a few years' time she found herself in a bedroom with a man.

Montaigne was faulting our conventional portraits for leaving out so much of what we are. It was in part in order to correct this that he wrote his own book. When he retired at the age of thirty-eight, he wished to write, but was unsure what his theme should be.

Only gradually did an idea form in his mind for a book so unusual as to be unlike any of the thousand volumes on the semicircular shelves.

He abandoned millennia of authorial coyness to write about himself. He set out to describe as explicitly as possible the workings of his own mind and body – declaring his intention in the preface to the *Essays*, two volumes of which were published in Bordeaux in 1580, with a third added in a Paris edition eight years later:

> Had I found myself among those peoples who are said still to live under the sweet liberty of Nature's primal laws, I can assure you that I would most willingly have portrayed myself whole, and wholly naked.

No author had hitherto aspired to present himself to his readers without any clothes on. There was no shortage of official, fully clothed portraits, accounts of the lives of saints and popes, Roman emperors and Greek statesmen. There was even an official portrait of Montaigne by Thomas de Leu (1562 – c. 1620), which showed him dressed in the mayoral robes of the city, with the chain of the order of Saint-Michel offered to him by Charles IX in 1571, wearing an inscrutable, somewhat severe expression.

But this robed, Ciceronian self was not what Montaigne wished his *Essays* to reveal. He was concerned with the whole man, with the creation of an alternative to the portraits which had left out most of what man was. It was why his book came to include discussions of his meals, his penis, his stools, his sexual conquests and his farts – details which had seldom featured in a serious book before, so gravely did they flout man's image of himself as a rational creature. Montaigne informed his readers:

> *That the behaviour of his penis constituted an essential part of his identity:*
>
> Every one of my members, each as much as another, makes me myself; and none makes me more properly a man than that

one. I owe to the public my portrait complete.

That he found sex noisy and messy:

Everywhere else you can preserve some decency; all other activities accept the rules of propriety; this other one can only be thought of as flawed or ridiculous. Just try and find a wise and discreet way of doing it!

That he liked quiet when sitting on the toilet:

Of all the natural operations, that is the one during which I least willingly tolerate being disrupted.

And that he was very regular about going:

My bowels and I never fail to keep our rendezvous, which is (unless some urgent business or illness disturbs us) when I jump out of bed.

If we accord importance to the kind of portraits which surround us, it is because we fashion our lives according to their example, accepting aspects of ourselves if they concur with what others mention of themselves. What we see evidence for in others, we will attend to within, what others are silent about, we may stay blind to or experience only in shame.

When I picture to myself the most reflective and the most wise of men in [sexual] postures, I hold it as an effrontery that he should claim to be reflective and wise.

It is not that wisdom is impossible, rather it is the definition of wisdom that Montaigne was seeking to nuance. True wisdom must involve an accommodation with our baser selves, it must adopt a modest view about the role that intelligence and high culture can play in any life and accept the urgent and at times deeply unedifying demands of our mortal frame. Epicurean and Stoic philosophies had suggested that we could achieve mastery over our bodies, and never be swept away by our physical and passionate selves. It is noble advice that taps into our highest aspirations. It is also impossible, and therefore counter-productive:

What is the use of those high philosophical peaks on which no

human being can settle and those rules which exceed our
practice and our power?
It is not very clever of [man] to tailor his obligations to the
standards of a different kind of being.

The body cannot be denied nor overcome, but there is at least, as
Montaigne wished to remind the ' old crone ', no need to choose
between our dignity and an interest in *fouteau*:

May we not say that there is nothing in us during this earthly
prison either purely corporeal or purely spiritual and that it is
injurious to tear a living man apart?

3

On Cultural Inadequacy

Another cause of a sense of inadequacy is the speed and arrogance
with which people seem to divide the world into two camps, the
camp of the *normal* and that of the *abnormal*. Our experiences
and beliefs are liable frequently to be dismissed with a quizzical,
slightly alarmed, ' Really? How weird! ' , accompanied by a
raised eyebrow, amounting in a small way to a denial of our
legitimacy and humanity.

In the summer of 1580, Montaigne acted on the desire of a
lifetime, and made his first journey outside France, setting off on
horseback to Rome via Germany, Austria and Switzerland. He
travelled in the company of four young noblemen, including his
brother, Bertrand de Mattecoulon, and a dozen servants. They
were to be away from home for seventeen months, covering
3,000 miles. Among other towns, the party rode through Basle,
Baden, Schaffhausen, Augsburg, Innsbruck, Verona, Venice,
Padua, Bologna, Florence and Siena − finally reaching Rome
towards evening on the last day of November 1580.

As the party travelled, Montaigne observed how people's ideas of what was normal altered sharply from province to province. In inns in the Swiss cantons, they thought it normal that beds should be raised high off the ground, so that one needed steps to climb into them, that there should be pretty curtains around them and that travellers should have rooms to themselves. A few miles away, in Germany, it was thought normal that beds should be low on the ground, have no curtains around them and that travellers should sleep four to a room. Innkeepers there offered feather quilts rather than the sheets one found in French inns. In Basle, people didn't mix water with their wine and had six or seven courses for dinner, and in Baden they ate only fish on Wednesdays. The smallest Swiss village was guarded by at least two policemen; the Germans rang their bells every quarter of an hour, in certain towns, every minute. In Lindau, they served soup made of quinces, the meat dish came before the soup, and the bread was made with fennel.

French travellers were prone to be very upset by the differences. In hotels, they kept away from sideboards with strange foods, requesting the normal dishes they knew from home. They tried not to talk to anyone who had made the error of not speaking their language, and picked gingerly at the fennel bread. Montaigne watched them from his table:

> Once out of their villages, they feel like fish out of water. Wherever they go they cling to their ways and curse foreign ones. If they come across a fellow-countryman ... they celebrate the event ... With a morose and taciturn prudence they travel about wrapped up in their cloaks and protecting themselves from the contagion of an unknown clime.

In the middle of the fifteenth century, in the southern German states, a new method of heating homes had been developed: the *Kastenofen*, a freestanding box-shaped iron stove made up of rectangular plates bolted together, in which coal or wood could be burnt. In the long winters, the advantages were great. Closed stoves could dispense four times the heat of an open fire, yet demanded less fuel and no chimney-sweeps. The heat was absorbed by the casing and spread slowly and evenly through the air. Poles were fixed around the stoves for airing and drying laundry, and families could use their stoves as seating areas throughout the winter.

But the French were not impressed. They found open fires cheaper to build; they accused German stoves of not providing a source of light and of withdrawing too much moisture from the air, lending an oppressive feeling to a room.

The subject was a matter of regional incomprehension. In Augsburg in October 1580, Montaigne met a German who delivered a lengthy critique of the way French people heated their houses with open fires, and who then went on to adumbrate the advantages of the iron stove. On hearing that Montaigne would be spending only a few days in the town (he had arrived on the 15th and was to leave on the 19th), he expressed pity for him, citing among the chief inconveniences of leaving Augsburg the 'heavy-headedness' he would suffer on returning to open fires – the very same 'heavy-headedness' which the French had long condemned iron stoves for provoking.

Montaigne examined the issue at close quarters. In Baden, he was assigned a room with an iron stove, and once he had grown used to a certain smell it released, spent a comfortable night. He noted that the stove enabled him to dress without putting on a furred gown, and months later, on a cold night in Italy, expressed regret at the absence of stoves in his inn.

On his return home, he weighed up the respective qualities of each heating system:
It is true that the stoves give out an oppressive heat and that the

> materials of which they are built produce a smell when hot
> which causes headaches in those who are not used to them ...
> On the other hand, since the heat they give out is even,
> constant and spread all-over, without the visible flame, smoke
> and the draught produced by our chimneys, it has plenty of
> grounds for standing comparison with ours.

So what annoyed Montaigne were the firm, unexamined convictions of both the Augsburg gentleman and the French that their own system of heating was superior. Had Montaigne returned from Germany and installed in his library an iron stove from Augsburg, his countrymen would have greeted the object with the suspicion they accorded anything new:

> Each nation has many customs and practices which are not only
> unknown to another nation but barbarous and a cause of
> wonder.

When there was of course nothing barbarous nor wondrous about either a stove or a fireplace. The definition of normality proposed by any given society seems to capture only a fraction of what is in fact reasonable, unfairly condemning vast areas of experience to an alien status. By pointing our to the man from Augsburg and his Gascon neighbours that an iron stove and an open fireplace had a legitimate place in the vast realm of acceptable heating systems, Montaigne was attempting to broaden his readers' provincial conception of the normal − and following in the footsteps of his favourite philosopher:

> When they asked Socrates where he came from, he did not say
> 'From Athens', but 'From the world.'

This world had recently revealed itself to be far more peculiar than anyone in Europe had ever expected. On Friday 12 October 1492, forty-one years before Montaigne's birth, Christopher Columbus reached one of the islands on the archipelago of the Bahamas at the entrance of the gulf of Florida, and made contact with some Guanahani Indians, who had never heard of Jesus and walked about without any clothes on.

Montaigne took an avid interest. In the round library were several books on the life of the Indian tribes of America, among them Francisco Lopez de Gomara's *L'histoire générale des Indes*, Girolamo Benzoni's *Historia de mondo novo* and Jean de Léry's *Le voyage au Btésil*. He read that in South America, people liked to eat spiders, grasshoppers, ants, lizards and bats: ' They cook them and serve them up in various sauces. ' There were American tribes in which virgins openly displayed their private parts, brides had orgies on their wedding day, men were allowed to marry each other, and the dead were boiled, pounded into a gruel, mixed with wine and drunk by their relatives at spirited parties. There were countries in which women stood up to pee and men squatted down, in which men let their hair grow on the front of their body, but shaved their back. There were countries in which men were circumcised, while in others, they had a horror of the tip of the penis ever seeing the light of day and so ' scrupulously stretched the foreskin right over it and tied it together with little cords '. There were nations in which you greeted people by turning your back to them, in which when the king spat, the court favourite held out a hand, and when he discharged his bowels, attendants ' gathered up his faeces in a linen cloth '. Every country seemed to have a different conception of beauty:

In Peru, big ears are beautiful: they stretch them as far as they can, artificially. A man still alive today says that he saw in the East a country where this custom of stretching ears and loading them with jewels is held in such esteem that he was often able to thrust his arm, clothes and all, through the holes women pierced in their lobes. Elsewhere there are whole nations which carefully blacken their teeth and loathe seeing white ones. Elsewhere they dye them red ... The women of Mexico count low foreheads as a sign of beauty: so, while they pluck the hair from the rest of their body, there they encourage it to grow thick and propagate it artificially. They hold large breasts in such high esteem that they affect giving suck to their children over their shoulders.

From Jean de Léry, Montaigne learned that the Tupi tribes of Brazil walked around in Edenic nudity, and showed no trace of shame (indeed, when Europeans tried to offer the Tupi women clothes, they giggled and turned them down, puzzled why anyone would burden themselves with anything so uncomfortable).

De Léry's engraver (who had spent eight years with the tribes) took care to correct the rumour rife in Europe that the Tupis were as hairy as animals (de Léry: *'Ils ne sont point naturellement poilus que nous ne sommes en ce pays'*). The men shaved their heads, and the women grew their hair long, and tied it together with pretty red braids. The Tupi Indians loved to wash; any time they saw a river, they would jump into it and rub each other down. They might wash as many as twelve times a day.

They lived in long barn-like structures which slept 200 people. Their beds were woven from cotton and slung between pillars like hammocks (when they went hunting, the Tupis took their beds with them, and had afternoon naps suspended between trees). Every six months, a village would move to a new location, because the inhabitants felt a change of scene would do them good (*'Ils n'ont d'autre réponse, sinon de dire que changeant l'air, ils se portent mieux'* – de Léry). The Tupis' existence was so well ordered, they frequently lived to be a hundred and never had white or grey hair in old age. They were also extremely hospitable. When a newcomer arrived in a village, the women would cover their faces, start crying, and exclaim, 'How are you? You've taken such trouble to come and visit us!' Visitors would immediately be offered the favourite Tupi drink, made from the root of a plant and coloured like claret, which tasted sharp but was good for the stomach.

Tupi men were allowed to take more than one wife, and were said to be devoted to them all. ' Their entire system of ethics contains only the same two articles: resoluteness in battle and love of their wives, ' reported Montaigne. And the wives were apparently happy with the arrangement, showing no jealousy (sexual relations were relaxed, the only prohibition being that one should never sleep with close relatives). Montaigne, with his wife downstairs in the castle, relished the detail:

> One beautiful characteristic of their marriages is worth noting: just as our wives are zealous in thwarting our love and tenderness for other women, theirs are equally zealous in obtaining them for them. Being more concerned for their husband's reputation than for anything else, they take care and trouble to have as many fellow-wives as possible, since that is a testimony to their husband's valour.

It was all undeniably peculiar. Montaigne did not find any of it abnormal.

He was in a minority. Soon after Columbus's discovery, Spanish and Portuguese colonists arrived from Europe to exploit the new lands and decided that the natives were little better than animals. The Catholic knight Villegagnon spoke of them as ' beasts with a human face' (' ce sont des bêtes portant figure humaine') ; the Calvinist minister Richer argued they had no moral sense (' l'hébétude crasse de leur esprit ne distingue pas le bien du mal') ; and the doctor Laurent Joubert, after examining five Brazilian women, asserted that they had no periods and therefore categorically did not belong to the human race.

Having stripped them of their humanity, the Spanish began to slaughter them like animals. By 1534, forty-two years after Columbus's arrival, the Aztec and Inca empires had been destroyed, and their peoples enslaved or murdered. Montaigne read of the barbarism in Bartolomeo Las Casas's *Brevissima Relación de la Destrucción de las Indias* (printed in Seville in

1552, translated into French in 1580 by Jacques de Miggrode as *Tyrannies et cruautés des Espagnols perpétrées es Indes occidentales qu'on dit le Nouveau Monde*). The Indians were undermined by their own hospitality and by the weakness of their arms. They opened their villages and cities to the Spanish, to find their guests turning on them when they were least prepared. Their primitive weapons were no match for Spanish cannons and swords, and the *conquistadores* showed no mercy towards their victims. They killed children, slit open the bellies of pregnant women, gouged out eyes, roasted whole families alive and set fire to villages in the night.

They trained dogs to go into the jungles where the Indians had fled and to tear them to pieces.

Men were sent to work in gold- and silver-mines, chained together by iron collars. When a man died, his body was cut from the chain, while his companions on either side continued working. Most Indians did not last more than three weeks in the mines. Women were raped and disfigured in front of their husbands.

The favoured form of mutilation was to slice chins and noses. Las Casas told how one woman, seeing the Spanish armies advancing with their dogs, hanged herself with her child. A soldier arrived, cut the child in two with his sword, gave one half to his dogs, then asked a friar to administer last rites so that the infant would be assured a place in Christ's heaven.

With men and women separated from each other, desolate and anxious, the Indians committed suicide in large numbers. Between Montaigne's birth in 1533 and the publication of the third book of his *Essays* in 1588, the native population of the New World is estimated to have dropped from 80 to 10 million inhabitants.

The Spanish had butchered the Indians with a clean conscience because they were confident that they knew what a normal human being was. Their reason told them it was someone who wore breeches, had one wife, didn't eat spiders and slept in a bed:

> We could understand nothing of their language; their manners and even their features and clothing were far different from ours. Which of us did not take them for brutes and savages? Which of us did not attribute their silence to dullness and brutish ignorance? After all, they ... were unaware of our hand-kissings and our low and complex bows.

They might have seemed like human beings: ' Ah! But they wear no breeches ... '

Behind the butchery lay messy reasoning. Separating the normal from the abnormal typically proceeds through a form of inductive logic, whereby we infer a general law from particular instances (as logicians would put it, from observing that A1 is ø, A2 is ø and A3 is ø, we come to the view that ' All As are ø'). Seeking to judge whether someone is intelligent, we look for features common to everyone intelligent we have met hitherto. If we met an intelligent person who looked like 1, another who looked like 2, and a third like 3, we are likely to decide that intelligent people read a lot, dress in black and look rather solemn. There is a danger we will dismiss as stupid, and perhaps later kill, someone who looks like 4.

French travellers who reacted in horror to German stoves in their bedrooms would have known a number of good fireplaces in their country before arriving in Germany. One would perhaps have looked like 1, another like 2, a third like 3, and from this they would have concluded that the essence of a good heating system was an open hearth.

Montaigne bemoaned the intellectual arrogance at play. There *were* savages in South America; they were not the ones eating spiders:

> Every man calls barbarous anything he is not accustomed to;
> we have no other criterion of truth or right-reason than the
> example and form of the opinions and customs of our own
> country. There we always find the perfect religion, the perfect
> polity, the most developed and perfect way of doing anything!

He was not attempting to do away with the distinction between
barbarous and civilized; there were differences in value between
the customs of countries (cultural relativism being as crude as
nationalism). He was correcting the way we made the distinction.
Our country might have many virtues, but these did not depend on
it being *our* country. A foreign land might have many faults, but
these could not be identified through the mere fact that its customs
were unusual. Nationality and familiarity were absurd criteria by
which to decide on the good.

French custom had decreed that if one had an impediment in the
nasal passage, one should blow it into a handkerchief. But
Montaigne had a friend who, having reflected on the matter, had
come to the view that it might be better to blow one's nose straight
into one's fingers:

> Defending his action ... he asked me why that filthy mucus
> should be so privileged that we should prepare fine linen to
> receive it and then should wrap it up and carry it carefully
> about on our persons . . . I considered that what he said was not
> totally unreasonable, but habit had prevented me from noticing
> just that strangeness which we find so hideous in similar
> customs in another country.

Careful reasoning rather than prejudice was to be the means of
evaluating behaviour, Montaigne's frustration caused by those
who blithely equated the unfamiliar with the inadequate and so
ignored the most basic lesson in intellectual humility offered by
the greatest of the ancient philosophers:

> The wisest man that ever was, when asked what he knew,
> replied that the one thing he did know was that he knew nothing.

What, then, should we do if we find ourselves facing a veiled suggestion of abnormality manifested in a quizzical, slightly alarmed ' Really? How weird!', accompanied by a raised eyebrow, amounting in its own small way to a denial of legitimacy and humanity − a reaction which Montaigne's friend had encountered in Gascony when he blew his nose into his fingers, and which had, in its most extreme form, led to the devastation of the South American tribes?

Perhaps we should remember the degree to which accusations of abnormality are regionally and historically founded. To loosen their hold on us, we need only expose ourselves to the diversity of customs across time and space. What is considered abnormal in one group at one moment may not, and will not always be deemed so. We may cross borders in our minds.

Montaigne had filled his library with books that helped him cross the borders of prejudice. There were history books, travel journals, the reports of missionaries and sea captains, the literatures of other lands and illustrated volumes with pictures of strangely clad tribes eating fish of unknown names. Through these books, Montaigne could gain legitimacy for parts of himself of which there was no evidence in the vicinity − the Roman parts, the Greek parts, the sides of himself that were more Mexican and Tupi than Gascon, the parts that would have liked to have six wives or have a shaved back or wash twelve times a day; he could feel less alone with these by turning to copies of Tacitus's *Annals*, Gonçalez de Mendoza's history of China, Goulart's history of Portugal, Lebelski's history of Persia, Leo Africanus's travels around Africa, Lusignano's history of Cyprus, Postel's collection of Turkish and oriental histories and Muenster's universal cosmography (which promised pictures of ' animaulx estranges').

If he felt oppressed by the claims made by others to universal truth, he could in a similar way line up the theories of the universe held by all the great ancient philosophers and then witness, despite the confidence of each thinker that he was in possession of the whole truth, the ludicrous divergence that resulted. After such comparative study, Montaigne sarcastically confessed to having no clue whether to accept:

the 'Ideas' of Plato, the atoms of Epicurus, the plenum and vacuum of Leucippus and Democritus, the water of Thales, the infinity of Nature of Anaximander, or the aether of Diogenes, the numbers and symmetry of Pythagoras, the infinity of Parmenides, the Unity of Musaeus, the fire and water of Apollodorus, the homogeneous particles of Anaxagoras, the discord and concord of Empedocles, the fire of Heraclitus, or any other opinion drawn from the boundless confusion of judgement and doctrines produced by our fine human reason, with all its certainty and perspicuity.

The discoveries of new worlds and ancient texts powerfully undermined what Montaigne described as ' that distressing and combative arrogance which has complete faith and trust in itself':

Anyone who made an intelligent collection of the asinine stupidities of human wisdom would have a wondrous tale to tell ... We can judge what we should think of Man, of his sense and of his reason, when we find such obvious and gross errors even in these important characters who have raised human intelligence to great heights.

It also helped to have spent seventeen months journeying around Europe on horseback. Testimony of other countries and ways of life alleviated the oppressive atmosphere of Montaigne's own region. What one society judged to be strange, another might more sensibly welcome as normal.

Other lands may return to us a sense of possibility stamped out by provincial arrogance; they encourage us to grow more acceptable to ourselves. The conception of the normal proposed by any particular province – Athens, Augsburg, Cuzco, Mexico, Rome, Seville, Gascony – has room for only a few aspects of our nature, and unfairly consigns the rest to the barbaric and bizarre. Every man may bear the whole form of the human condition, but it seems that no single country can tolerate the complexity of this condition.

Among the fifty-seven inscriptions that Montaigne had painted on the beams of his library ceiling, was a line from Terence:

Homo sum, humani a me nihil alienum puto.

I am a man, nothing human is foreign to me.

By travelling across frontiers, on horseback and in the imagination, Montaigne invited us to exchange local prejudices and the selfdivision they induced for less constraining identities as citizens of the world.

Another consolation for accusations of abnormality is friendship, a friend being, among other things, someone kind enough to consider more of us normal than most people do. We may share judgements with friends that would in ordinary company be censured for being too caustic, sexual, despairing, daft, clever or vulnerable – friendship a minor conspiracy against what other people think of as reasonable.

Like Epicurus, Montaigne believed friendship to be an essential component of happiness:

In my judgement the sweetness of well-matched and compatible fellowship can never cost too dear. O! a friend! How true is that ancient judgement, that the frequenting of one is more sweet than the element water, more necessary than the element fire.

For a time, he was fortunate enough to know such fellowship. At the age of twenty-five, he was introduced to a twenty-eight-year-old writer and member of the Bordeaux Parlement, Étienne de La Boétie. It was friendship at first sight:

> We were seeking each other before we set eyes on each other
> because of the reports we had heard ... we embraced each
> other by our names. And at our first meeting, which chanced
> to be at a great crowded town-festival, we found ourselves so
> taken with each other, so well acquainted, so bound together,
> that from that time on nothing was so close to us as each other.

The friendship was of a kind, Montaigne believed, that only
occurred once every 300 years; it had nothing in common with the
tepid alliances frequently denoted by the term:

> What we normally call friends and friendships are no more than
> acquaintances and familiar relationships bound by some chance
> or some suitability, by means of which our souls support each
> other. In the friendship which I am talking about, souls are
> mingled and confounded in so universal a blending that they
> efface the seam which joins them together so that it cannot be
> found.

The friendship would not have been so valuable if most people had
not been so disappointing − if Montaigne had not had to hide so
much of himself from them. The depth of his attachment to La
Boétie signalled the extent to which, in his interactions with
others, he had been forced to present only an edited image of
himself to avoid suspicion and raised eyebrows. Many years later,
Montaigne analysed the source of his affections for La Boétie:

Luy seul jouyssoit de ma vraye image.

He alone had the privilege of my true portrait.

That is, La Boétie − uniquely among Montaigne's acquaintances −
understood him properly. He allowed him to be himself; through
his psychological acuity, he enabled him to be so. He offered
scope for valuable and yet until then neglected dimensions of
Montaigne's character − which suggests that we pick our friends
not only because they are kind and enjoyable company, but also,
perhaps more importantly, because they understand us for who we
think we are.

The idyll was painfully brief. Four years after the first meeting, in August 1563, La Boétie fell ill with stomach cramps and died a few days later. The loss was to haunt Montaigne for ever:

> In truth if I compare the rest of my life ... to those four years which I was granted to enjoy the sweet companionship and fellowship of a man like that, it is but smoke and ashes, a night dark and dreary. Since that day when I lost him ... I merely drag wearily on.

Throughout the *Essays*, there were expressions of longing for a soul mate comparable to the dead companion. Eighteen years after La Boétie's death, Montaigne was still visited by periods of grief. In May 1581, in La Villa near Lucca, where he had gone to take the waters, he wrote in his travel journal that he had spent an entire day beset by ' painful thoughts about Monsieur de La Boétie. I was in this mood so long, without recovering, that it did me much harm. '

He was never to be blessed again in his friendships, but he discovered the finest form of compensation. In the *Essays*, he recreated in another medium the true portrait of himself that La Boétie had recognized. He became himself on the page as he had been himself in the company of his friend.

Authorship was prompted by disappointment with those in the vicinity, and yet it was infused with the hope that someone elsewhere would understand; his book an address to everyone and no one in particular. He was aware of the paradox of expressing his deepest self to strangers in bookshops:

> Many things that I would not care to tell any individual man I tell to the public, and for knowledge of my most secret thoughts, I refer my most loyal friends to a bookseller's stall.

And yet we should be grateful for the paradox. Booksellers are the most valuable destination for the lonely, given the numbers of books that were written because authors couldn't find anyone to talk to.

Montaigne might have begun writing to alleviate a personal sense of loneliness, but his book may serve in a small way to alleviate our own. One man's honest, unguarded portrait of himself – in which he mentions impotence and farting, in which he writes of his dead friend and explains that he needs quiet when sitting on the toilet – enables us to feel less singular about sides of ourselves that have gone unmentioned in normal company and normal portraits, but which, it seems, are no less a part of our reality.

4

On Intellectual Inadequacy

There are some leading assumptions about what it takes to be a clever person:

What clever people should know

One of them, reflected in what is taught in many schools and universities, is that clever people should know how to answer questions like:

1. Find the lengths or angles marked x in the following triangles.

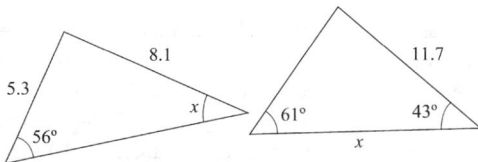

2. What are the subject term, predicate term, copula and quantifiers (if any) in the following sentences: Dogs are man's best friend; Lucilius is wicked; All bats are members of the class of rodents; Nothing green is in the room?

3. What is Thomas Aquinas's First Cause argument?

4. Translate:

Πᾶσα τέχνη καὶ πᾶσα μέθοδος, ὁμοίως δὲ πρᾶξίς τε καὶ προαίρεσις, ἀγαθοῦ τινὸς ἐφίεσθαι δοκεῖ· διὸ καλῶς ἀπεφήναντο τἀγαθὸν οὗ πάντ' ἐφίεται. (διαφορὰ δέ τις φαίνεται τῶν τελῶν· τὰ μὲν γάρ εἰσιν ἐνέργειαι, τὰ δὲ παρ' αὐτὰς ἔργα τινά· ὧν δ' εἰσὶ τέλη τινὰ παρὰ τὰς πράξεις, ἐν τούτοις βελτίω πέφυκε τῶν ἐνεργειῶν τὰ ἔργα.) πολλῶν δὲ πράξεών οὐσῶν καὶ τεχνῶν καὶ ἐπιστημῶν πολλὰ γίνεται καὶ τὰ τέλη· ἰατρικῆς μὲν γὰρ ὑγίεια, ναυπηγικῆς δὲ πλοῖον, στρατηγικῆς δὲ νίκη, οἰκονομικῆς δὲ πλοῦτος.

(Aristotle, *Nicomachean Ethics*, I i – iv)

5. Translate:

> *In capitis mei levitatem iocatus est et in oculorum valitudinem et in crurum gracilitatem et in staturam. Quae contumelia est quod apparet audire? Coram uno aliquid dictum ridemus, coram pluribus indignamur, et eorum aliis libertatem non relinquimus, quae ipsi in nos dicere adsuevimus; iocis temperatis delectamur, immodicis irascimur.*

(Seneca, *De Constantia*, XVI. 4)

Montaigne had faced many such questions and answered them well. He was sent to one of France's best educational establishments, the Collège de Guyenne in Bordeaux, founded in 1533 to replace the city's old and inadequate Collège des Arts. By the time Michel started attending classes there at the age of six, the school had developed a national reputation as a centre of learning. The staff included an enlightened principal, André de Gouvéa, a renowned Greek scholar, Nicolas de Grouchy, an Aristotelian scholar, Guillaume Guerente, and the Scottish poet George Buchanan.

If one tries to define the philosophy of education underpinning the Collège de Guyenne, or indeed that of most schools and universities before and after it, one might loosely suggest it to be based on the idea that the more a student learns about the world (history, science, literature), the better. But Montaigne, after following the curriculum at the Collège dutifully until graduation, added an important proviso:

If man were wise, he would gauge the true worth of anything
by its usefulness and appropriateness to his life.

Only that which makes us feel better may be worth understanding.

Two great thinkers of antiquity were likely to have featured prominently in the curriculum at the Collège de Guyenne and been held up as exemplars of intelligence. Students would have been introduced to Aristotle's *Prior* and *Posterior Analytics*, in which the Greek philosopher pioneered logic, and stated that if A is predicated of every B, and B of every C, necessarily A is predicated of every C. Aristotle argued that if a proposition says or denies P of S, then S and P are its terms, with P being the predicate term and S the subject term, and added that all propositions are either universal or particular, affirming or denying P of every S or part of S. Then there was the Roman scholar Marcus Terentius Varro, who assembled a library for Julius Caesar and wrote six hundred books, including an encyclopedia on the liberal arts and twenty-five books on etymology and linguistics.

Montaigne was not unmoved. It is a feat to write a shelf of books on the origins of words and to discover universal affirmatives. And yet if we were to find that those who did so were no happier or were indeed a little more unhappy than those who had never heard of philosophical logic, we might wonder. Montaigne considered the lives of Aristotle and Varro, and raised a question:

What good did their great erudition do for Varro and Aristotle?

Did it free them from human ills? Did it relieve them of misfortunes such as befall a common porter? Could logic console them for the gout … ?

To understand why the two men could have been both so erudite and so unhappy, Montaigne distinguished between two categories of knowledge: *learning* and *wisdom*. In the category of learning he placed, among other subjects, logic, etymology, grammar, Latin and Greek. And in the category of wisdom, he placed a far broader, more elusive and more valuable kind of knowledge, everything that could help a person to live well, by which Montaigne meant, help them to live happily and morally.

The problem with the Collège de Guyenne, despite its professional staff and principal, was that it excelled at imparting learning but failed entirely at imparting wisdom − repeating at an institutional level the errors that had marred the personal lives of Varro and Aristotle:

I gladly come back to the theme of the absurdity of our education: its end has not been to make us good and wise, but learned. And it has succeeded. It has not taught us to seek virtue and to embrace wisdom: it has impressed upon us their derivation and their etymology …

We readily inquire, 'Does he know Greek or Latin?' 'Can he write poetry and prose?' But what matters most is what we put last: 'Has he become better and wiser?' We ought to find out not who understands *most* but who understands *best*. We work merely to fill the memory, leaving the understanding and the sense of right and wrong empty.

He had never been good at sport: ' At dancing, tennis and wrestling I have not been able to acquire more than a slight, vulgar skill; and at swimming, fencing, vaulting and jumping, no skill at all. ' Nevertheless, so strong was Montaigne's objection to the lack of wisdom imparted by most schoolteachers, that he did not shrink from suggesting a drastic alternative to the classroom for the youth of France.

He would of course have preferred students to go to school, but schools that taught them wisdom rather than the etymology of the word and could correct the long-standing intellectual bias towards abstract questions. Thales from Miletus in Asia Minor was an early example of the bias, celebrated throughout the ages for having in the sixth century BC tried to measure the heavens and for having determined the height of the Great Pyramid of Egypt according to the theorem of similar triangles – a complicated and dazzling achievement, no doubt, but not what Montaigne wished to see dominate his curriculum. He had greater sympathy with the implicit educational philosophy of one of Thales's impudent young acquaintances:

> I have always felt grateful to that girl from Miletus who, seeing the local philosopher ... with his eyes staring upwards, constantly occupied in contemplating the vault of heaven, tripped him up, to warn him that there was time enough to occupy his thoughts with things above the clouds when he had accounted for everything lying before his feet ... You can make exactly the same reproach as that woman made against Thales against anyone concerned with philosophy: he fails to see what lies before his feet.

Montaigne noted in other areas a similar tendency to privilege extraordinary activities over humbler but no less important ones – and just like the girl from Miletus, tried to bring us back to earth:

> Storming a breach, conducting an embassy, ruling a nation are glittering deeds. Rebuking, laughing, buying, selling, loving, hating and living together gently and justly with your household – and with yourself – not getting slack nor being false to yourself, is something more remarkable, more rare and more difficult. Whatever people may say, such secluded lives sustain in that way duties which are at least as hard and as tense as those of other lives.

So what would Montaigne have wished pupils to learn at school?
What kind of examinations could have tested for the wise
intelligence he had in mind, one so far removed from the mental
skills of the unhappy Aristotle and Varro?

The examinations would have raised questions about the
challenges of quotidian life: love, sex, illness, death, children,
money and ambition.

An examination in Montaignean wisdom

1. About seven or eight years ago, some two leagues from here, there
   was a villager, who is still alive; his brain had long been battered
   by his wife's jealousy; one day he came home from work to be
   welcomed by her usual nagging; it made him so mad that, taking
   the sickle he still had in his hand he suddenly lopped off the
   members which put her into such a fever and chucked them in her
   face. (*Essays*, II. 29)
   a) How should one settle domestic disputes?
   b) Was the wife nagging or expressing affection?

2. Consider these two quotations:
   I want death to find me planting my cabbages, neither worrying
   about it nor the unfinished gardening. (*Essays*, I. 20)
   I can scarcely tell my cabbages from my lettuces. (*Essays*, II. 17)
   What is a wise approach to death?

3. It is perhaps a more chaste and fruitful practice to bring women to
   learn early what the living reality [of penis size] is rather than to
   allow them to make conjectures according to the licence of a heated
   imagination: instead of our organs as they are, their hopes and
   desires lead them to substitute extravagant ones three times as big .
   .. What great harm is done by those graffiti of enormous genitals
   which boys scatter over the corridors and staircases of our royal
   palaces! From them arises a cruel misunderstanding of our natural
   capacities. (*Essays*, III. 5)
   How should a man with a small 'living reality' bring up the

subject?

4. I know of a squire who had entertained a goodly company in his
   hall and then, four or five days later, boasted as a joke (for there
   was no truth in it) that he had made them eat cat pie; one of the
   young ladies in the party was struck with such a horror at this that
   she collapsed with a serious stomach disorder and a fever: it was
   impossible to save her. (*Essays*, I. 21)

   Analyse the distribution of moral responsibility.

5. If only talking to oneself did not look mad, no day would go by
   without my being heard growling to myself, against myself, ' You
   silly shit!' (*Essays*, I. 38)

   The most uncouth of our afflictions is to despise our being.
   (*Essays*, III. 13)

   How much love should one have for oneself?

Setting people examination papers measuring wisdom rather than
learning would probably result in an immediate realignment of the
hierarchy of intelligence – and a surprising new élite. Montaigne
delighted in the prospect of the incongruous people who would
now be recognized as cleverer than the lauded but often unworthy
traditional candidates.

What clever people should sound and look like

It is common to assume that we are dealing with a highly
intelligent book when we cease to understand it. Profound ideas
cannot, after all, be explained in the language of children. Yet
the association between difficulty and profundity might less
generously be described as a manifestation in the literary sphere of
a perversity familiar from emotional life, where people who are
mysterious and elusive can inspire a respect in modest minds that
reliable and clear ones do not.

Montaigne had no qualms bluntly admitting his problem with
mysterious books. ' I cannot have lengthy commerce with

[them] , ' he wrote, ' I only like pleasurable, easy [ones] which tickle my interest. '

> I am not prepared to bash my brains for anything, not even for learning's sake, however precious it may be. From books all I seek is to give myself pleasure by an honourable pastime ... If I come across difficult passages in my reading I never bite my nails over them: after making a charge or two I let them be ... If one book wearies me I take up another.

Which was nonsense, or rather playful posturing on the part of a man with a thousand volumes on his shelf and an encyclopedic knowledge of Greek and Latin philosophy. If Montaigne enjoyed presenting himself as a dim gentleman prone to somnolence during philosophical expositions, it was disingenuousness with a purpose. The repeated declarations of laziness and slowness were tactical ways to undermine a corrupt understanding of intelligence and good writing.

There are, so Montaigne implied, no legitimate reasons why books in the humanities should be difficult or boring; wisdom does not require a specialized vocabulary or syntax, nor does an audience benefit from being wearied. Carefully used, boredom can be a valuable indicator of the merit of books. Though it can never be a sufficient judge (and in its more degenerate forms, slips into wilful indifference and impatience) , taking our levels of boredom into account can temper an otherwise excessive tolerance for balderdash. Those who do not listen to their boredom when reading, like those who pay no attention to pain, may be increasing their suffering unnecessarily. Whatever the dangers of being wrongly bored, there are as many pitfalls in never allowing ourselves to lose patience with our reading matter.

Every difficult work presents us with a choice of whether to judge the author inept for not being clear, or ourselves stupid for not grasping what is going on. Montaigne encouraged us to blame the author. An incomprehensible prose-style is likely to have resulted more from laziness than cleverness; what reads easily is rarely so written. Or else such prose masks an absence of content; being incomprehensible offers unparalleled protection against having nothing to say:

> Difficulty is a coin which the learned conjure with so as not to reveal the vanity of their studies and which human stupidity is keen to accept in payment.

There is no reason for philosophers to use words that would sound out of place in a street or market:

> Just as in dress it is the sign of a petty mind to seek to draw attention by some personal or unusual fashion, so too in speech; the search for new expressions and little-known words derives from an adolescent schoolmasterish ambition. If only I could limit myself to words used in Les Halles in Paris.

But writing with simplicity requires courage, for there is a danger that one will be overlooked, dismissed as simpleminded by those with a tenacious belief that impassable prose is a hallmark of intelligence. So strong is this bias, Montaigne wondered whether the majority of university scholars would have appreciated Socrates, a man they professed to revere above all others, if he had approached them in their own towns, devoid of the prestige of Plato's dialogues, in his dirty cloak, speaking in plain language:

> The portrait of the conversations of Socrates which his friends have bequeathed to us receives our approbation only because we are overawed by the general approval of them. It is not from our own knowledge; since they do not follow our practices: if something like them were to be produced nowadays there are few who would rate them highly. We can appreciate no graces which are not pointed, inflated and magnified by artifice. Such graces as flow on under the name of naivety and simplicity readily go unseen by so coarse an insight as ours ... For us, is not naivety close kin to

simplemindedness and a quality worthy of reproach? Socrates makes his soul move with the natural motion of the common people: thus speaks a peasant; thus speaks a woman ... His inductions and comparisons are drawn from the most ordinary and bestknown of men's activities; anyone can understand him. Under so common a form we today would never have discerned the nobility and splendour of his astonishing concepts; we who judge any which are not swollen up by erudition to be base and commonplace and who are never aware of riches except when pompously paraded.

It is a plea to take books seriously, even when their language is unintimidating and their ideas clear – and, by extension, to refrain from considering ourselves as fools if, because of a hole in our budget or our education, our cloaks are simple and our vocabulary no larger than that of a stallholder in Les Halles.

What clever people should know

They should know the facts, and if they do not and if they have in addition been so foolish as to get these wrong in a book, they should expect no mercy from scholars, who will be justified in slapping them down, and pointing out, with supercilious civility, that a date is wrong or a word misquoted, a passage is out of context or an important source forgotten.

Yet in Montaigne's schema of intelligence, what matters in a book is usefulness and appropriateness to life; it is less valuable to convey with precision what Plato wrote or Epicurus meant than to judge whether what they have said is interesting and could in the early hours help us over anxiety or loneliness. The responsibility of authors in the humanities is not to quasi-scientific accuracy, but to happiness and health. Montaigne vented his irritation with those who refused the point:

The scholars whose concern it is to pass judgement on books recognize no worth but that of learning and allow no intellectual activity other than that of scholarship and erudition. Mistake one Scipio for the other, and you have nothing left worth saying, have you! According to them, fail to know your Aristotle and you fail to know yourself.

The *Essays* were themselves marked by frequent misquotations, misattributions, illogical swerves of argument and a failure to define terms. The author wasn't bothered:

> I do my writing at home, deep in the country, where nobody can help or correct me and where I normally never frequent anybody who knows even the Latin of the Lord's prayer let alone proper French.

Naturally there were errors in the book ('I am full of them,' he boasted), but they weren't enough to doom the *Essays*, just as accuracy could not ensure their worth. It was a greater sin to write something which did not attempt to be wise than to confuse Scipio Aemilianus (*c.* 185—129 BC) with Scipio Africanus (236—183 BC).

Where clever people should get their ideas from

From people even cleverer than they are. They should spend their time quoting and producing commentaries about great authorities who occupy the upper rungs of the tree of knowledge. They should write treatises on the moral thought of Plato or the ethics of Cicero.

Montaigne owed much to the idea. There were frequent passages of commentary in the *Essays*, and hundreds of quotations from authors who Montaigne felt had captured points more elegantly and more acutely than he was able to. He quoted Plato 128 times, Lucretius 149 and Seneca 130.

It is tempting to quote authors when they express our very own thoughts but with a clarity and psychological accuracy we cannot match. They know us better than we know ourselves. What is shy and confused in us is succinctly and elegantly phrased in them, our pencil lines and annotations in the margins of their books and our borrowings from them indicating where we find a piece of ourselves, a sentence or two built of the very substance of which our own minds are made — a congruence all the more striking if the work was written in an age of togas and animal sacrifices. We invite these words into our books as a homage for reminding us of who we are.

But rather than illuminating our experiences and goading us on to our own discoveries, great books may come to cast a problematic shadow. They may lead us to dismiss aspects of our lives of which there is no printed testimony. Far from expanding our horizons, they may unjustly come to mark their limits. Montaigne knew one man who seemed to have bought his bibliophilia too dearly:

> Whenever I ask [this] acquaintance of mine to tell me what he knows about something, he wants to show me a book: he would not venture to tell me that he has scabs on his arse without studying his lexicon to find out the meanings of *scab* and *arse*.

Such reluctance to trust our own, extra-literary, experiences might not be grievous if books could be relied upon to express all our potentialities, if they knew all our scabs. But as Montaigne recognized, the great books are silent on too many themes, so that if we allow them to define the boundaries of our curiosity, they will hold back the development of our minds. A meeting in Italy crystallized the issue:

> In Pisa I met a decent man who is such an Aristotelian that the most basic of his doctrines is that the touchstone and the measuring-scale of all sound ideas and of each and every truth must lie in conformity with the teachings of Aristotle, outside of which all is inane and chimerical: Aristotle has seen everything, done everything.

He had, of course, done and seen a lot. Of all the thinkers of antiquity, Aristotle was perhaps the most comprehensive, his works ranging over the landscape of knowledge (*On Generation and Corruption*, *On the Heavens*, *Meteorology*, *On the Soul*, *Parts of Animals*, *Movements of Animals*, *Sophistical Refutations*, *Nicomachean Ethics*, *Physics*, *Politics*).

But the very scale of Aristotle's achievement bequeathed a problematic legacy. There are authors too clever for our own good. Having said so much, they appear to have had the last word. Their genius inhibits the sense of irreverence vital to creative work in their successors. Aristotle may, paradoxically, prevent those who most respect him from behaving like him. He rose to greatne only by doubting much of the knowledge that had been built up before him, not by refusing to read Plato or Heraclitus, but by mounting a salient critique of some of their weaknesses based on an appreciation of their strengths. To act in a truly Aristotelian spirit, as Montaigne realized and the man from Pisa did not, may mean allowing for some intelligent departures from even the most accomplished authorities.

Yet it is understandable to prefer to quote and write commentaries rather than speak and think for ourselves. A commentary on a book written by someone else, though technically laborious to produce, requiring hours of research and exegesis, is immune from the most cruel attacks that can befall original works. Commentators may be criticized for failing to do justice to the ideas of great thinkers; they cannot be held responsible for the ideas themselves — which was a reason why Montaigne included so many quotations and passages of commentary in the *Essays*:

> I sometimes get others to say what I cannot put so well myself because of the weakness of my language, and sometimes because of the weakness of my intellect ... [*and*] *sometimes ... to rein in the temerity of those hasty criticisms which leap to attack writings of every kind, especially recent writings by men still alive ... I have to hide my weaknesses beneath those great*

reputations.

It is striking how much more seriously we are likely to be taken after we have been dead a few centuries. Statements which might be acceptable when they issue from the quills of ancient authors are likely to attract ridicule when expressed by contemporaries. Critics are not inclined to bow before the grander pronouncements of those with whom they attended university. It is not these individuals who will be allowed to speak *as though they were ancient philosophers.* ' No man has escaped paying the penalty for being born, ' wrote Seneca, but a man struck by a similar sentiment in later ages would not be advised to speak like this unless he manifested a particular appetite for humiliation. Montaigne, who did not, took shelter, and at the end of the *Essays*, made a confession, touching for its vulnerability:

> If I had had confidence to do what I really wanted, I would
> have spoken utterly alone, come what may.

If he lacked confidence, it was because the closer one came to him in time and place, the less his thoughts were likely to be treated as though they might be as valid as those of Seneca and Plato:

> In my own climate of Gascony, they find it funny to see me in
> print. I am valued the more the farther from home knowledge
> of me has spread.

In the behaviour of his family and staff, those who heard him snoring or changed the bedlinen, there was none of the reverence of his Parisian reception, let alone his posthumous one:

> A man may appear to the world as a marvel: yet his wife and
> his manservant see nothing remarkable about him. Few men
> have been wonders to their families.

We may take this in two ways: that no one is genuinely marvellous, but that only families and staff are close enough to discern the disappointing truth. Or that many people are interesting, but that if they are too close to us in age and place, we are likely not to take them too seriously, on account of a curious bias against what is at hand.

Montaigne was not pitying himself; rather, he was using the criticism of more ambitious contemporary works as a symptom of a deleterious impulse to think that the truth always has to lie far from us, in another climate, in an ancient library, in the books of people who lived long ago. It is a question of whether access to genuinely valuable things is limited to a handful of geniuses born between the construction of the Parthenon and the sack of Rome, or whether, as Montaigne daringly proposed, they may be open to you and me as well.

A highly peculiar source of wisdom was being pointed out, more peculiar still than Pyrrho's seafaring pig, a Tupi Indian or a Gascon ploughman: the reader. If we attend properly to our experiences and learn to consider ourselves plausible candidates for an intellectual life, it is, implied Montaigne, open to all of us to arrive at insights no less profound than those in the great ancient books.

The thought is not easy. We are educated to associate virtue with submission to textual authorities, rather than with an exploration of the volumes daily transcribed within ourselves by our perceptual mechanisms. Montaigne tried to return us to ourselves:

> We know how to say, ' This is what Cicero said ' ; ' This is morality for Plato ' ; ' These are the *ipsissima verba* of Aristotle. ' But what have we got to say? What judgements do we make? What are we doing? A parrot could talk as well as we do.

Parroting wouldn't be the scholar's way of describing what it takes to write a commentary. A range of arguments could show the value of producing an exegesis on the moral thought of Plato or the ethics of Cicero. Montaigne emphasized the cowardice and tedium in the activity instead. There is little skill in secondary works (' Invention takes incomparably higher precedence over quotation '), the difficulty is technical, a matter of patience and a quiet library. Furthermore, many of the books which academic tradition encourages us to parrot are not fascinating in themselves. They are accorded a central place in the syllabus because they are the work of prestigious authors, while many equally or far more valid themes languish because no grand intellectual authority ever elucidated them. The relation of art to reality has long been considered a serious philosophical topic, in part because Plato first raised it; the relation of shyness to personal appearance has not, in part because it did not attract the attention of any ancient philosopher.

In light of this unnatural respect for tradition, Montaigne thought it worth while to admit to his readers that, in truth, he thought Plato could be limited and dull:

> Will the licence of our age excuse my audacious sacrilege in thinking that [his] *Dialogues* drag slowly along stifling his matter, and in lamenting the time spent on those long useless preparatory discussions by a man who had so many better things to say?

(A relief to come upon this thought in Montaigne, one prestigious writer lending credence to timid, silent suspicions of another.) As for Cicero, there was no need even to apologize before attacking:

> His introductory passages, his definitions, his sub-divisions and his etymologies eat up most of his work ... If I spend an hour reading him (which is a lot for me) and then recall what pith and substance I have got out of him, most of the time I find nothing but wind.

If scholars paid such attention to the classics, it was, suggested Montaigne, from a vainglorious wish to be thought intelligent through association with prestigious names. The result for the reading public was a mountain of very learned, very unwise books:

> There are more books on books than on any other subject: all we do is gloss each other. All is a-swarm with commentaries:

of authors there is a dearth.

But interesting ideas are, Montaigne insisted, to be found in every life. However modest our stories, we can derive greater insights from ourselves than from all the books of old:

> Were I a good scholar, I would find enough in my own experience to make me wise. Whoever recalls to mind his last bout of anger ... sees the ugliness of this passion better than in Aristotle. Anyone who recalls the ills he has undergone, those which have threatened him and the trivial incidents which have moved him from one condition to another, makes himself thereby ready for future mutations and the exploring of his condition. Even the life of Caesar is less exemplary for us than our own; a life whether imperial or plebeian is always a life affected by everything that can happen to a man.

Only an intimidating scholarly culture makes us think otherwise:

> We are richer than we think, each one of us.

We may all arrive at wise ideas if we cease to think of ourselves as so unsuited to the task because we aren't 2,000 years old, aren't interested in Plato's dialogues and live quietly in the country:

> You can attach the whole of moral philosophy to a commonplace private life just as well as to one of richer stuff.

It was perhaps to bring the point home that Montaigne offered so much information on exactly how commonplace and private his own life had been – why he wanted to tell us:

> *That he didn't like apples:*
> I am not overfond ... of any fruit except melons.
> *That he had a complex relationship with radishes:*
> I first of all found that radishes agreed with me; then they did not; now they do again.
> *That he practised the most advanced dental hygiene:*
> My teeth ... have always been exceedingly good ... Since boyhood I learned to rub them on my napkin, both on waking up and before and after meals.

That he ate too fast:
In my haste I often bite my tongue and occasionally my fingers.

And liked wiping his mouth:
I could dine easily enough without a tablecloth, but I feel very uncomfortable dining without a clean napkin ... I regret that we have not continued along the lines of the fashion started by our kings, changing napkins likes plates with each course.

Trivia, perhaps, but symbolic reminders that there was a thinking 'I' behind his book, that a moral philosophy had issued − and so could issue again − from an ordinary, fruit-resistant soul.

There is no need to be discouraged if, from the outside, we look nothing like those who have ruminated in the past.

In Montaigne's redrawn portrait of the adequate, semi-rational human being, it is possible to speak no Greek, fart, change one's mind after a meal, get bored with books, know none of the ancient philosophers and mistake Scipios.

A virtuous, ordinary life, striving for wisdom but never far from folly, is achievement enough.

V Consolation for a Broken Heart

1

For the griefs of love, he may be the finest among philosophers:

1788 Arthur Schopenhauer is born in Danzig. In later years, he looks back on the event with regret: ' We can regard our life as a uselessly disturbing episode in the blissful repose of nothingness. '

' Human existence must be a kind of error, ' he specifies, ' it may be said of it, " It is bad today and every day it will get worse, until the worst of all happens. " ' Schopenhauer's father Heinrich, a wealthy merchant, and his mother Johanna, a dizzy socialite twenty years her husband's junior, take little interest in their son, who grows into one of the greatest pessimists in the history of philosophy: ' Even as a child of six, my parents, returning from a walk one evening, found me in deep despair. '

1803—5 After the apparent suicide of his father (discovered floating in a canal beside the family Warehouse), the seventeen-year-old Schopenhauer is left with a fortune that ensures he will never have to work. The thought affords no comfort. He later recalls: ' In my seventeenth year, without any learned school education, I was gripped by the *misery of life* as Buddha was in his youth when he saw sickness, old age, pain and death. The truth ... was that this world could not have been the work of an all-loving Being, but rather that of a devil, who had brought creatures into existence in order to delight in the sight of their sufferings; to this the data pointed, and the belief that it is so won the upper hand. '

Schopenhauer is sent to London to learn English at a boarding-school, Eagle House in Wimbledon. After receiving a letter from him, his friend Lorenz Meyer replies, ' I am sorry that your stay in England has induced you to hate the entire *nation*. ' Despite the hatred, he acquires an almost perfect command of the language, and is often mistaken for an Englishman in conversation.

Schopenhauer travels through France, he visits the city of Nîmes, to which, 1,800 or so years before, Roman engineers had piped water across the majestic Pont du Gard to ensure that citizens would always have enough water to bathe in. Schopenhauer is unimpressed by what he sees of the Roman remains: 'These traces soon lead one's thoughts to the thousands of long-decomposed humans.'

Schopenhauer's mother complains of her son's passion for 'pondering on human misery'.

1809—1811 Schopenhauer studies at the university of Göttingen and decides to become a philosopher: 'Life is a sorry business, I have resolved to spend it reflecting upon it.'

On an excursion to the countryside, a male friend suggests they should attempt to meet women. Schopenhauer quashes the plan, arguing that 'life is so short, questionable and evanescent that it is not worth the trouble of major effort.'

1813 He visits his mother in Weimar. Johanna Schopenhauer has befriended the town's most famous resident, Johann Wolfgang von Goethe, who visits her regularly (and likes talking with Sophie, Johanna's housemaid, and Adele, Arthur's younger sister). After an initial meeting, Schopenhauer describes Goethe as 'serene, sociable, obliging, friendly: praised be his name for ever and ever!' Goethe reports, 'Young Schopenhauer appeared to me to be a strange and interesting young man.' Arthur's feelings for the writer are never wholly reciprocated. When the philosopher leaves Weimar, Goethe composes a couplet for him:

> *Willst du dich des Lebens freuen,*
> *So musst der Welt du Werth verleihen.*
> If you wish to draw pleasure out of life,
> You must attach value to the world.

Schopenhauer is unimpressed, and in his notebook beside Goethe's tip, appends a quotation from Chamfort: '*Il vaut mieux laisser les hommes pour ce qu'ils sont, que les prendre pour ce qu'ils ne sont pas.* ' (Better to accept men for what they are, than to take them to be What they are not.)

1814—15   Schopenhauer moves to Dresden and writes a thesis (*On the Fourfold Root of the Principle of Sufficient Reason*). He has few friends and enters into conversations with reduced expectations: ' Sometimes I speak to men and women just as a little girl speaks to her doll. She knows, of course, that the doll does not understand her, but she creates for herself the joy of communication through a pleasant and conscious self-deception. '
He becomes a regular in an Italian tavern which serves his favourite meats – Venetian salami, truffled sausage and Parma ham.

1818   He finishes *The World as Will and Representation*, which he knows to be a masterpiece. It explains his lack of friends: ' A man of genius can hardly be sociable, for what dialogues could indeed be so intelligent and entertaining as his own monologues? '

1818—19   To celebrate the completion of his book, Schopenhauer travels to Italy. He delights in art, nature and the climate, though his mood remains fragile: ' We should always be mindful of the fact that no man is ever very far from the state in which he would readily want to seize a sword or poison in order to bring his existence to an end; and those who are far from believing this could easily be convinced of the opposite by an accident, an illness, a violent change of fortune – or of the weather. ' He visits Florence, Rome, Naples and Venice and meets a number of attractive women at receptions: ' I was very fond of them – if only they would have had me. ' Rejection helps to inspire a view that.
' Only the male intellect, clouded by the sexual impulse, could call the undersized, narrow-shouldered, broad-hipped, and short-legged sex the fair sex. '

1819   *The World as Will and Representation* is published. It sells 230 copies. ' Every life history is a history of suffering ' ; ' If only I could get rid of the illusion of regarding the generation of vipers and toads as my equals, it would be a great help to me. '

1820 Schopenhauer attempts to gain a university post in philosophy in Berlin. He offers lectures on ' The whole of philosophy, i. e. the theory of the essence of the world and of the human mind. ' Five students attend. In a nearby building, his rival, Hegel, can be heard lecturing to an audience of 300. Schopenhauer assesses Hegel's philosophy: ' [I] ts fundamental ideas are the absurdest fancy, a world turned upside down, a philosophical buffoonery ... its contents being the hollowest and most senseless display of words ever lapped up by blockheads, and its presentation ... being the most repulsive and nonsensical gibberish, recalling the rantings of a bedlamite. ' The beginnings of disenchantment with academia: ' That one can be serious about philosophy has as a rule not occurred to anyone, least of all to a lecturer on philosophy, just as no one as a rule believes less in Christianity than does the Pope. '

1821 Schopenhauer falls in love with Caroline Medon, a nineteen-year-old singer. The relationship lasts intermittently for ten years, but Schopenhauer has no wish to formalize the arrangement: ' To marry means to do everything possible to become an object of disgust to each other. ' He nevertheless has fond thoughts of polygamy: ' Of the many advantages of polygamy, one is that the husband would not come into such close contact with his in-laws, the fear of which at present prevents innumerable marriages. Ten mothers-in-law instead of one! '

1822 Travels to Italy for a second time (Milan, Florence, Venice). Before setting out, he asks his friend Friedrich Osann to look out for ' any mention of me in books, journals, literary periodicals and such like. ' Osann does not find the task time-consuming.

1825 Having failed as an academic, Schopenhauer attempts to become a translator. But his offers to turn Kant into English and

Tristram Shandy into German are rejected by publishers. He confides in a letter a melancholy wish to have ' a position in bourgeois society ', though will never attain one. ' If a God has made this world, then I would not like to be the God; its misery and distress would break my heart. ' Fortunately, he can rely on a comfortable sense of his own worth in darker moments: ' How often must I learn ... that in the affairs of everyday life ... my spirit and mind are what a telescope is in an opera-house or a cannon at a harehunt?'

1828 Turns forty. ' After his fortieth year, ' he consoles himself, ' any man of merit ... will hardly be free from a certain touch of misanthropy. '

1831 Now forty-three, living in Berlin, Schopenhauer thinks once again of getting married. He turns his attentions to Flora Weiss, a beautiful, spirited girl who has just turned seventeen. During a boating party, in an attempt to charm her, he smiles and offers her a bunch of white grapes. Flora later confides in her diary: ' I didn't want them. I felt revolted because old Schopenhauer had touched them, and so I let them slide, quite gently, into the water behind me. ' Schopenhauer leaves Berlin in a hurry: ' Life has no genuine intrinsic worth, but is kept in motion merely by want and illusion. '

1833 He settles in a modest apartment in Frankfurt am Main, a town of some 50,000 inhabitants. He describes the city, the banking centre of continental Europe, as ' a small, stiff, internally crude, municipally puffed-up, peasant-proud nation of Abderites, whom I do not like to approach '.

His closest relationships are now with a succession of poodles, who he feels have a gentleness and humility humans lack: ' The sight of any animal immediately gives me pleasure and gladdens my heart. ' He lavishes affection on these poodles, addressing them as ' Sir ', and takes a keen interest in animal welfare: ' The highly intelligent dog, man's truest and most faithful friend, is put on a chain by him! Never do I see such a dog without feelings of the deepest sympathy for him and of profound indignation against his master. I think with satisfaction of a case, reported some years ago in *The Times*, where Lord X kept a large dog on a chain. One day as he was walking through the yard, he took it into his head to go and pat the dog, whereupon the animal tore his arm open from top to bottom, and quite right, too! What he meant by this was: "You are not my master, but my devil who makes a hell of my brief existence!" May this happen to all who chain up dogs. '

The philosopher adopts a rigid daily routine. He writes for three hours in the morning, plays the flute (Rossini) for an hour, then dresses in white tie for lunch in the Englischer Hof on the Rossmarkt. He has an enormous appetite, and tucks a large white napkin into his collar. He refuses to acknowledge other diners when eating, but occasionally enters into conversation over coffee. One of them describes him as 'comically disgruntled, but in fact harmless and good-naturedly gruff'.

Another reports that Schopenhauer frequently boasts of the excellent condition of his teeth as evidence that he is superior to other people, or as he puts it, superior to the 'common biped'.

After lunch, Schopenhauer retires to the library of his club, the nearby Casino Society, where he reads *The Times* – the newspaper which he feels will best inform him of the miseries of the world. In mid-afternoon, he takes a two-hour walk with his dog along the banks of the Main, muttering under his breath. In the evening, he visits the opera or the theatre, where he is often enraged by the noise of late-comers, shufflers and coughers – and writes to the authorities urging strict measures against them. Though he has read and much admires Seneca, he does not agree with the Roman philosopher's verdict on noise: 'I have for a long time been of the opinion that the quantity of noise anyone can comfortably endure is in inverse proportion to his mental powers ... The man who habitually slams doors instead of shutting them with the hand ... is not merely ill-mannered, but also coarse and narrow-minded ... We shall be quite civilized only when ... it is no longer anyone's right to cut through the consciousness of every thinking being ... by means of whistling, howling, bellowing, hammering, whipcracking ... and so on. '

1840 He acquires a new white poodle and names her Atma, after the world-soul of the Brahmins. He is attracted to Eastern religions in general and Brahmanism in particular (he reads a few pages of the Upanishads every night). He describes Brahmins as, ' the noblest and oldest of people ', and threatens to sack his cleaning lady, Margaretha Schnepp, when she disregards orders not to dust the Buddha in his study.

He spends increasing amounts of time alone. His mother worries about him: ' Two months in your room without seeing a single person, that is not good, my son, and saddens me, a man cannot and should not isolate himself in that manner. ' He takes to sleeping for extended periods during the day: ' If life and existence were an enjoyable state, then everyone would reluctantly approach the unconscious state of sleep and would gladly rise from it again. But the very opposite is the case, for everyone very willingly goes to sleep and unwillingly gets up again. ' He justifies his appetite for sleep by comparing himself to two of his favourite thinkers: ' Human beings require more sleep the more developed ... and the more active their brain is. Montaigne relates of himself that he had always been a heavy sleeper; that he had spent a large part of his life in sleeping; and that at an advanced age he still slept from eight to nine hours at a stretch. It is also reported of Descartes that he slept a great deal. '

1843 Schopenhauer moves to a new house in Frankfurt, number 17 Schöne Aussicht, near the river Main in the centre of town (English translation: Pretty view). He is to live in the street for the rest of his life, though in 1859, he moves to number 16 after a quarrel with his landlord over his dog.

1844 He publishes a second edition and a further volume of *The World as Will and Representation*. He remarks in the preface: 'Not to my contemporaries or my compatriots, but to mankind I consign my now complete work, confident that it will not be without value to humanity, even if this value should be recognized only tardily, as is the inevitable fate of the good in whatever form.' The work sells under 300 copies: 'Our greatest pleasure consists in being admired; but the admirers, even if there is every cause, are not very keen to express their admiration. And so the happiest man is he who has managed sincerely to admire himself, no matter how.'

1850 Atma dies. He buys a brown poodle called Butz, who becomes his favourite poodle. When a regimental band passes his house, Schopenhauer is known to stand up in the middle of conversations and put a seat by the window from which Butz can look out. The creature is referred to by the children of the neighbourhood as 'young Schopenhauer'.

1851 He publishes a selection of essays and aphorisms, *Parerga and Paralipomena*. Much to the author's surprise, the book becomes a bestseller.

1853 His fame spreads across Europe ('the comedy of fame', as he puts it). Lectures on his philosophy are offered at the universities of Bonn, Breslau and Jena. He receives fan mail. A woman from Silesia sends him a long, suggestive poem. A man from Bohemia writes to tell him he places a wreath on his portrait every day. 'After one has spent a long life in insignificance and disregard, they come at the end with drums and trumpets and think that is something' is the response, but there is also satisfaction: 'Would anyone with a great mind ever have been able to attain his goal and create a permanent and perennial work, if he had taken as his guiding star the bobbing will-o'-the-wisp of

public opinion, that is to say the opinion of small minds?'
Philosophically minded Frankfurters buy poodles in homage.

1859 As fame brings more attention from women, his views on them soften. From having thought them ' suited to being the nurses and teachers of our earliest childhood precisely because they themselves are childish, silly and short-sighted, in a word, big-children, their whole lives long' , he now judges that they are capable of self-lessness and insight. An attractive sculptress and an admirer of his philosophy, Elizabeth Ney (a descendant of Napoleon's Maréchal) , comes to Frankfurt in October and stays in his apartment for a month making a bust of him.

' She works all day at my place. When I get back from luncheon we have coffee together, we sit together on the sofa and I feel as if I were married. '

1860 Increasing ill-health suggests the end is near: ' I can bear the thought that in a short time worms will eat away my body; but the idea of philosophy professors nibbling at my philosophy makes me shudder. ' At the end of September, after a walk by the banks of the Main, he returns home, complains of breathlessness and dies, still convinced that ' human existence must be a kind of error. '

∞

Such was the life of a philosopher who may offer the heart unparalleled assistance.

2

A contemporary love story

WITH SCHOPENHAUERIAN NOTES

A *man is attempting to work on a train between Edinburgh and London. It is early in the afternoon on a warm spring day.*

Papers and a diary are on the table before him, and a book is open on the armrest. But the man has been unable to hold a coherent thought since Newcastle, when a woman entered the carriage and seated herself across the aisle. After looking impassively out of the window for a few moments, she turned her attention to a pile of magazines. She has been reading Vogue *since Darlington. She reminds the man of a portrait by Christen Købke of Mrs Høegh-Guldberg (though he cannot recall either of these names), which he saw, and felt strangely moved and saddened by, in a museum in Denmark a few years before.*

But unlike Mrs Høegh-Guldberg, she has short brown hair and wears jeans, a pair of trainers and a canary-yellow V-neck sweater over a T-shirt. He notices an incongruously large digital sports-watch on her pale, freckle-dotted wrist. He imagines running his hand through her chestnut hair, caressing the back of her neck, sliding his hand inside the sleeve of her pullover, watching her fall asleep beside him, her lips slightly agape. He imagines living with her in a house in south London, in a cherry-tree-lined street. He speculates that she may be a cellist or a graphic designer, or a doctor specializing in genetic research.

His mind turns over strategies for conversation. He considers asking her for the time, for a pencil, for directions to the bathroom, for reflections on the weather, for a look at one of her magazines. He longs for a train crash, in which their carriage would be thrown into one of the vast barley-fields through which they are passing. In the chaos, he would guide her safely outside, and repair with her to a nearby tent set up by the ambulance service, where they would be offered lukewarm tea and stare into each other's eyes. Years later, they would attract interest by revealing that they had met in the tragic Edinburgh Express collision. But because the train seems disinclined to derail, and though he knows it to be louche and absurd, the man cannot help

*clearing his throat and leaning over to ask the angel if she might
have a spare ballpoint. It feels like jumping off the side of a very
high bridge.*

1. philosophers have not traditionally been impressed: the
   tribulations of love have appeared too childish to warrant
   investigation, the subject better left to poets and hysterics. It
   is not for philosophers to speculate on hand-holding and
   scented letters. Schopenhauer was puzzled by the indifference:

   > We should be surprised that a matter that generally plays
   > such an important part in the life of man has hitherto been
   > almost entirely disregarded by philosophers, and lies before
   > us as raw and untreated material.

   The neglect seemed the result of a pompous denial of a side of
   life which violated man's rational self-image. Schopenhauer
   insisted on the awkward reality:

   > Love ... interrupts at every hour the most serious
   > occupations, and sometimes perplexes for a while even the
   > greatest minds. It does not hesitate ... to interfere with the
   > negotiations of statesmen and the investigations of the
   > learned. It knows how to slip its love-notes and ringlets even
   > into ministerial portfolios and philosophical manuscripts ... It
   > sometimes demands the sacrifice of ... health, sometimes of
   > wealth, position and happiness.

2. Like the Gascon essayist born 255 years before him,
   Schopenhauer was concerned with what made man –
   supposedly the most rational of all creatures – less than
   reasonable. There was a set of Montaigne's works in the
   library of the apartment at Schöne Aussicht. Schopenhauer had
   read how reason could be dethroned by a fart, a big lunch or
   an ingrowing toenail, and concurred with Montaigne's view
   that our minds were subservient to our bodies, despite our
   arrogant faith in the contrary.

3. But Schopenhauer went further. Rather than alighting on loose

examples of the dethronement of reason, he gave a name to a force within us which he felt invariably had precedence over reason, a force powerful enough to distort all of reason's plans and judgements, and which he termed the will-to-life (*Wille zum Leben*)⁻ defined as an inherent drive within human beings to stay alive and reproduce. The will-to-life led even committed depressives to fight for survival when they were threatened by a shipwreck or grave illness. It ensured that the most cerebral, career-minded individuals would be seduced by the sight of gurgling infants, or if they remained unmoved, that they were likely to conceive a child anyway, and love it fiercely on arrival. And it was the will-to-life that drove people to lose their reason over comely passengers encountered across the aisles of long-distance trains.

4. Schopenhauer might have resented the disruption of love (it isn't easy to proffer grapes to schoolgirls) ; but he refused to conceive of it as either disproportionate or accidental. It was entirely commensurate with love's function:

Why all this noise and fuss? Why all the urgency, uproar,
anguish and exertion? ... Why should such a trifle play so
important a role ... ? It is no trifle that is here in question; on
the contrary, the importance of the matter is perfectly in
keeping with the earnestness and ardour of the effort. The
ultimate aim of all love-affairs ... is actually more important
than all other aims in man's life; and therefore it is quite
worthy of the profound seriousness with which everyone
pursues it.

And what is the aim? Neither communion nor sexual release, understanding nor entertainment. The romantic dominates life because:

What is decided by it is nothing less than the composition of
the next generation ... the existence and special constitution
of the human race in times to come.

It is because love directs us with such force towards the second of the will-to-life's two great commands that Schopenhauer judged it the most inevitable and understandable of our obsessions.

5. The fact that the continuation of the species is seldom in our minds when we ask for a phone number is no objection to the theory. We are, suggested Schopenhauer, split into conscious and unconscious selves, the unconscious governed by the will-to-life, the conscious subservient to it and unable to learn of all its plans. Rather than a sovereign entity, the conscious mind is a partially sighted servant of a dominant, child-obsessed will-to-life:

> [The intellect] does not penetrate into the secret workshop of the will's decisions. It is, of course, a confidant of the will, yet a confidant that does not get to know everything.

The intellect understands only so much as is necessary to promote reproduction – which may mean understanding very little:

> [It] remains ... much excluded from the real resolutions and secret decisions of its own will.

An exclusion which explains how we may consciously feel nothing more than an intense desire to see someone again, while unconsciously being driven by a force aiming at the reproduction of the next generation.

Why should such deception even be necessary? Because, for Schopenhauer, we would not reliably assent to reproduce unless we first had lost our minds.

6. The analysis surely violates a rational self-image, but at least it counters suggestions that romantic love is an avoidable departure from more serious tasks, that it is forgivable for youngsters with too much time on their hands to swoon by moonlight and sob beneath bedclothes, but that it is unnecessary and demented for their seniors to neglect their work *because they have glimpsed a face on a train*. By conceiving of

love as biologically inevitable, key to the continuation of the species, Schopenhauer's theory of the will invites us to adopt a more forgiving stance towards the eccentric behaviour to which love so often makes us subject.

T *he man and woman are seated at a window-table in a Greek restaurant in north London. A bowl of olives lies between them, but neither can think of a way to remove the stones with requisite dignity and so they are left untouched.*

She had not been carrying a ballpoint on her, but had offered him a pencil. After a pause, she said how much she hated long train-journeys, a superfluous remark which had given him the slender encouragement he needed. She was not a cellist, nor a graphic designer, rather a lawyer specializing in corporate finance in a city firm. She was originally from Newcastle, but had been living in London for the past eight years. By the time the train pulled into Euston, he had obtained a phone number and an assent to a suggestion of dinner.

A waiter arrives to take their order. She asks for a salad and the sword-fish. She has come directly from work, and is wearing a light-grey suit and the same watch as before.

They begin to talk. She explains that at weekends, her favourite activity is rock-climbing. She started at school, and has since been on expeditions to France, Spain and Canada. She describes the thrill of hanging hundreds of feet above a valley floor, and camping in the high mountains, where in the morning, icicles have formed inside the tent. Her dinner companion feels dizzy on the second floor of apartment buildings. Her other passion is dancing, she loves the energy and sense of freedom. When she can, she stays up all night. He favours proximity to a bed by eleven thirty. They talk of work. She has been involved in a patent case. A kettle designer from Frankfurt has alleged copyright infringement against a British company. The company is liable under section 60,1, *a of the Patents Act of* 1977.

He does not follow the lengthy account of a forthcoming case, but is convinced of her high intelligence and their superlative compatibility.

1. One of the most profound mysteries of love is ' Why him?', and ' Why her?' Why, of all the possible candidates, did our desire settle so strongly on this creature, why did we come to treasure them above all others when their dinner conversation was not always the most enlightening, nor their habits the most suitable? And why, despite good intentions, were we unable to develop a sexual interest in certain others, who were perhaps objectively as attractive and might have been more convenient to live with?

2. The choosiness did not surprise Schopenhauer. We are not free to fall in love with everyone because we cannot produce healthy children with everyone. Our will-to-life drives us towards people who will raise our chances of producing beautiful and intelligent offspring, and repulses us away from those who lower these same chances. Love is nothing but the conscious manifestation of the will-to-life's discovery of an ideal co-parent:

> The moment when [two people] begin to love each other – *to fancy each other*, as the very apposite English expression has it – is actually to be regarded as the very first formation of a new individual.

In initial meetings, beneath the quotidian patter, the unconscious of both parties will assess whether a healthy child could one day result from intercourse:

> There is something quite peculiar to be found in the deep, unconscious seriousness with which two young people of the opposite sex regard each other when they meet for the first time, the searching and penetrating glance they cast at each other, the careful inspection all the features and parts of their respective persons have to undergo. This scrutiny and

examination is the meditation of the genius of the species concerning the individual possible through these two.

3. And what is the will-to-life seeking through such examination? Evidence of healthy children. The will-to-life must ensure that the next generation will be psychologically and physiologically fit enough to survive in a hazardous world, and so it seeks that children be well-proportioned in limb (neither too short nor too tall, too fat nor too thin), and stable of mind (neither too timid nor too reckless, neither too cold nor too emotional, etc.).

Since our parents made errors in their courtships, we are unlikely to be ideally balanced ourselves. We have typically come out too tall, too masculine, too feminine; our noses are large, our chins small. If such imbalances were allowed to persist, or were aggravated, the human race would, within a short time, founder in oddity. The will-to-life must therefore push us towards people who can, on account of their imperfections, cancel out our own (a large nose combined with a button nose promises a perfect nose), and hence help us restore physical and psychological balance in the next generation:

> Everyone endeavours to eliminate through the other individual his own weaknesses, defects, and deviations from the type, lest they be perpetuated or even grow into complete abnormalities in the child which will be produced.

The theory of neutralization gave Schopenhauer confidence in predicting pathways of attraction. Short women will fall in love with tall men, but rarely tall men with tall women (their unconscious fearing the production of giants). Feminine men who don't like sport will often be drawn to boyish women who have short hair (and wear sturdy watches):

> The neutralization of the two individualities ... requires that the particular degree of *his* manliness shall correspond exactly to the particular degree of *her* womanliness, so that the one-sidedness of each exactly cancels that of the other.

4. Unfortunately, the theory of attraction led Schopenhauer to a conclusion so bleak, it may be best if readers about to be married left the next few paragraphs unread in order not to have to rethink their plans; namely, that a person who is highly suitable for our child is almost never (though we cannot realize it at the time because we have been blindfolded by the will-to-life) very suitable for us.

'That convenience and passionate love should go hand in hand is the rarest stroke of good fortune,' observed Schopenhauer. The lover who saves our child from having an enormous chin or an effeminate temperament is seldom the person who will make us happy over a lifetime. The pursuit of personal happiness and the production of healthy children are two radically contrasting projects, which love maliciously confuses us into thinking of as one for a requisite number of years. We should not be surprised by marriages between people who would never have been friends:

> Love ... casts itself on persons who, apart from the sexual relation, would be hateful, contemptible, and even abhorrent to the lover. But the will of the species is so much more powerful than that of the individual, that the lover shuts his eyes to all the qualities repugnant to him, overlooks everything, misjudges everything, and binds himself for ever to the object of his passion. He is thus completely infatuated by that delusion, which vanishes as soon as the will of the species is satisfied, and leaves behind a detested partner for life. Only from this is it possible to explain why we often see very rational, and even eminent, men tied to termagants and matrimonial fiends, and cannot conceive how they could have made such a choice ... A man in love may even clearly recognize and bitterly feel in his bride the intolerable faults of temperament and character which promise him a life of misery, and yet not be frightened away ... for ultimately he

seeks not *his* interest, but that of a third person who has yet to come into existence, although he is involved in the delusion that what he seeks is his own interest.

The will-to-life's ability to further its own ends rather than our happiness may, Schopenhauer's theory implies, be sensed with particular clarity in the lassitude and tristesse that frequently befall couples immediately after love-making:

> Has it not been observed how *illico post coitum cachinnus auditur Diaboli?* (Directly after copulation the devil's laughter is heard.)

So one day, a boyish woman and a girlish man will approach the altar with motives neither they, nor anyone (save a smattering of Schopenhauerians at the reception), will have fathomed. Only later, when the will's demands are assuaged and a robust boy is kicking a ball around a suburban garden, will the ruse be discovered. The couple will part or pass dinners in hostile silence. Schopenhauer offered us a choice –

> It seems as if, in making a marriage, either the individual or the interest of the species must come off badly

– though he left us in little doubt as to the superior capacity of the species to guarantee its interests:

> The coming generation is provided for at the expense of the present.

T he man pays for dinner and asks, with studied casualness, if it might be an idea to repair to his flat for a drink. She smiles and stares at the floor. Under the table, she is folding a paper napkin into ever smaller squares. ' That would be lovely, it really would,' she says, ' but I have to get up very early to catch a flight to Frankfurt for this meeting. Five thirty or, like, even earlier. Maybe another time though. It would be lovely. Really, it would. ' Another smile. The napkin disintegrates under pressure.

Despair is alleviated by a promise that she will call from

Germany, and that they must meet again soon, perhaps on the very day of her return. But there is no call until late on the appointed day, when she rings from a booth at Frankfurt airport. In the background are crowds and metallic voices announcing the departure of flights to the Orient. She tells him she can see huge planes out of the window and that this place is like hell.

She says that the fucking Lufthansa flight has been delayed, that she will try to get a seat on another airline but that he shouldn't wait. There follows a pause before the worst is confirmed. Things are a little complicated in her life right now really, she goes on, she doesn't quite know what she wants, but she knows she needs space and some time, and if it is all right with him, she will be the one to call once her head is a little clearer.

1. The philosopher might have offered unflattering explanations of why we fall in love, but there was consolation for rejection – the consolation of knowing that our pain is normal. We should not feel confused by the enormity of the upset that can ensue from only a few days of hope. It would be unreasonable if a force powerful enough to push us towards child-rearing could – if it failed in its aim – vanish without devastation. Love could not induce us to take on the burden of propagating the species without promising us the greatest happiness we could imagine. To be shocked at how deeply rejection hurts is to ignore what acceptance involves. We must never allow our suffering to be compounded by suggestions that there is something odd in suffering so deeply. There would be something amiss if we didn't.

2. What is more, we are not inherently unlovable. There is nothing wrong with us *per se*. Our characters are not repellent, nor our faces abhorrent. The union collapsed because we were unfit to produce a balanced child *with one particular person*. There is no need to hate ourselves. One day we will come

across someone who can find us wonderful and who will feel exceptionally natural and open with us (because our chin and their chin make a desirable combination from the will-to-life's point of view).

3. We should in time learn to forgive our rejectors. The break-up was not their choice. In every clumsy attempt by one person to inform another that they need more space or time, that they are reluctant to commit or are afraid of intimacy, the rejector is striving to intellectualize an essentially unconscious negative verdict formulated by the will-to-life. Their reason may have had an appreciation of our qualities, their will-to-life did not and told them so in a way that brooked no argument — by draining them of sexual interest in us. If they were seduced away by people less intelligent than we are, we should not condemn them for shallowness. We should remember, as Schopenhauer explains, that:

> What is looked for in marriage is not intellectual entertainment,
> but the procreation of children.

4. We should respect the edict from nature against procreation that every rejection contains, as we might respect a flash of lightning or a lava flow — an event terrible but mightier than ourselves. We should draw consolation from the thought that a lack of love:

> between a man and a woman is the announcement that what
> they might produce would only be a badly organized,
> unhappy being, wanting in harmony in itself.

We might have been happy with our beloved, but nature was not — a greater reason to surrender our grip on love.

For a time, the man is beset by melancholy. At the weekend, he takes a walk in Battersea Park, and sits on a bench overlooking the Thames. He has with him a paperback edition of Goethe's The Sorrows of Young Werther, *first published in*

Leipzig in 1774.

There are couples pushing prams and leading young children by the hand. A little girl in a blue dress covered in chocolate, points up to a plane descending towards Heathrow. ' Daddy, is God in there?' she asks, but Daddy is in a hurry and in a mood, and picks her up and says he doesn't know, as though he had been asked for directions. A four-year-old boy drives his tricycle into a shrub and wails for his mother, who has just shut her eyes on a rug spread on a tattered patch of grass. She requests that her husband assist the child. He gruffly replies that it is her turn. She snaps that it is his. He says nothing. She says he's crap and stands up. An elderly couple on an adjacent bench silently share an egg-and-cress sandwich.

1. Schopenhauer asks us not to be surprised by the misery. We should not ask for a point to being alive, in a couple or a parent.
2. There were many works of natural science in Schopenhauer's library – among them William Kirby and William Spence's *Introduction to Entomology*, François Huber's *Des Abeilles* and Cadet de Vaux's *De la taupe, de ses moeurs, de ses habitudes et des moyens de la détruire.* The philosopher read of ants, beetles, bees, flies, grasshoppers, moles and migratory birds, and observed, with compassion and puzzlement, how all these creatures displayed an ardent, senseless commitment to life. He felt particular sympathy for the mole, a stunted monstrosity dwelling in damp narrow corridors, who rarely saw the light of day and whose offspring looked like gelatinous worms – but who still did everything in its power to survive and perpetuate itself:

   To dig strenuously with its enormous shovel-paws is the business of its whole life; permanent night surrounds it; it has its embryo eyes merely to avoid the light ... what does it attain by this course of life that is full of trouble and devoid of pleasure? ... The cares and troubles of life are out of all proportion to the yield or profit from it.

Every creature on earth seemed to Schopenhauer to be equally committed to an equally meaningless existence:

> Contemplate the restless industry of wretched little ants ... the life of most insects is nothing but a restless labour for preparing nourishment and dwelling for the future offspring that will come from their eggs. After the offspring have consumed the nourishment and have turned into the chrysalis stage, they enter into life merely to begin the same task again from the beginning ... we cannot help but ask what comes of all of this ... there is nothing to show but the satisfaction of hunger and sexual passion, and ... a little momentary gratification ... now and then, between ... endless needs and exertions.

3. The philosopher did not have to spell out the parallels. We pursue love affairs, chat in cafés with prospective partners and have children, with as much choice in the matter as moles and ants – and are rarely any happier.

4. He did not mean to depress us, rather to free us from expectations which inspire bitterness. It is consoling, when love has let us down, to hear that happiness was never part of the plan. The darkest thinkers may, paradoxically, be the most cheering:

> There is only one inborn error, and that is the notion that we exist in order to be happy ... So long as we persist in this inborn error ... the world seems to us full of contradictions. For at every step, in great things and small, we are bound to experience that the world and life are certainly not arranged for the purpose of maintaining a happy existence ... hence the countenances of almost all elderly persons wear the expression of what is called *disappointment*.

They would never have grown so disappointed if only they had entered love with the correct expectations:

> What disturbs and renders unhappy ... the age of youth ... is

the hunt for happiness on the firm assumption that it must be met with in life. From this arises the constantly deluded hope and so also dissatisfaction. Deceptive images of a vague happiness of our dreams hover before us in capriciously selected shapes and we search in vain for their original ... Much would have been gained if through timely advice and instruction young people could have had eradicated from their minds the erroneous notion that the world has a great deal to offer them.

3

We do have one advantage over moles. We may have to fight for survival and hunt for partners and have children as they do, but we can in addition go to the theatre, the opera and the concert hall, and in bed in the evenings, we can read novels, philosophy and epic poems − and it is in these activities that Schopenhauer located a supreme source of relief from the demands of the will-to-life. What we encounter in works of art and philosophy are objective versions of our own pains and struggles, evoked and defined in sound, language or image. Artists and philosophers not only show us what we have felt, they present our experiences more poignantly and intelligently than we have been able; they give shape to aspects of our lives that we recognize as our own, yet could never have understood so clearly on our own. They explain our condition to us, and thereby help us to be less lonely with, and confused by it. We may be obliged to continue burrowing underground, but through creative works, we can at least acquire moments of insight into our woes, which spare us feelings of alarm and isolation (even persecution) at being afflicted by them. In their different ways, art and philosophy help us, in Schopenhauer's words, to turn pain into knowledge.

The philosopher admired his mother's friend Johann Wolfgang von Goethe because he had turned so many of the pains of love into knowledge, most famously in the novel he had published at the age of twenty-five, and which had made his name throughout Europe. *The Sorrows of Young Werther* described the unrequited love felt by a particular young man for a particular young woman (the charming Lotte, who shared Werther's taste for *The Vicar of Wakefield* and wore white dresses with pink ribbons at the sleeves), but it simultaneously described the love affairs of thousands of its readers (Napoleon was said to have read the novel nine times). The greatest works of art speak to us without knowing of us. As Schopenhauer put it:

> The ... poet takes from life that which is quite particular and individual, and describes it accurately in its individuality; but in this way he reveals the whole of human existence ... though he appears to be concerned with the particular, he is actually concerned with that which is everywhere and at all times. From this it arises that sentences, especially of the dramatic poets, even without being general apophthegms, find frequent application in real life.

Goethe's readers not only *recognized* themselves in *The Sorrows of Young Werther*, they also *understood* themselves better as a result, for Goethe had clarified a range of the awkward, evanescent moments of love, moments that his readers would previously have lived through, though would not necessarily have fathomed. He laid bare certain laws of love, what Schopenhauer termed essential 'Ideas' of romantic psychology. He had, for example, perfectly captured the apparently kind – yet infinitely cruel – manner with which the person who does not love deals with the one who does. Late in the novel, tortured by his feelings, Werther breaks down in front of Lotte:

> 'Lotte' he cried, 'I shall never see you again!' – 'Why ever not?' she replied: 'Werther, you may and must see us again, but do be less agitated in your manner. Oh, why did you have to be born with this intense spirit, this uncontrollable passion

for everything you are close to! I implore you,' she went on, taking his hand, 'be calmer. Think of the many joys your spirit, your knowledge and your gifts afford you!'

We need not have lived in Germany in the second half of the eighteenth century to appreciate what is involved. There are fewer stories than there are people on earth, the plots repeated ceaselessly while the names and backdrops alter. 'The essence of art is that its one case applies to thousands,' knew Schopenhauer.

In turn, there is consolation in realizing that our case is *only* one of thousands. Schopenhauer made two trips to Florence, in 1818 and again in 1822. He is likely to have visited the Brancacci chapel in Santa Maria del Carmine, in which Masaccio had painted a series of frescos between 1425 and 1426.

The distress of Adam and Eve at leaving paradise is not theirs alone. In the faces and posture of the two figures, Masaccio has captured the essence of distress, the very Idea of distress, his fresco a universal symbol of our fallibility and fragility. We have all been expelled from the heavenly garden.

But by reading a tragic tale of love, a rejected suitor raises himself above his own situation; he is no longer one man suffering alone, singly and confusedly, he is part of a vast body of human beings who have throughout time fallen in love with other humans in the agonizing drive to propagate the species. His suffering loses a little of its sting, it grows more comprehensible, less of an individual curse. Of a person who can achieve such objectivity, Schopenhauer remarks:

In the course of his own life and in its misfortunes, he will look less at his own individual lot than at the lot of mankind as a whole, and accordingly will conduct himself... more as a *knower* than as a *sufferer*.

We must, between periods of digging in the dark, endeavour always to transform our tears into knowledge.

Ⅵ Consolation for Difficulties

1

Few philosophers have thought highly of feeling wretched. A wise life has traditionally been associated with an attempt to reduce suffering: anxiety, despair, anger, self-contempt and heartache.

2

Then again, pointed out Friedrich Nietzsche, the majority of philosophers have always been 'cabbage-heads'. 'It is my fate to have to be the first *decent* human being,' he recognized with a degree of embarrassment in the autumn of 1888. 'I have a terrible fear that I shall one day be pronounced *holy*'; and he set the date somewhere around the dawn of the third millennium: 'Let us assume that people will be *allowed* to read [my work] in about the year 2000.' He was sure they would enjoy it when they did:

> It seems to me that to take a book of mine into his hands is one of the rarest distinctions that anyone can confer upon himself. I even assume that he removes his shoes when he does so – not to speak of boots.

A distinction because, alone among the cabbage-heads, Nietzsche had realized that difficulties of every sort were to be welcomed by those seeking fulfilment:

> You want if possible – and there is no madder 'if possible' – *to abolish suffering*; and we? – it really does seem that *we* would rather increase it and make it worse than it has ever been!

Though punctilious in sending his best wishes to friends, Nietzsche knew in his heart what they needed:

> To those human beings who are of any concern to me I wish suffering, desolation, sickness, ill-treatment, indignities – I wish that they should not remain unfamiliar with profound self-contempt, the torture of self-mistrust, the wretchedness of the vanquished.

Which helped to explain why his work amounted to, even if he said so himself:

The greatest gift that [mankind] has ever been given.

3

We should not be frightened by appearances.

In the eyes of people who are seeing us for the first time ...
usually we are nothing more than a single individual trait
which leaps to the eye and determines the whole impression
we make. Thus the gentlest and most reasonable of men
can, if he wears a large moustache ... usually be seen as
no more than the appurtenance *of a large moustache, that*
is to say a military type, easily angered and occasionally
violent – and as such he will be treated.

4

He had not always thought so well of difficulty. For his initial
views, he had been indebted to a philosopher he had discovered at
the age of twenty-one as a student at Leipzig University. In the
autumn of 1865, in a second-hand bookshop in Leipzig's
Blumengasse, he had by chance picked up an edition of *The*
World as Will and Representation, whose author had died five
years previously in an apartment in Frankfurt 300 kilometres to the
west:

I took [Schopenhauer's book] in my hand as something totally
unfamiliar and turned the pages. I don't know which daimon
was whispering to me: 'Take this book home.' In any case,
it happened, which was contrary to my custom of otherwise
never rushing into buying a book. Back at the house I threw
myself into the corner of a sofa with my new treasure, and
began to let that dynamic, dismal genius work on me. Each
line cried out with renunciation, negation, resignation.

The older man changed the younger one's life. The essence of
philosophical wisdom was, Schopenhauer explained, Aristotle's

remark in the *Nicomachean Ethics*:

> The prudent man strives for freedom from pain, not pleasure.

The priority for all those seeking contentment was to recognize the impossibility of fulfilment and so to avoid the troubles and anxiety that we typically encounter in its pursuit:

> [We should] direct our aim not to what is pleasant and
> agreeable in life, but to the avoidance, as far as possible, of its
> numberless evils ... The happiest lot is that of the man who has
> got through life without any very great pain, bodily or mental.

When he next wrote home to his widowed mother and his nineteen-year-old sister in Naumburg, Nietzsche replaced the usual reports on his diet and the progress of his studies with a summary of his new philosophy of renunciation and resignation:

> We know that life consists of suffering, that the harder we try
> to enjoy it, the more enslaved we are by it, and so we
> [should] discard the goods of life and practise abstinence.

It sounded strange to his mother, who wrote back explaining that she didn't like 'that kind of display or that kind of opinion so much as a proper letter, full of news', and advised her son to entrust his heart to God and to make sure he was eating properly.

But Schopenhauer's influence did not subside. Nietzsche began to live cautiously. Sex figured prominently in a list he drew up under the heading 'Delusions of the Individual'. During his military service in Naumburg, he positioned a photograph of Schopenhauer on his desk, and in difficult moments cried out, 'Schopenhauer, help!' At the age of twenty-four, on taking up the Chair of Classical Philology at Basle University, he was drawn into the intimate circle of Richard and Cosima Wagner through a common love of the pessimistic, prudent sage of Frankfurt.

5

Then, after more than a decade of attachment, in the autumn of 1876, Nietzsche travelled to Italy and underwent a radical change of mind. He had accepted an invitation from Malwida von Meysenbug, a wealthy middle-aged enthusiast of the arts, to spend a few months with her and a group of friends in a villa in Sorrento on the Bay of Naples.

'I never saw him so lively. He laughed aloud from sheer joy,' reported Malwida of Nietzsche's first response to the Villa Rubinacci, which stood on a leafy avenue on the edge of Sorrento. From the living room there were views over the bay, the island of Ischia and Mount Vesuvius, and in front of the house, a small garden with fig and orange trees, cypresses and grape arbours led down to the sea.

The house guests went swimming, and visited Pompeii, Vesuvius, Capri and the Greek temples at Paestum. At mealtimes, they ate light dishes prepared with olive oil, and in the evenings, read together in the living room: Jacob Burckhardt's lectures on Greek civilization, Montaigne, La Rochefoucauld, Vauvenargues, La Bruyère, Stendhal, Goethe's ballad *Die Braut von Korinth*, and his play *Die natürliche Tochter*, Herodotus, Thucydides, and Plato's *Laws* (though, perhaps spurred on by Montaigne's confessions of distaste, Nietzsche grew irritated with the latter: 'The Platonic dialogue, that dreadfully self-satisfied and childish kind of dialectics, can only have a stimulating effect if one has never read any good Frenchmen ... Plato is boring').

And as he swam in the Mediterranean, ate food cooked in olive oil rather than butter, breathed warm air and read Montaigne and Stendhal ('These little things – nutriment, place, climate, recreation, the whole casuistry of selfishness – are beyond all conception of greater importance than anything that has been considered of importance hitherto'), Nietzsche gradually changed his philosophy of pain and pleasure, and with it, his perspective on difficulty. Watching the sun set over the Bay of Naples at the end of October 1876, he was infused with a new, quite un-Schopenhauerian faith in existence. He felt that he had been old at the beginning of his life, and shed tears at the thought that he had been saved at the last moment.

6

He made a formal announcement of his conversion in a letter to Cosima Wagner at the end of 1876: 'Would you be amazed if I confess something that has gradually come about, but which has more or less suddenly entered my consciousness: a disagreement with Schopenhauer's teaching? On virtually all general propositions I am not on his side.'

One of these propositions being that, because fulfilment is an illusion, the wise must devote themselves to avoiding pain rather than seeking pleasure, living quietly, as Schopenhauer counselled, 'in a small fireproof room' – advice that now struck Nietzsche as both timid and untrue, a perverse attempt to dwell, as he was to put it pejoratively several years later, 'hidden in forests like shy deer'. Fulfilment was to be reached not by avoiding pain, but by recognizing its role as a natural, inevitable step on the way to reaching anything good.

7

What had, besides the food and the air, helped to change Nietzsche's outlook was his reflection on the few individuals throughout history who appeared genuinely to have known fulfilled lives; individuals who could fairly have been described – to use one of the most contested terms in the Nietzschean lexicon – as *Übermenschen*.

The notoriety and absurdity of the word owe less to Nietzsche's own philosophy than to his sister Elisabeth's subsequent enchantment with National Socialism ('that vengeful anti-Semitic goose', as Friedrich described her long before she shook the Führer's hand), and the unwitting decision by Nietzsche's earliest Anglo-Saxon translators to bequeath to the *Übermensch* the name of a legendary cartoon hero.

But Nietzsche's *Übermenschen* had little to do with either airborne aces or fascists. A better indication of their identity came in a passing remark in a letter to his mother and sister:

> Really, there is nobody living about whom I care *much*. The people I like have been dead for a long, long time − for example, the Abbé Galiani, or Henri Beyle, or Montaigne.

He could have added another hero, Johann Wolfgang von Goethe. These four men were perhaps the richest clues for what Nietzsche came in his maturity to understand by a fulfilled life.

They had much in common. They were curious, artistically gifted, and sexually vigorous. Despite their dark sides, they laughed, and many of them danced, too; they were drawn to 'gentle sunlight, bright and buoyant air, southerly vegetation, the breath of the sea [and] fleeting meals of flesh, fruit and eggs'. Several of them had a gallows humour close to Nietzsche's own − a joyful, wicked laughter arising from pessimistic hinterlands. They had explored their possibilities, they possessed what Nietzsche called ' life ', which suggested courage, ambition, dignity, strength of character, humour and independence (and a parallel absence of sanctimoniousness, conformity, resentment and prissiness).

They had been involved in the world. Montaigne had been mayor of Bordeaux for two terms and journeyed across Europe on horseback. The Neapolitan Abbé Galiani had been Secretary to the Embassy in Paris and written works on money supply and grain distribution (which Voltaire praised for combining the wit of Molière and the intelligence of Plato). Goethe had worked for a decade as a civil servant in the Court in Weimar; he had proposed reforms in agriculture, industry and poor relief, undertaken diplomatic missions and twice had audiences with Napoleon.

On his visit to Italy in 1787, he had seen the Greek temples at

Paestum and made three ascents of Mount Vesuvius, coming close enough to the crater to dodge eruptions of stone and ash.

Nietzsche called him 'magnificent', 'the last German I hold in reverence' : 'He made use of ... practical activity ... he did not divorce himself from life but immersed himself in it ... [he] took as much as possible upon himself ... What he wanted was totality; he fought against the disjunction of reason, sensuality, feeling, will.'

Stendhal had accompanied Napoleon's armies around Europe, he had visited the ruins of Pompeii seven times and admired the Pont du Gard by a full moon at five in the morning ('The Coliseum in Rome hardly plunged me into a reverie more profound ...').

Nietzsche's heroes had also fallen in love repeatedly. 'The whole movement of the world tends and leads towards copulation,' Montaigne had known. At the age of seventy-four, on holiday in Marienbad, Goethe had become infatuated with Ulrike von Levetzow, a pretty nineteen-year-old, whom he had invited out for tea and on walks, before asking for (and being refused) her hand in marriage. Stendhal, who had known and loved *Werther*, had been as passionate as its author, his diaries detailing conquests across decades. At twenty-four, stationed with the Napoleonic armies in Germany, he had taken the innkeeper's daughter to bed and noted proudly in his diary that she was 'the first German woman I ever saw who was totally exhausted after an orgasm. I made her passionate with my caresses; she was very frightened.'

And finally, these men had all been artists ('Art is the great stimulant to life,' recognized Nietzsche), and must have felt extraordinary satisfaction upon completing the *Essais*, *Il Socrate immaginario*, *Römische Elegien* and *De l'amour*.

8

These were, Nietzsche implied, some of the elements that human beings naturally needed for a fulfilled life. He added an important detail; that it was impossible to attain them without feeling very miserable some of the time:

> What if pleasure and displeasure were so tied together that whoever *wanted* to have as much as possible of one *must* also have as much as possible of the other ... you have the choice: either *as little displeasure as possible*, painlessness in brief ... or *as much displeasure as possible* as the price for the growth of an abundance of subtle pleasures and joys that have rarely been relished yet? If you decide for the former and desire to diminish and lower the level of human pain, you also have to diminish and lower the level of their *capacity for joy*.

The most fulfilling human projects appeared inseparable from a degree of torment, the sources of our greatest joys lying awkwardly close to those of our greatest pains:

> Examine the lives of the best and most fruitful people and peoples and ask yourselves whether a tree that is supposed to grow to a proud height can dispense with bad weather and storms; whether misfortune and external resistance, some kinds of hatred, jealousy, stubbornness, mistrust, hardness, avarice, and violence do not belong among the *favourable* conditions without which any great growth even of virtue is scarcely possible.

9

Why? Because no one is able to produce a great work of art without experience, nor achieve a worldly position immediately, nor be a great lover at the first attempt; and in the interval between initial failure and subsequent success, in the gap between who we wish one day to be and who we are at present, must come pain, anxiety, envy and humiliation. We suffer because we cannot spontaneously master the ingredients of fulfilment.

Nietzsche was striving to correct the belief that fulfilment must come easily or not at all, a belief ruinous in its effects, for it leads us to withdraw prematurely from challenges that might have been overcome if only we had been prepared for the savagery legitimately demanded by almost everything valuable.

We might imagine that Montaigne's *Essays* had sprung fully formed from his mind and so could take the clumsiness of our own first attempts to write a philosophy of life as signs of a congenital incapacity for the task. We should look instead at the evidence of colossal authorial struggles behind the final masterpiece, the plethora of additions and revisions the *Essays* demanded.

Le Rouge et le noir, *Vie de Henry Brulard* and *De l'amour* had been no easier to write. Stendhal had begun his artistic career by sketching out a number of poor plays. One had centred on the landing of an émigré army at Quiberon (the characters were to include William Pitt and Charles James Fox), another had charted Bonaparte's rise to power and a third – tentatively titled *L'Homme qui craint d'être gouverné* – had depicted the slide of an old man into senility. Stendhal had spent weeks at the Bibliothèque Nationale, copying out dictionary definitions of words like '*plaisanterie*', '*ridicule*' and '*comique*' – but it had not been enough to transform his leaden play-writing. It was many decades of toil before the masterpieces emerged.

If most works of literature are less fine than *Le Rouge et le noir*, it is – suggested Nietzsche – not because their authors lack genius, but because they have an incorrect idea of how much pain is required. This is how hard one should try to write a novel:

> The recipe for becoming a good novelist ... is easy to give, but to carry it out presupposes qualities one is accustomed to overlook when one says 'I do not have enough talent.' One has only to make a hundred or so sketches for novels, none longer than two pages but of such distinctness that every word in them is necessary; one should write down anecdotes every day until one has learnt how to give them the most pregnant

and effective form; one should be tireless in collecting and describing human types and characters; one should above all relate things to others and listen to others relate, keeping one's eyes and ears open for the effect produced on those present, one should travel like a landscape painter or costume designer ... one should, finally, reflect on the motives of human actions, disdain no signpost for instruction about them and be a collector of these things by day and night. One should continue in this many-sided exercise *for some ten years*; what is then created in the workshop ... will be fit to go out into the world.

The philosophy amounted to a curious mixture of extreme faith in human potential (fulfilment is open to us all, as is the writing of great novels) and extreme toughness (we may need to spend a miserable decade on the first book).

It was in order to accustom us to the legitimacy of pain that Nietzsche spent so much time talking about mountains.

10

It is hard to read more than a few pages without coming upon an alpine reference:

Ecce Homo: He who knows how to breathe the air of my writings knows that it is an air of heights, a *robust* air. One has to be made for it, otherwise there is no small danger one will catch cold. The ice is near, the solitude is terrible – but how peacefully all things lie in the light! how freely one breathes! how much one feels *beneath* one! Philosophy, as I have hitherto understood and lived it, is a voluntary living in ice and high mountains.

On the Genealogy of Morals: We would need *another* sort of spirit than those we are likely to encounter in this age [to understand my philosophy] ... they would need to be acclimatized to thinner air higher up, to winter treks, ice and mountains in every sense.

Human*, *All Too Human: In the mountains of truth you will never climb in vain: either you will get up higher today or you will exercise your strength so as to be able to get up higher tomorrow.

Untimely Meditations: To climb as high into the pure icy Alpine air as a philosopher ever climbed, up to where all the mist and obscurity cease and where the fundamental constitution of things speaks in voice rough and rigid but ineluctably comprehensible!

He was – in both a practical and spiritual sense – of the mountains. Having taken citizenship in April 1869, Nietzsche may be considered Switzerland's most famous philosopher. Even so, he on occasion succumbed to a sentiment with which few Swiss are unacquainted. 'I am distressed to be Swiss!' he complained to his mother a year after taking up citizenship.

Upon resigning his post at Basle University at the age of thirty-five, he began spending winters by the Mediterranean, largely in Genoa and Nice, and summers in the Alps, in the small village of Sils-Maria, 1,800 metres above sea-level in the Engadine region of south-eastern Switzerland, a few kilometres from St Moritz, where the winds from Italy collide with cooler northern gusts and turn the sky an aquamarine blue.

Nietzsche visited the Engadine for the first time in June 1879 and at once fell in love with the climate and topography. 'I now have Europe's best and mightiest air to breathe,' he told Paul Rée, 'its nature is akin to my own.' To Peter Gast, he wrote, 'This is not Switzerland ... but something quite different, at least much more southern – I would have to go to the high plateaux of Mexico overlooking the Pacific to find anything similar (for example, Oaxaca), and the vegetation there would of course be tropical. Well, I shall try to keep this Sils-Maria for myself.' And to his old schoolfriend Carl von Gersdorff, he explained, 'I feel that here and nowhere else is my real home and breeding ground. '

Nietzsche spent seven summers in Sils-Maria in a rented room in a chalet with views on to pine trees and mountains. There he wrote all or substantial portions of *The Gay Science*, *Thus Spake Zarathustra*, *Beyond Good and Evil*, *On the Genealogy of Morals* and *Twilight of the Idols*. He would rise at five in the morning and work until midday, then take walks up the huge peaks that necklace the village, Piz Corvatsch, Piz Lagrev, Piz de la Margna, jagged and raw mountains that look as if they had only recently thrust through the earth's crust under atrocious tectonic pressures. In the evening, alone in his room, he would eat a few slices of ham, an egg and a roll and go to bed early. ('How can anyone become a thinker if he does not spend at least a third of the day without passions, people and books?')

Today, inevitably, there is a museum in the village. For a few francs, one is invited to visit the philosopher's bedroom, refurbished, the guidebook explains, ' as it looked in Nietzsche's time, in all its unpretentiousness'.

Yet to understand why Nietzsche felt there to be such an affinity between his philosophy and the mountains, it may be best to skirt the room and visit instead one of Sils-Maria's many sports shops in order to acquire walking boots, a rucksack, a water-bottle, gloves, a compass and a pick.

A hike up Piz Corvatsch, a few kilometres from Nietzsche's house, will explain better than any museum the spirit of his philosophy, his defence of difficulty, and his reasons for turning away from Schopenhauerian deer-like shyness.

At the base of the mountain one finds a large car park, a row of recycling bins, a depot for rubbish trucks and a restaurant offering oleaginous sausages and rösti.

The summit is, by contrast, sublime. There are views across the entire Engadine: the turquoise lakes of Segl, Silvaplana and St

Moritz, and to the south, near the border with Italy, the massive Sella and Roseg glaciers. There is an extraordinary stillness in the air, it seems one can touch the roof of the world. The height leaves one out of breath but curiously elated. It is hard not to start grinning, perhaps laughing, for no particular reason, an innocent laughter that comes from the core of one's being and expresses a primal delight at being alive to see such beauty.

But, to come to the moral of Nietzsche's mountain philosophy, it isn't easy to climb 3,451 metres above sea-level. It requires five hours at least, one must cling to steep paths, negotiate a way around boulders and through thick pine-forests, grow breathless in the thin air, add layers of clothes to fight the wind and crunch through eternal snows.

11

Nietzsche offered another alpine metaphor. A few steps from his room in Sils-Maria a path leads to the Fex Valley, one of the most fertile of the Engadine. Its gentle slopes are extensively farmed. In summer, families of cows stand reflectively munching the almost luminously rich-green grass, their bells clanging as they move from one patch to another.

Streams trickle through the fields with the sound of sparkling water being poured into glasses. Beside many small, immaculate farms (each one flying the national and cantonal flags) stand carefully tended vegetable gardens from whose loamy soils sprout vigorous cauliflowers, beetroots, carrots and lettuces, which tempt one to kneel down and take rabbit-like bites out of them.

If there are such nice lettuces here, it is because the Fex Valley is glacial, with the characteristic mineral richness of soil once a glacial mantle has retreated. Much further along the valley, hours of strenuous walking from the tidy farms, one comes upon the glacier itself, massive and terrifying. It looks like a tablecloth waiting for a tug to straighten out its folds, but these folds are the size of houses and are made of razor-sharp ice, and occasionally release agonized bellows as they rearrange themselves in the summer sun.

It is hard to conceive, when standing at the edge of the cruel glacier, how this frozen bulk could have a role to play in the gestation of vegetables and lush grass only a few kilometres along the valley, to imagine that something as apparently antithetical to a green field as a glacier could be responsible for the field's fertility.

Nietzsche, who often walked in the Fex Valley carrying a pencil and leather-bound notebook (' Only thoughts which come from *walking* have any value ') , drew an analogy with the dependence of positive elements in human life on negative ones, of fulfilment on difficulties:

> When we behold those deeply-furrowed hollows in which glaciers have lain, we think it hardly possible that a time will come when a wooded, grassy valley, watered by streams, will spread itself out upon the same spot. So it is, too, in the history of mankind: the most savage forces beat a path, and are mainly destructive; but their work was none-the-less necessary, in order that later a gentler civilization might raise its house. The frightful energies − those which are called evil − are the cyclopean architects and road-makers of humanity.

12

But frightful difficulties are sadly, of course, not enough. All lives are difficult; what makes some of them fulfilled as well is the manner in which pains have been met. Every pain is an indistinct signal that something is wrong, which may engender either a good or bad result depending on the sagacity and strength of mind of the sufferer. Anxiety may precipitate panic, or an accurate analysis of what is amiss. A sense of injustice may lead to murder, or to a ground-breaking work of economic theory. Envy may lead to bitterness, or to a decision to compete with a rival and the production of a masterpiece.

As Nietzsche's beloved Montaigne had explained in the final chapter of the *Essays*, the art of living lies in finding uses for our adversities:

> We must learn to suffer whatever we cannot avoid. Our life is composed, like the harmony of the world, of discords as well as of different tones, sweet and harsh, sharp and flat, soft and loud. If a musician liked only some of them, what could he sing? He has got to know how to use all of them and blend them together. So too must we with good and ill, which are of one substance with our life.

And some 300 years later, Nietzsche returned to the thought:

> If only we were fruitful fields, we would at bottom let nothing perish unused and see in every event, thing and man welcome manure.

How then to be fruitful?

13

Born in Urbino in 1483, Raphael from an early age displayed such an interest in drawing that his father took the boy to Perugia to work as an apprentice to the renowned Pietro Perugino. He was soon executing works of his own and by his late teens had painted several portraits of members of the court of Urbino, and altarpieces for churches in Città di Castello, a day's ride from Urbino across the mountains on the road to Perugia.

But Raphael, one of Nietzsche's favourite painters, knew he was not then a great artist, for he had seen the works of two men, Michelangelo Buonarroti and Leonardo da Vinci. They had shown him that he was unable to paint figures in motion, and despite an aptitude for pictorial geometry, that he had no grasp of linear perspective. The envy could have grown monstrous. Raphael turned it into manure instead.

In 1504, at the age of twenty-one, he left Urbino for Florence in order to study the work of his two masters. He examined their cartoons in the Hall of the Great Council where Leonardo had worked on the Battle of Anghiari and Michelangelo on the Battle of Cascina. He imbibed the lessons of Leonardo and Michelangelo's anatomical drawings and followed their example of dissecting and drawing corpses. He learned from Leonardo's *Adoration of the Magi* and his cartoons of the Virgin and Child, and looked closely at an unusual portrait Leonardo had been asked to execute for a nobleman, Francesco del Giocondo, who had wanted a likeness of his wife, a young beauty with a somewhat enigmatic smile.

The results of Raphael's exertions were soon apparent. We can compare *Portrait of a Young Woman* which Raphael had drawn before moving to Florence with *Portrait of a Woman* completed a few years after.

Mona had given Raphael the idea of a half-length seated pose in which the arms provided the base of a pyramidal composition. She had taught him how to use contrasting axes for the head, shoulder and hands in order to lend volume to a figure. Whereas the woman drawn in Urbino had looked awkwardly constricted in her clothes, her arms unnaturally cut off, the woman from Florence was mobile and at ease.

Raphael had not spontaneously come into possession of his talents; he had become great by responding intelligently to a sense of inferiority that would have led lesser men to despair.

The career path offered a Nietzschean lesson in the benefits of wisely interpreted pain:

Don't talk about giftedness, inborn talents! One can name all kinds of great men who were not very gifted. They *acquired* greatness, became 'geniuses' (as we put it) through qualities

about whose lack no man aware of them likes to speak; all of
them had that diligent seriousness of a craftsman, learning first
to construct the parts properly before daring to make a great
whole. They allowed themselves time for it, because they took
more pleasure in making the little, secondary things well than
in the effect of a dazzling whole.

Raphael had been able – to use Nietzsche's terms – to sublimate
(*sublimieren*), spiritualize (*vergeistigen*) and raise (*aufheben*)
to fruitfulness the difficulties in his path.

14

The philosopher had a practical as well as a metaphorical interest
in horticulture. On resigning from Basle University in 1879,
Nietzsche had set his heart on becoming a professional gardener.
'You know that my preference is for a simple, natural way of
life,' he informed his surprised mother, 'and I am becoming
increasingly eager for it. There is no other cure for my health. I
need real *work*, which takes time and induces *tiredness* without
mental strain.' He remembered an old tower in Naumburg near
his mother's house, which he planned to rent while looking after
the adjoining garden. The gardening life began with enthusiasm in
September 1879 – but there were soon problems. Nietzsche's poor
eyesight prevented him from seeing what he was trimming, he had
difficulty bending his back, there were too many leaves (it was
autumn) and after three weeks, he felt he had no alternative but
to give up.

Yet traces of his horticultural enthusiasm survived in his
philosophy, for in certain passages, he proposed that we should
look at our difficulties like gardeners. At their roots, plants can be
odd and unpleasant, but a person with knowledge and faith in
their potential will lead them to bear beautiful flowers and fruit –
just as, in life, at root level, there may be difficult emotions and
situations which can nevertheless result, through careful

cultivation, in the greatest achievements and joys.

> One can dispose of one's drives like a gardener and, though few know it, cultivate the shoots of anger, pity, curiosity, vanity as productively and profitably, as a beautiful fruit tree on a trellis.

But most of us fail to recognize the debt we owe to these shoots of difficulty. We are liable to think that anxiety and envy have nothing legitimate to teach us and so remove them like emotional weeds. We believe, as Nietzsche put it, that ' the higher *is not allowed* to grow out of the lower, *is not allowed* to have grown at all ... everything first-rate must be *causa sui* [the cause of itself]. '

Yet ' good and honoured things ' were, Nietzsche stressed, ' artfully related, knotted and crocheted to ... wicked, apparently antithetical things'. ' Love and hate, gratitude and revenge, good nature and anger ... belong together, ' which does not mean that they have to be *expressed* together, but that a positive may be the result of a negative successfully gardened. Therefore:

> The emotions of hatred, envy, covetousness and lust for domination [are] life-conditioning emotions ... which must fundamentally and essentially be present in the total economy of life.

To cut out every negative root would simultaneously mean choking off positive elements that might arise from it further up the stem of the plant.

We should not feel embarrassed by our difficulties, only by our failure to grow anything beautiful from them.

15

It was for their apparent appreciation of the point that Nietzsche looked back in admiration to the ancient Greeks.

It is tempting when contemplating their serene temples at dusk, like those at Paestum, a few kilometres from Sorrento – which Nietzsche visited with Malwida von Meysenbug in early 1877 – to imagine that the Greeks were an unusually measured people whose temples were the outward manifestations of an order they felt within themselves and their society.

This had been the opinion of the great classicist Johann Winckelmann (1717—68) and had won over successive generations of German university professors. But Nietzsche proposed that far from arising out of serenity, classical Greek civilization had arisen from the sublimation of the most sinister forces:

> The greater and more terrible the passions are that an age, a people, an individual can permit themselves, because they are capable of employing them as *a means*, *the higher stands their culture*.

The temples might have looked calm, but they were the flowers of well-gardened plants with dark roots. The Dionysiac festivals showed both the darkness and the attempt to control and cultivate it:

> Nothing astonishes the observer of the Greek world more than when he discovers that from time to time the Greeks made as it were a festival of all their passions and evil natural inclinations and even instituted a kind of official order of proceedings in the celebration of what was all-too-human in them ... They took this all-too-human to be inescapable and, instead of reviling it, preferred to accord it a kind of right of the second rank through regulating it within the usages of society and religion: indeed, everything in man possessing *power* they called divine and inscribed it on the walls of their Heaven. They do not repudiate the natural drive that finds expression in the evil qualities but regulate it and, as soon as they have discovered sufficient prescriptive measures to provide these wild waters with the least harmful means of channeling and outflow, confine them to

definite cults and days. This is the root of all the moral freemindedness of antiquity. One granted to the evil and suspicious ... a moderate discharge, and did not strive after their total annihilation.

The Greeks did not cut out their adversities; they cultivated them:
All passions have a phase when they are merely disastrous, in which they draw their victims down by weight of stupidity – and a later, very much later one in which they marry the spirit, 'spiritualize' themselves. In former times, because of the stupidity of passion, people waged war on passion itself: they plotted to destroy it ... *Destroying* the passions and desires merely in order to avoid their stupidity and the disagreeable consequences of their stupidity seems to us nowadays to be itself simply an acute form of stupidity. We no longer marvel at dentists who *pull out* teeth to stop them hurting.

Fulfilment is reached by responding wisely to difficulties that could tear one apart. Squeamish spirits may be tempted to pull the molar out at once or come off Piz Corvatsch on the lower slopes. Nietzsche urged us to endure.

16

And far from coincidentally, never to drink.

Dear Mother,
If I write to you today, it is about one of the most unpleasant and painful incidents I have ever been responsible for. In fact, I have misbehaved very badly, and I don't know whether you can or will forgive me. I pick up my pen most reluctantly and with a heavy heart, especially when I think back to our pleasant life together during the Easter holidays, which was never spoiled by any discord. Last Sunday, I got drunk, and I have no excuse, except that I did not know how much I could take, and I was rather excited in the afternoon.

So wrote eighteen-year-old Friedrich to his mother Franziska after four glasses of beer in the halls of Attenburg near his school in the spring of 1863. A few years later, at Bonn and Leipzig universities, he felt irritation with his fellow students for their love of alcohol: 'I often found the expressions of good fellowship in the clubhouse extremely distasteful ... I could hardly bear certain individuals because of their beery materialism.'

The attitude remained constant throughout the philosopher's adult life:

Alcoholic drinks are no good for me; a glass of wine or beer a day is quite enough to make life for me a 'Vale of Tears' – Munich is where my antipodes live.

'How much *beer* there is in the German intelligence!' he complained. 'Perhaps the modern European discontent is due to the fact that our forefathers were given to drinking through the entire Middle Ages ... The Middle Ages meant the alcohol poisoning of Europe.'

In the spring of 1871, Nietzsche went on holiday with his sister to the Hôtel du Parc in Lugano. The hotel bill for 2 – 9 March shows that he drank fourteen glasses of milk.

It was more than a personal taste. Anyone seeking to be happy was strongly advised never to drink anything alcoholic at all. Never:

I cannot advise all *more spiritual* natures too seriously to abstain from alcohol absolutely. *Water* suffices.

Why? Because Raphael had not drunk to escape his envy in Urbino in 1504, he had gone to Florence and learned how to be a great painter. Because Stendhal had not drunk in 1805 to escape his despair over *L'Homme qui craint d'être gouverné*, he had gardened the pain for seventeen years and published *De l'amour* in 1822:

If you refuse to let your own suffering lie upon you even for an hour and if you constantly try to prevent and forestall all possible distress way ahead of time; if you experience suffering and displeasure as evil, hateful, worthy of annihilation, and as a defect of existence, then it is clear that [you harbour in your heart]... the *religion of comfortableness.* How little you know of human *happiness*, you comfortable... people, for happiness and unhappiness are sisters and even twins that either grow up together or, as in your case, *remain small* together.

17

Nietzsche's antipathy to alcohol explains simultaneously his antipathy to what had been the dominant British school of moral philosophy: Utilitarianism, and its greatest proponent, John Stuart Mill. The Utilitarians had argued that in a world beset by moral ambiguities, the way to judge whether an action was right or wrong was to measure the amount of pleasure and pain it gave rise to. Mill proposed that:

[A] ctions are right in proportion as they tend to promote happiness, wrong as they tend to produce the reverse of happiness. By happiness is intended pleasure, and the absence of pain; by unhappiness, pain, and the privation of pleasure.

The thought of Utilitarianism, and even the nation from which it had sprung, enraged Nietzsche:

European vulgarity, the plebeianism of modern ideas [is the work and invention of] *England.*

Man does *not* strive for happiness; only the English do that.

He was, of course, also striving for happiness; he simply believed that it could not be attained as painlessly as the Utilitarians appeared to be suggesting:

All these modes of thought which assess the value of things according to *pleasure* and *pain*, that is to say according to attendant and secondary phenomena, are foreground modes of thought and naïveties which anyone conscious of *creative* powers and an artist's conscience will look down on with derision.

An artist's conscience because artistic creation offers a most explicit example of an activity which may deliver immense fulfilment but always demands immense suffering. Had Stendhal assessed the value of his art according to the ' pleasure ' and ' pain' it had at once brought him, there would have been no advance from L' *Homme qui craint d' être gouverné* to the summit of his powers.

Instead of drinking beer in the lowlands, Nietzsche asked us to accept the pain of the climb. He also offered a suggestion for townplanners:

> The secret for harvesting from existence the greatest fruitfulness and the greatest enjoyment is – to *live dangerously*! Build your cities on the slopes of Vesuvius!

And if one were still tempted to have a drink, but had no high opinion of Christianity, Nietzsche added a further argument to dissuade one from doing so. Anyone who liked drinking had, he argued, a fundamentally Christian outlook on life:

> To believe that wine *makes cheerful* I would have to be a Christian, that is to say believe what is for me in particular an absurdity.

18

He had more experience of Christianity than of alcohol. He was born in the tiny village of Röcken near Leipzig in Saxony. His father, Carl Ludwig Nietzsche, was the parson, his deeply devout mother was herself the daughter of a parson, David Ernst Oehler, who took services in the village of Pobles an hour away. Their son was baptized before an assembly of the local clergy in Röcken church in October 1844.

Friedrich loved his father, who died when he was only four, and revered his memory throughout his life. On the one occasion when he had a little money, after winning a court case against a publisher in 1885, he ordered a large headstone for his father's grave on which he had carved a quotation from Corinthians (1 Cor 13.8):

Die Liebe höret nimmer auf
Charity never faileth

'He was the perfect embodiment of a country pastor,' Nietzsche recalled of Carl Ludwig. 'A tall, delicate figure, a fine-featured face, amiable and beneficent. Everywhere welcomed and beloved as much for his witty conversation as for his warm sympathy, esteemed and loved by the farmers, extending blessings by word and deed in his capacity as a spiritual guide.'

Yet this filial love did not prevent Nietzsche from harbouring the deepest reservations about the consolation that his father, and Christianity in general, could offer those in pain:

I bring against the Christian Church the most terrible charge any prosecutor has ever uttered. To me it is the extremest thinkable form of corruption ... [it] has left nothing untouched by its depravity ... I call Christianity the *one* great curse, the *one* great intrinsic depravity ...

One does well to put gloves on when reading the New Testament. The proximity of so much uncleanliness almost forces one to do so ... Everything in it is cowardice, everything is self-deception and closing one's eyes to oneself ... Do I still have to add that in the entire New Testament there is only *one* solitary figure one is obliged to respect? Pilate, the Roman governor.

Quite simply:

It is indecent to be a Christian today.

19

How does the New Testament console us for our difficulties? By suggesting that many of these are not difficulties at all but rather virtues:

> *If one is worried about timidity, the New Testament points out:*
> Blessed are the meek; for they shall inherit the earth.
> (Matthew 5.5)
>
> *If one is worried about having no friends, the New Testament suggests:*
> Blessed are ye, when men shall hate you, and when they shall
> separate you from their company, and shall reproach you, and
> cast out your name as evil ... your reward is great in heaven.
> (Luke 6.22−3)
>
> *If one is worried about an exploitative job, the New Testament advises:*
> Servants, obey in all things your masters according to the
> flesh ... Knowing that of the Lord ye shall receive the reward of
> the inheritance; for ye serve the Lord Christ. (Colossians
> 3.22−4)
>
> *If one is worried at having no money, the New Testament tells us:*
> It is easier for a camel to go through the eye of a needle, than
> for a rich man to enter into the kingdom of God. (Mark
> 10.25)

There may be differences between such words and a drink but
Nietzsche insisted on an essential equivalence. Both Christianity
and alcohol have the power to convince us that what we previously
thought deficient in ourselves and the world does not require
attention; both weaken our resolve to garden our problems; both
deny us the chance of fulfilment:

The two great European narcotics, alcohol and Christianity.

Christianity had, in Nietzsche's account, emerged from the minds
of timid slaves in the Roman Empire who had lacked the stomach
to climb to the tops of mountains, and so had built themselves a
philosophy claiming that their bases were delightful. Christians
had wished to enjoy the real ingredients of fulfilment (a position

in the world, sex, intellectual mastery, creativity) but did not have the courage to endure the difficulties these goods demanded. They had therefore fashioned a hypocritical creed denouncing what they wanted but were too weak to fight for while praising what they did not want but happened to have. Powerlessness became ' goodness ', baseness ' humility ', submission to people one hated ' obedience ' and, in Nietzsche's phrase, ' not-being-able-to-take-revenge' turned into ' forgiveness '. Every feeling of weakness was overlaid with a sanctifying name, and made to seem ' a voluntary achievement, something wanted, chosen, a *deed*, an *accomplishment*'. Addicted to 'the religion of comfortableness', Christians, in their value system, had given precedence to what was easy, not what was desirable, and so had drained life of its potential.

20

Having a ' Christian ' perspective on difficulty is not limited to members of the Christian church; it is for Nietzsche a permanent psychological possibility. We all become Christians when we profess indifference to what we secretly long for but do not have; when we blithely say that we do not need love or a position in the world, money or success, creativity or health − while the corners of our mouths twitch with bitterness; and we wage silent wars against what we have publicly renounced, firing shots over the parapet, sniping from the trees.

How would Nietzsche have preferred us to approach our setbacks? To continue to believe in what we wish for, *even when we do not have it, and may never.* Put another way, to resist the temptation to denigrate and declare evil certain goods because they have proved hard to secure − a pattern of behaviour of which Nietzsche's own, infinitely tragic life offers us perhaps the best model.

Epicurus had from an early age been among his favourite ancient philosophers; he called him 'the soul-soother of later antiquity', 'one of the greatest men, the inventor of an heroic-idyllic mode of philosophizing'. What especially appealed to him was Epicurus's idea that happiness involved a life among friends. But he was rarely to know the contentment of community: 'It is our lot to be intellectual hermits and occasionally to have a conversation with someone like-minded.' At thirty, he composed a hymn to loneliness, '*Hymnus auf die Einsamkeit*', which he did not have the heart to finish.

The search for a wife was no less sorrowful, the problem partly caused by Nietzsche's appearance – his extraordinarily large walrus moustache – and his shyness, which bred the gauche stiff manner of a retired colonel. In the spring of 1876, on a trip to Geneva, Nietzsche fell in love with a twenty-three-year-old, green-eyed blonde, Mathilde Trampedach. During a conversation on the poetry of Henry Longfellow, Nietzsche mentioned that he had never come across a German version of Longfellow's 'Excelsior'. Mathilde said she had one at home and offered to copy it out for him. Encouraged, Nietzsche invited her out for a walk. She brought her landlady as a chaperone. A few days later, he offered to play the piano for her, and the next she heard from the thirty-one-year-old Professor of Classical Philology at Basle University was a request for marriage. 'Do you not think that together each of us will be better and more free than either of us could be alone – and so *excelsior*?' asked the playful colonel. 'Will you dare to come with me ... on all the paths of living and thinking?' Mathilde didn't dare.

A succession of similar rejections took their toll. In the light of his depression and ill health, Richard Wagner decided that there were two possible remedies: 'He must either marry or write an opera. ' But Nietzsche couldn't write an opera, and apparently lacked the talent to produce even a decent tune. (In July 1872, he sent the conductor Hans von Bülow a piano duet he had written, asking for an honest appraisal. It was, replied von Bülow, ' the most extreme fantastical extravagance, the most irritating and antimusical set of notes on manuscript paper I have seen for a long time' , and he wondered whether Nietzsche might have been pulling his leg. ' You designated your music as " frightful " - it truly is. ')

Wagner grew more insistent. ' For Heaven's sake, marry a rich woman! ' he intoned, and entered into communication with Nietzsche's doctor, Otto Eiser, with whom he speculated that the philosopher's ill health was caused by excessive masturbation. It was an irony lost on Wagner that the one rich woman with whom Nietzsche was truly in love was Wagner's own wife, Cosima. For years, he carefully disguised his feelings for her under the cloak of friendly solicitude. It was only once he had lost his reason that the reality emerged. ' Ariadne, I love you, ' wrote Nietzsche, or, as he signed himself, Dionysus, in a postcard sent to Cosima from Turin at the beginning of January 1889.

Nevertheless, Nietzsche intermittently agreed with the Wagnerian thesis on the importance of marriage. In a letter to his married friend Franz Overbeck, he complained, ' Thanks to your wife, things are a hundred times better for you than for me. You have a nest together. I have, at best, a *cave* ... Occasional contact with people is like a holiday, a redemption from " me ". '

In 1882, he hoped once more that he had found a suitable wife, Lou Andreas-Salomé, his greatest, most painful love. She was twenty-one, beautiful, clever, flirtatious and fascinated by his philosophy. Nietzsche was defenceless. ' I want to be lonely no longer, but to learn again to be a human being. Ah, here I have practically everything to learn! ' he told her. They spent two weeks together in the Tautenburg forest and in Lucerne posed with their mutual friend Paul Rée for an unusual photograph.

But Lou was more interested in Nietzsche as a philosopher than as a husband. The rejection threw him into renewed prolonged, violent depression. ' My lack of confidence is now immense, ' he told Overbeck, ' everything I hear makes me think that people despise me. ' He felt particular bitterness towards his mother and sister, who had meddled in the relationship with Lou, and now broke off contact with them, deepening his isolation. (' I do not like my mother, and it is painful for me to hear my sister's voice. I always became ill when I was with them. ')

There were professional difficulties, too. None of his books sold more than 2,000 copies in his sane life-time; most sold a few hundred. With only a modest pension and some shares inherited from an aunt on which to survive, the author could rarely pay for new clothes, and ended up looking, in his words, ' scraped like a mountain sheep '. In hotels, he stayed in the cheapest rooms, often fell into arrears with the rent and could afford neither heating nor the hams and sausages he loved.

His health was as problematic. From his schooldays, he had suffered from a range of ailments: headaches, indigestion, vomiting, dizziness, near blindness and insomnia, many of these the symptoms of the syphilis he had almost certainly contracted in a Cologne brothel in February 1865 (though Nietzsche claimed he had come away without touching anything except a piano). In a letter to Malwida von Meysenbug written three years after his trip to Sorrento, he explained, ' As regards torment and self-denial, my life during these past years can match that of any ascetic of any time... ' And to his doctor he reported, ' Constant pain, a feeling of being half-paralysed, a condition closely related to seasickness, during which I find it difficult to speak − this feeling lasts several hours a day. For my diversion I have raging seizures (the most recent one forced me to vomit for three days and three nights; I thirsted after death). Can't read! Only seldom can I write! Can't deal with my fellows! Can't listen to music!'

Finally, at the beginning of January 1889, Nietzsche broke down in Turin's Piazza Carlo Alberto and embraced a horse, was carried back to his boarding-house, where he thought of shooting the Kaiser, planned a war against anti-Semites, and grew certain that he was – depending on the hour – Dionysus, Jesus, God, Napoleon, the King of Italy, Buddha, Alexander the Great, Caesar, Voltaire, Alexander Herzen and Richard Wagner; before he was bundled into a train and taken to an asylum in Germany to be looked after by his elderly mother and sister until his death eleven years later at the age of fifty-five.

22

And yet through appalling loneliness, obscurity, poverty and ill health, Nietzsche did not manifest the behaviour of which he had accused Christians; he did not take against friendship, he did not attack eminence, wealth, or well-being. The Abbé Galiani and Goethe remained heroes. Though Mathilde had wished for no more than a conversation about poetry, he continued to believe that 'for the male sickness of self-contempt the surest cure is to be loved by a clever woman.' Though sickly and lacking Montaigne or Stendhal's dexterity on a horse, he remained attached to the idea of an active life: 'Early in the morning, at break of day, in all the freshness and dawn of one's strength, to read a *book* – I call that vicious!'

He fought hard to be happy, but where he did not succeed he did not turn against what he had once aspired to. He remained committed to what was in his eyes the most important characteristic of a noble human being: to be someone who '*no longer denies*'.

23

After seven hours of walking, much of it in the rain, it was in a state of extreme exhaustion that I reached the summit of Piz Corvatsch, high above the clouds that decked the Engadine valleys below. In my rucksack I carried a water-bottle, an Emmental sandwich and an envelope from the Hotel Edelweiss in Sils-Maria on which I had that morning written a quote from the mountain philosopher, with the intention of facing Italy and reading it to the wind and the rocks at 3,400 metres.

Like his pastor father, Nietzsche had been committed to the task of consolation. Like his father, he had wished to offer us paths to fulfilment. But unlike pastors, and dentists who pull out throbbing teeth and gardeners who destroy plants with ill-favoured roots, he had judged difficulties to be a critical prerequisite of fulfilment, and hence knew saccharine consolations to be ultimately more cruel than helpful:

> The worst sickness of men has originated in the way they have combated their sicknesses. What seemed a cure has in the long run produced something worse than what it was supposed to overcome. The means which worked immediately, anaesthetizing and intoxicating, *the so-called consolations*, were ignorantly supposed to be actual cures. The fact was not noticed ... that these instantaneous alleviations often had to be paid for with a general and profound worsening of the complaint.

Not everything which makes us feel better is good for us. Not everything which hurts may be bad.

图书在版编目(CIP)数据

哲学的慰藉:中英双语插图本 /(英)德波顿(de
Botton,A.)著;资中筠译.—上海:上海译文出版社,
2010.1(2024.6 重印)
书名原文:The Consolations of Philosophy
ISBN 978-7-5327-4937-9

Ⅰ.哲... Ⅱ.①德...②资... Ⅲ.①英语—汉语—对照读
物②文学—通俗读物 Ⅳ.H319.4:I

中国版本图书馆 CIP 数据核字(2009)第 209650 号

Alain de Botton
The Consolations of Philosophy
Penguin Group, 2000
This edition arranged with INTERCONTINENTAL LITERARY AGENCY(ILA)
through BIG APPLE TUTTLE-MORI AGENCY, LABUAN, MALAYSIA.
Chinese and English edition Copyright © 2010 by Shanghai Translation Publishing
House
All Rights Reserved
作者个人网站:www. alaindebotton.com

图字:09-2009-616 号

哲学的慰藉
〔英〕阿兰·德波顿/著 资中筠/译
责任编辑/衷雅琴 装帧设计/张志全工作室

上海译文出版社有限公司出版、发行
网址:www.yiwen.com.cn
201101 上海市闵行区号景路 159 弄 B 座
苏州市越洋印刷有限公司印刷

开本 787×1092 1/32 印张 15.25 插页 5 字数 264,000
2010 年 1 月第 1 版 2024 年 6 月第 13 次印刷
印数:45,401—47,400 册
ISBN 978-7-5327-4937-9/I·2764
定价:65.00 元